THE CHANGING FACE OF DEATH

Also by Glennys Howarth and Peter C. Jupp

CONTEMPORARY ISSUES IN THE SOCIOLOGY OF DEATH, DYING AND DISPOSAL (*editors*)

Also by Glennys Howarth

LAST RITES

THE UNKNOWN COUNTRY: EXPERIENCES OF DEATH IN AUSTRALIA, BRITAIN AND THE USA
(*editor with Kathy Charmaz and Allan Kellehear*)

Also by Peter C. Jupp

POSTMODERNITY, SOCIOLOGY AND RELIGION
(*editor with Kieran Flanagan*)

The Changing Face of Death

Historical Accounts of Death and Disposal

Edited by

Peter C. Jupp
Institute of Community Studies
London

and

Glennys Howarth
School of Cultural and Community Studies
University of Sussex

First published in Great Britain 1997 by
MACMILLAN PRESS LTD
Houndmills, Basingstoke, Hampshire RG21 6XS
and London
Companies and representatives
throughout the world

A catalogue record for this book is available
from the British Library.

ISBN 0–333–63863–8

First published in the United States of America 1997 by
ST. MARTIN'S PRESS, INC.,
Scholarly and Reference Division,
175 Fifth Avenue,
New York, N.Y. 10010

ISBN 0–312–16403–3

Library of Congress Cataloging-in-Publication Data
The changing face of death : historical accounts of death and disposal
/ edited by Peter C. Jupp and Glennys Howarth.
p.   cm.
Includes bibliographical references and index.
ISBN 0–312–16403–3 (cloth)
1. Funeral rites and ceremonies—Great Britain—History.
2. Funeral rites and ceremonies—History.   3. Mourning customs–
–Social aspects—Great Britain—History.   4. Mourning customs–
–History.   5. Death.   I. Howarth, Glennys.   II. Jupp, Peter C.
GT3243.C53   1996
393'.0941—dc20   96–25766
                                                   CIP

10 9   8   7   6   5   4   3   2   1
06 05 04 03 02 01 00 99 98 97

Printed and bound in Great Britain by
The Ipswich Book Co. Ltd

Peter C. Jupp dedicates this book to
Elisabeth, Edmund and Miles
Glennys Howarth dedicates it to
Elizabeth, Sheila and Martin

Contents

Acknowledgements

The Changing Face of Death originated at Mansfield College, Oxford in April 1993 where the Editors had organised the first international conference: *The Social Context of Death, Dying and Disposal.* We are grateful to Mansfield for its hospitality, to Judith Russell for her administrative flair and, above all, to the enthusiasm and commitment of those scholars and professionals who took part. During our research work at the London School of Economics in the late 1980s, we had become indebted to the work of an increasing number of death scholars from various disciplines, and the conference was organised to enable them to meet. Over 40 papers were presented, and this book, like its companion *Contemporary Issues in the Sociology of Death, Dying and Disposal* (Macmillan, 1996), and the journal *Mortality* (launched this year), is part of the visible result.

Our commitment to the study of death owes an enormous amount to the sustained support of our families and to the many, many friends and colleagues with whom we have had, over the years, many stimulating conversations. We particularly wish to mention Douglas Davies, David Field, Jenny Hockey, Maura Naylor, Lindsay Prior, Tony Walter and Michael Young; and colleagues on the Council of the National Funerals College, the Churches' Group on Funeral Services at Cemeteries and Crematoria, and who work as bereavement counsellors, as funeral directors and in the cemetery and crematorium services.

We are especially grateful to Ms Annabelle Buckley, our Editor at Macmillan, for her constant patience and encouragement. We thank our contributors, not only for their scholarship but also for the unflagging good will and humour with which they have responded to our requests for reduction and redrafting. We thank Ms Katharine Riley for her tireless energies in the word-processing and collation of the texts.

We believe that our common mortality is the critical element in the human condition and in human societies. We offer this book to our readers in the hope that it may provide illumination both scholarly and personal. The death of Ernest Jupp (1904–1995) during the work on this volume has served to confirm – as we hope he thought it might – that the two elements are not only contrasting but complementary.

Peter C. Jupp and Glennys Howarth

Notes on Contributors

Stephen Collins was educated at Bristol University and the London School of Economics, trained and worked as a probation officer, and was involved for many years in social work training; now Lecturer in the Human Sciences in the Department of Social and Economic Studies, Bradford University. Author of *Step-parents and their Children* (Souvenir Press, 1988) *Social Work with Young Offenders* (Butterworth, 1981 with David Behan) and of academic papers on psychoanalysis and family history. Current research is on the historical development of the ideological basis of family life.

Clare Gittings is Education Officer at the National Portrait Gallery, London. She published *Brasses and Brass Rubbing* (Blandford Press, 1970), *Death, Burial and the Individual in Early Modern England* (Croom Helm/Routledge) in 1984 and contributed to *Death in Towns* (Leicester University Press, 1993) and *Death, Passion and Politics* (Dulwich Picture Gallery, 1995). Educated at the University of East Anglia and St Anne's College, Oxford, she has also been a primary school teacher and a VSO volunteer. She is currently on the Council of the Museums Association and a school governor.

Glennys Howarth is a Lecturer in Sociology at the University of Sussex. Before that, she was T. H. Marshall Fellow in the Department of Sociology at the London School of Economics. Recent research has included studies of the funeral industry and the social implications of the coroner system. She is the author of *Last Rites* (Baywood Publishers, and co-editor, with Peter Jupp, of the journal *Mortality* (Carfax).1996)

Malcolm Johnson was appointed Director of the School for Policy Studies in the University of Bristol in 1995. Since 1984 he had been Professor of Health and Social Welfare and Dean of the School of Health, Welfare and Community Education at the Open University, where he co-ordinated the course *Death and Dying*. He was the founding Editor of *Ageing and Society* and founding Associate Editor of *Sociology of Health and Illness*. He has researched and published widely on gerontology, social policy analysis and health studies.

Peter C. Jupp is a United Reformed Church minister. He works for the Institute of Community Studies in London as Director of the National Funerals College. His doctoral thesis investigated the development of cremation in England. He was the Convenor of the Sociology of Religion Study Group in the British Sociological Association, 1991–4. With Kieran Flanagan, he is the co-editor of *Postmodernity, Sociology and Religion* and with Glennys Howarth, co-editor of *Contemporary Issues in the Sociology of Death, Dying and Disposal* and the journal *Mortality* (Carfax).

Christine King is Vice-Chancellor of Staffordshire University. She has degrees in History and Theology and the History of Religion. Her research and writings have included a major investigation into the history of religious groups during the Third Reich. Her work on Elvis brings her back to an earlier interest, that of medieval pilgrimage. She confesses to being an Elvis fan.

Julian Litten has specialised in the history of the funerary trade 1450–1800 and intramural burial. He was consultant for the funeral of the Unknown Mariner of the Mary Rose at Portsmouth Cathedral (1984) and was in-house consultant to the Art of Death Exhibition at the V&A Museum (1991). His *The English Way of Death: The Common Funeral since 1450* was published in 1991, and he contributed to Harvey and Mortimer (eds), *The Funeral Effigies in Westminster Abbey* in 1994. He is an FSA, FSA(Scot), and a member of the General Synod of the Church of England, a member of the Cathedrals Fabric Commission for England, Westminster Abbey Architectural Advisory Panel, President of the Friends of Kensal Green Cemetery.

Elizabeth Musgrave is a Senior Lecturer in History at Nene College, Northampton. Recent research has focused on the history of the building industries of early modern Brittany, France, including the social meaning and function of buildings. She is now working on rural industries and artisans of the Saintonge region of western France in the early modern period.

John Pinfold is Librarian of Rhodes House Library, Oxford. Formerly he was Reference Librarian at the British Library of Political and Economic Science (London School of Economics) where his interest in local history led to his study of the 'Green Ground'.

Lindsay Prior is a Senior Lecturer in Social Research Methods at the University of Cardiff. He is author of *The Social Organization of Death* (Macmillan, 1989) and *The Social Organization of Mental Illness* (Sage, 1993). He is currently working, among other things, on a study of fatal accidents.

Julie Rugg has worked with the Cemetery Research Group at the University of York since the beginning of 1991. She has two main research interests:

the history of nineteenth-century cemetery development and current local authority cemetery policy. She is the joint author, with Julie Dunk, of *The Management of Old Cemetery Land*.

Stephen White was formerly a Senior Lecturer at the Cardiff Law School of the University of Wales. He has written extensively about Criminal Law and is currently engaged in research into the development of the law relating to cremation in the nineteenth century.

Alan Wilkinson, an Anglican priest, is Diocesan Theologian of Portsmouth Cathedral, an honorary Canon of Chichester and Ripon Cathedrals and a Tutor for the Open University. He is the author of *The Church of England and the First World War* (SPCK, 1978), *Dissent or Conform? War, Peace and the English Churches 1900–45* (SCM, 1986) and *The Community of the Resurrection, A Centenary History* (SCM, 1992).

Foreword

The extraordinary extension of life during the twentieth century and the mixture of illusion and reality that medicine can cure all ills, has misled the developed world into half believing in human immortality. The dramatic reduction in premature death is to be celebrated. The demographic revolution which allows most people to live healthily into old age is a spectacular gain for humankind – not a burden as the long-faced politicians and morbid policymakers would have it. Yet the comparative rarity of death in childhood, early adulthood or middle age has largely removed distressing death from everyday experience. With the willing help of the death professions – doctors, funeral directors and clergy in particular – the intimate experience of the end of life has been replaced by something more distant, more managed and more institutionalised. Death has been placed in the dark attic room of the contemporary, developed world.

In their wonderfully rich book Peter Jupp and Glennys Howarth provide abundant evidence of the many different pageants of death which heralded and signified the conclusion of life. Largely through historical accounts, the reader discovers how death rituals evolve and change even within the same culture as beliefs, fashions and entrepreneurial energy have reshaped the social, economic and spiritual dimensions of dying, grieving and remembering. What shines out of the dozen very different, but equally fascinating, chapters is the omnipresence of death in earlier times. Along with its unwanted commonness came a readiness to look mortality in the face. Humble lives were reflected by modest coffins and funerals; exalted ones with elaborate practices and ostentatious memorials. Rural rituals differed from those of the town. Were there more comparisons of death beyond these shores (than the two in this book) they would reveal a wonderful variety of behaviour surrounding death which reflect cultures and beliefs.

The Changing Face of Death is a volume of contemporary relevance despite its grounding in historical scholarship, for like all good history it puts the present distaste of death into stark relief. Simply by absorbing the many vignettes of death in all its variety, one is struck by the emotional and symbolic poverty of the British way of death. The great and the good may be equally mourned; those who die young are grieved for by many. But the average funeral of an ordinary old person is a miserable, colourless and anonymous affair.

If Ariès' claim that we are a death-denying society is an imperfect descriptor, the phrase has a powerful ring of truth. There is no lack of writing and talk about death. Has there ever been an age when this was not so? But our unwillingness to acknowledge the finiteness of our existence has left several generations with little opportunity to talk of death without being considered to have an inappropriate interest in a socially unwelcome topic. Those who are members of belief communities are still able to discuss what is beyond the human span. For the growing majority, there has, until recently, been a curious and unhealthy silence.

If others share my view that societies which have no public discourse about death and which have discarded centuries of valuable ritual are unhealthy, they may also welcome the evident signs of a greater openness. This collection of essays is one manifestation of the change. The sparse scholarly interest has burgeoned over the past decade. It has been paralleled by a more reflective attitude amongst health professionals. In part prompted by the development of palliative medicine from within the hospice movement, it is also a response to a new salience of ethical considerations and litigation in relation to death.

There is at the same time a welcome shift in media attention. Television studio discussions, radio 'phone-ins and newspaper articles about every aspect of dying and death are more common than ever before. The cultural triggers for the new interest may be assisted suicide, AIDS, or the price of funerals, but the opportunity to relate personal hopes, fears and expectations is a positive development. Research into the grieving process shows that in addition to the well-being and guilt which derive from biographical reflection, there is much that is healing in the more open processes of talking, listening and remembering.

It would be a great pity if the readership of this book were confined to the small – if growing – cadre of thanatological historians. The contributors tell their stories with vitality and style, leading the reader to see the procession of history from a new vantage point. All who have any professional involvement with dying, dead or bereaved people will gain insight and inspiration. In turn it would enable them to see more clearly that if the line in Edith Sitwell's poem 'Eurydice' '... all in the end is harvest' is to be achieved, much depends on them. It is in all our interests that the face of death is changed. This volume makes a signal contribution.

Professor Malcolm Johnson
University of Bristol
June 1996

Introduction
Peter C. Jupp

DEATH AS A SOCIAL AND HISTORICAL ACTOR

Sooner or later, every one of us will die. Death is the critical actor in the drama of personal and social life, both off- and centre-stage.

The certainty of death provokes response. This may range from outright avoidance to foolhardy bravado. The range of attitudes may be publicly articulated, either in the political rhetoric of a war or its aftermath (Fussell, 1975, 1989), or as private assent in the inner mind to common folk beliefs (Bennett, 1987; Richardson, 1987, ch. 1). Both death and the fear of it take different forms in different ages and societies. The recourse to suicide, for example, receives different legitimation according to era or culture. Yet nearly all individuals take their cue from the range of responses their specific society deems acceptable. As the following chapters will show, the interpretation of death and the image of its terrors, the arrangements for disposal and the domestic, economic and political consequences, vary in and differentiate each human society.

The decision to confront death requires the operation of choice. The highwayman demands, 'Your money or your life.' Thus death enforces a prioritisation of values (Goody, 1975): 'If you were to die tomorrow, how would you spend today?' The Christian Scriptures indicate how nature creates a particularly short-lived vacuum in the economic arena: 'Thou fool, this night thy soul shall be required of thee, then whose shall those things be which thou hast provided?' (Luke 12:19–20).

Death is the ultimate enforcer of change. Whatever arrangement we make for the conduct of our affairs, death will eventually bring about their cessation or replacement. The social advantages of death are discussed thus by Michael Young,

> death ensures that the multiple connections over time between one generation and another are not too close. If they were, the adaptability of human beings, and all other forms of life, would be greatly weakened... If the individual members of any species were everlasting there would be no evolution. (Young, 1988, p. 255)

Death guarantees change. It brings an end to every parent, every employer, every ruler. Every subject people may look forward in the certain expectation of their oppressor's death. Indeed, the oppressor's downfall may be engineered by his rival's threat of self-death by martyrdom. Martyrdom is a special form of imparting post-mortem value to an individual death. Normal prospects of death prompt the construction of world views – universal, folk, personal or idiosyncratic – by which death's inevitability may be borne and interpreted. The more widely held the world view, the more it interacts with social structure. Bloch and Parry (1982) fruitfully explore concepts of the afterlife as symbols of the ideal social order. This highlights the traditional role of religion where social structure, interpretations of death and coping mechanisms work in harness, if not always in harmony.

The means to cope with death and to interpret it are two major weapons for human societies. Whilst the hypothesis that the fact of death accounts for the origin of religion has been rejected by Bowker (1991), the development of rituals and interpretations of death are prime responsibilities of organised religion (Rowell, 1977; Cohn-Sherbok and Lewis, 1995; Walter, 1996). In harness with religions, societies have codified rituals for the safe disposal of the dead; for the protection of the dead and their mourners from a variety of ills, both natural and supernatural; for the safe transmission of the 'soul' to an afterlife; and for the process of reincorporation of the bereaved into a readjusted stage of 'normal life'.

The transition to a next life may be envisaged, for example, through the medium of a resurrection of the body, the immortality of the soul, or reincarnation. Each inspires different sets of attitudes towards the corpse and its mode of disposal. The world of the dead may be characterised as either passive or dynamic (Walker, 1964) whereby relationships between the living and the dead may be conceived as beneficial or dangerous, and then either promoted or prosecuted. Differing Protestant and Catholic beliefs play a significant role in several chapters below. Archbishop Thomas à Becket knew the temptation that, 'Saint and martyr rule from the tomb' (Eliot, 1935). Many forms of power lie in the manipulation of the dead. The possession of relics (Finucane, 1977; Brown, 1981) and the ability to communicate with the dead (Barrow, 1986; Vitebsky, 1993) both constitute media of power. Beliefs about the afterlife may include concepts of rewards and sanctions for the maintenance of this-worldly behaviour (Goody, 1959, 1962; Rowell, 1974; le Goff, 1984). Ownership and control of access to burial grounds offer power both in political terms and in terms of moulding or remoulding interpretations of death (Curl, 1980; Brooks, 1989; Colvin, 1991; Sloane, 1991; Jupp, 1993; Kselman, 1993; Nicol, 1994; Parry, 1994).

Death insists on the transfer of power. Rulers cannot take infinite pains to ensure death neither ruffles their feathers, nor unfeathers their nests, but their attempts are considerable (Huntingdon and Metcalf, 1987; Cannadine and Price, 1987). Meanwhile power may fall into wrong or weaker hands.

Thus the prudent plan how to redirect their resources *after* their death by nominating heirs, writing wills and establishing trusts. Bureaucratic authority has developed modes of transferring power which minimise the threat of death (Marris, 1974). Far humbler people and in larger numbers may exert pressure on their survivors when feared, or honoured, as ghosts. Ancestor cults are a powerful tool for conservative or traditional societies, legitimating the power not only of the dead but also of the elderly.

The threat of death is regularly deployed by the powerful in order to govern. Throughout history capital punishment is the ultimate weapon of policing (Potter, 1993; Lessing, 1994; Evans, 1996). Both death and disposal are recruited as weapons in the policing of society. Criminals' activities may be marked out by forms of execution and their lasting status as outlaws perpetuated when they are buried in quick-lime, denied a grave-marker or otherwise refused a burial place alongside the law-abiding. The historians of genocide have shown how the categorisation of outlaw or alien is within the gift of governments, where the membership of the group to be destroyed is defined by the perpetrator (Gilbert, 1986; Bauman, 1989; Chalk & Jonassohn, 1990).

All societies perpetuate their social boundaries after death. Social distinctions, by gender, age, class or ethnicity, have always been identifiable in the degree of investment in the disposal of the dead and in mortality rates. Whilst complex funerary arrangements follow the death of a king, perfunctory funeral ceremonies will often indicate the social unimportance of the dead. These may be variously conceived as infants, the poor, or ethnic minorities. Such boundaries, being culturally formed, change with developments in society. Until the nineteenth century, the death of young children was so widespread as a consequence of malnutrition, inadequate medical knowledge and facilities, that the crime of infanticide was widespread and rarely prosecuted (Rose, 1986). With the overall rise in living standards, resort to large families as a defence against mortality declined. Within the last 20 years, new and sympathetic attitudes are accorded the parents who lose a child. Children (and pregnancies) today represent a considerable investment of time, money and emotion. At the other end of the life-cycle, the rise of living standards has promoted increased longevity (Mitchison, 1977).

Death threatens the disruption of every family. It is not merely the maker and breaker of imperial dynasties but of every private or domestic world. Yet longevity and prosperity may combine to remove some of the necessity for such preparations. Shorter has suggested that 'the larger lineage – that chain of generations stretching across time, of which individual nuclear families were once a part – has ceased to confer immortality' (Shorter, 1976, p. 8). Longevity, prosperity and religious secularisation have combined to offer wider forms of acceptable security than were hitherto available. The use of family identity – past and future – as a bulwark against death was partly underpinned by, for example, common religious faith, communal burial grounds and family graves, all three together strengthening the bond between family lineage and local community, especially within dominant élites (Colvin, 1991).

That family identity is no defence against death is evidenced from studies on child adoption and infanticide (Kertzer, 1993; Rose, 1986), from the widespread use of pauper graves and the contemporary western resort to cremation (Jupp, 1993). Transmission of wealth may adjust the focus. Ellis (1943) supported by Childe (1945) noted a period in Scandinavian history when a general increase in prosperity was accompanied by lesser investment in grave-goods. Her interpretation was that with new opportunities for wealth and with the adaptation of social classes to new trading alliances, prosperity came to depend less upon maintaining old family and kinship structures, for which grave maintenance had formerly provided a focus and a form of investment.

Pie is no longer rationed for postponed gratification 'in the sky/when you die'. Indeed, modern communications and the leisure industry have collaborated to make death and the threat of death a staple constituent of entertainment. The fact of death is turned into 'part of the magic world of the screen which is unconsciously bracketed as unreal' (Hick, 1976, p. 87).

New opportunities for work, leisure and prosperity have massive consequences for the role of women in society. In traditional societies women bear the burden of deathwork and mourning (Bloch, 1989; Danforth, 1982). Such mourning rituals may indicate a connection between the processes of death and birth and may seek to protect women from the pollution of contact with death (Watson, 1982). Gender roles have usually been allocated so that women, where not primarily involved in economic labour, bear the greater burden of mourning. Turning to modern western societies, Taylor claims the underlying meaning of Victorian mourning ritual was that a woman's sexual or emotional life had come to an end (1982, p. 270). If Taylor is correct, then social developments which bring changes in opportunities for women's work, education, marriage and divorce and child-rearing, will clearly reduce their traditional role in mourning. In our own era, many visible mourning rituals have been rejected as anachronistic, as obstructions in a busier and more mobile life and as inappropriate for societies grasping new opportunities for gender equalities. Gorer suggested (1955), in a hypothesis awaiting challenge, that the nineteenth-century taboo about sex and its expressiveness about death have merely exchanged places. Especially for women, in certain modern societies, the link – actual or ideological – between death and sex, between funerals and fertility, has been severed. At the same time, with the onset of AIDS, contemporary society is discovering that death and sex have become reconnected.

At a personal and domestic level, meanwhile, death eventually forces many people to make rational arrangements to limit the damage of their demise. Legal systems have developed for the writing, execution and resolution of wills. The insurance industry, which began as a defence against marine loss, developed into burial insurance, life assurance and the massive pensions industry. In modern times, the rise of the National Health Service in the UK and of unsocialised hospitals in the US, has marked the institutional separation of dying, turning it into a process requiring professional attentions and contexts families cannot be expected to provide. The institutional contexts of death have received increasing attention (Glaser and Strauss, 1965, 1968; Sudnow, 1967; Elias, 1985; Field, 1989; Hockey, 1990; Clark 1993a).

Death is big business and supplies employment. In successive generations, various trades have arisen to meet whatever obsequies have proved fashionable, marketable or necessary. The monumental brass industry flourished long before *Henry V*'s Chorus predicted that armourers would thrive. The chapters below indicate how whole hosts of professionals and artisans have, in successive eras, responded to the needs of bereaved people. They describe the contexts and institutions through which their services are provided. Over time, support for the bereaved family has shifted from neighbour, carpenter and village priest to medical personnel, funeral directors and local authority crematoria. Today's national and international funeral directing chains, for example, compete with pre-payment funeral plans, whilst various reform groups promote do-it-yourself funerals, cardboard coffins and woodland burial grounds. Far greater is private or commercial investment in pension-funds or state provision in Health Services, with their associated organisations for prevention and research. On an even larger canvas, the Armed Forces and defence industries, legitimate or otherwise, along with print and televisual journalism and the entertainment industry, all profit by the fact, or the threat, of death.

Death is not only script-writer and actor. It is also the chorus. It holds up a mirror to human society and shows us the specific prioritisation of values in every age (Ariès 1974, 1975, 1981, 1985). By the study of specific issues in mortality may attitudes about the value of human life and of deviant behaviour be measured and compared within and across societies. Abortion and contraception are traditional and contrasted resorts to family limitation, but are today made salient by a combination of longevity, poverty and prosperity, and the role of the law, the state and religion in a technologically-proficient medical system. Euthanasia and suicide have likewise always been utilised. But their study reveals, for example, the differing power and authority in religion, economic activity, social cohesion or concepts of self-worth. The health of a nation and of its constituent regions can be assessed by studies of the causes of death. Meanwhile those authorities which collect and analyse statistics thereby wield medical, political and ideological power (Prior, 1989). The analysis of specific forms of pestilence and epidemic, in chronicling a society's response, reveals the comparative strength and role of political, civil, medical and religious institutions (Evans, 1987).

War, like plague, alters attitudes to the corpse and to its disposal, and to common interpretations of death, in addition to its economic and political consequences which may re-order the priorities of life. War brings new technology, new values, new opportunities and a shake-up in social mood and order. Recent research into war memorials reveals successive stages of political and public attitudes to war deaths (Wilkinson, 1978; Borg, 1991; Davies, 1994). Meanwhile, behind the public attention accorded the Holocaust or Hiroshima, there lie, overshadowed, millions of more private tragedies. Character – national, sectional, and personal – is moulded and analysed by response to tragedy. The reality of nuclear weapons has added a new dimension (Morgenthau, 1967). The possibility of nuclear war has radically threatened that traditional concept of immortality whereby, whilst individuals are mortal, their significance abides in their own achievements and their survivors' memory. By the ultimate nuclear catastrophe, monuments, fame and memory will alike be destroyed.

OUTLINE OF THE BOOK

In the UK anthropology and medicine have always considered death as a crucial area of study. Historians and sociologists have followed more recently, after the French (from the 1950s) and the Americans (from the 1960s). In the 1980s a number of British sociologists and historians struck out quite independently into this terrain and some important work remains unpublished. As the decade progressed, contacts were increasingly made. A conference of the Social History Society on 'Death, Ritual and Bereavement' produced essays edited by Houlbrooke (1989). Independent conferences at Birmingham (1991) and Leicester (1991) led to books edited by Bassett (1993), Clark (1993b) and Field *et al.* (1996).

This book and its companion (Howarth and Jupp, 1996) developed from the conference 'The Social Context of Death, Dying and Disposal' at Mansfield College, Oxford, in April 1993. It was organised by the current editors as a further opportunity to bring together the growing number of scholars working on death. The 12 chapters in this volume follow a chronological order; each picks up certain themes from its predecessors. They illuminate selected aspects of the social context of death, dying and disposal between the Protestant Reformation and our own times: largely but not exclusively English. Two contributions examine specific issues in France and the United States.

Clare Gittings opens the collection with a study of grief in aristocratic families in early seventeenth-century England. We noted above that in modern western societies the family is the primary social unit affected by a death; and that the death of a partner, child or parent has repercussions for domestic life, sexual activity and intimate companionship, as well as for the economic or hierarchical organisation of the home. Gittings reveals the specific context in which this process began in England, the revolution in attitudes towards death, accompanied by a revolution in artistic expression of grief, following the Protestant Reformation.

By comparing artifacts such as tombs and elegies commissioned after the death of Sir Henry Unton with those commissioned for other aristocrats a generation later, she illuminates the revolution of attitudes and its contexts. She demonstrates how, in aristocratic circles, the focus of commemoration changed from a display of the dead person's position in the social hierarchy to an expression of the personal loss of those bereaved.

The first critical factor is the establishment of the Protestant religion. This, by outlawing the use of chantries, belief in Purgatory and intercessions for the dead, 'cut the connection between this life and the next' (Gittings, 1984, p. 80). As a result, emotional energy at death was redirected away from the soul in its post-mortem existence and upon the bereaved in their present state (Rowell, 1977; Duffy, 1992). Second, James I failed to exercise discipline upon aristocratic funerals through the Heralds, as his predecessor had done. The nobility was thus freer to organise funerals according to their own preferences. Third, increasing European contacts included the cult of melancholy. Associated with intellectual excellence, it combined with the Protestant uncertainty about legitimate responses to death and the career uncertainties associated with political and economic changes. By the comparison of successive funeral and memorial commissions against this background, Gittings reveals a critical shift of attitudes towards death which, given the permanence of the artifacts which celebrated these new attitudes, provided new models by which this revolution was enshrined.

The personal loss inflicted by death has different consequences according to social position and economic circumstance. In the second chapter, Stephen Collins traces the effect of death upon propertied families by a study of attitudes towards widows and to their remarriage. He seeks to explain the persistence of attitudes of ridicule and contempt towards widows over the period 1550 to 1800. The arguments against remarriage cluster around a high idealisation of widowhood and a ruthless criticism of women who remarried. These attitudes functioned to maintain traditional patriarchies and were indicative of men's sexual and economic insecurities. Collins explores five themes behind the anxiety felt about the 'loose cannon' role of experienced women enfranchised by death. While the five reinforced each other, principal among them is the role of wealth and its transmission in a hierarchical society. The widow's new economic power might make her an attraction for a second husband. The demands (or greed) of step-fathers and step-children threatened the smooth operation of primogeniture. The misogyny which denied that women could ever be chaste widows magnified the threat of sexuality to the social order. Women continued to seek remarriage nevertheless, and though by the end of the eighteenth century the metaphysical basis of the old sexual hierarchy had almost disappeared, new rationalisations for male insecurities had taken their place. The role of women in the social armour against fate would only radically change with women's emancipation – sexual, marital and economic – in the nineteenth and twentieth centuries, by which time the social meanings of sexuality, wealth and death had all undergone considerable change.

The third chapter, by Julian Litten, charts the rise of undertakers. Among the upper classes, the increasing desire that the funeral arrangements should help articulate private grief rather than social continuity led, after the Commonwealth, to opportunities for funeral innovation. The Commonwealth had reduced the influence of the College of Heralds. Within bereaved families mounting pressure for the expression of personal loss and for the operation of greater family control in funeral rituals was assisted by the emergence of a new entrepreneur. Whilst the first undertaker seems to have been William Boyce (*c.* 1675), the real innovator was William Russell who in 1689 concluded an agreement with the College of Arms that its members would attend certain funerals of rank that he had furnished. Analysing surviving material, like trade-cards, funeral invitations and pattern-books, Litten provides an overview of the trade, comparing the work of the coffin-maker, funeral-furnisher and undertaker. In a wider context, the rise of undertakers was due to a number of factors. The role of the Plague of 1665 in promoting different attitudes to death and to the corpse awaits further scholarly attention. Meanwhile, in the Post-Restoration era, the social hierarchy was readjusting; new guidelines were sought to express social status, especially in urban society. The role of the clergy at the deathbed (diminished since the Protestant Reformation) was increasingly taken by the doctor (Porter, 1989). The family's personal and emotional needs in funeral arrangements were met by the new trade of undertaking. Undertakers' power came speedily to lie in the family's surrender to them of the estimate of the family's rank and of what display – and cost – was appropriate. For Litten, the Hanoverian era was the undertakers' zenith. With the onset of industrialisation and the consequent increase in urban mortality, the mutual exploitation of bereaved family and undertaker would spread through all social classes.

In France, meanwhile, the Protestant Reformation had been unsuccessful. Elizabeth Musgrave discusses the culturally distinct region of Brittany, where official Catholic religion went hand in hand with folk beliefs. In this overwhelmingly rural society, the Church's control of death rituals and (largely) of the interpretation of death – of the significance of sin and death, purgatory, resurrection and judgement – lasted until the French Revolution. The Church in France thus acted as a dominant gatekeeper of death 250 years longer than in England.

The focus of her chapter is the charnel house (discontinued in England during the seventeenth century). In Brittany the charnel house was a response to the increasing shortage of burial space for parishioners within the church. The developing practice of the secondary burial of human bones thus established separate social space for the preservation of the dead and new rituals for their commemoration. The background to these practices and to the specific building projects that enabled them was partly the Counter-Reformation's organised educational programme about death and the dead. It was also the continuity of traditional Breton cults of the dead, informed by a combination of folk and Catholic beliefs, in which the worlds of the dead and of the living were contiguous. The Counter-Reformation both prolonged and developed the 'dynamic' as opposed to the 'passive' conception of the afterlife (Walker, 1964), by which the ties between the living and the dead were strengthened and maintained, the reverse of contemporary Protestant practice. Brittany however could not remain immune to external pressures and Musgrave examines certain secularising themes: the effect of increased royal taxation and the declining local economy upon Church building projects; changing attitudes towards the corpse as connections between burial and sanitation were explored in the eighteenth century; and the attack upon the Church culminating in the Revolution, with the consequent realignment of the responsibilities of church, local government and undertaker.

Three chapters by John Pinfold, Peter Jupp and Julie Rugg focus on the early nineteenth century in England, and the pressing need for reorganisation of space for the dead. Whilst certain European countries already forbade intramural burial and established new cemeteries outside city boundaries, the United Kingdom had not followed this growing trend. Urbanisation brought two relevant problems: it increased poor health and it put a premium on the availability of burial space. The Church of England was the major provider of burial ground, but it had generally failed to extend its churchyards in the eighteenth century to adjust for population growth. Pinfold's description of London's Green Ground draws upon local materials, such as maps and rate-books, to illustrate the decline of this inner-city neighbourhood after the wealthy moved towards the new West End. This tiny strip of ground became the repository of many of the poorest residents. The chapter describes the stratagems adopted by unscrupulous burial proprietors and their staff as the limited grave space was used repeatedly. Pinfold highlights the restrictions under which the poor buried their dead, and examines the reasons why reforms were delayed. Areas like the Green Ground revealed the connection between burial practices and sanitation. Pinfold introduces Dr George Walker, the local doctor who was one of the towering figures behind reform. Parliamentary legislation in responding to the second cholera outbreak in 1847–48 finally broke the web of local vested interests. It thereby set in motion the process by which the frame of reference for the disposal of the dead was switched from religious salvation to public health, and inaugurated the take-over by local authorities of responsibilities held by the Church for over one thousand years.

The failure to provide sufficient burial space is part of the context for my own discussion of Enon Chapel, a Baptist Church adjacent to the Green Ground. Built in 1821, Enon was closed by 1844. Enon provided a particular case for burial reformers who claimed that, within those 23 years, Enon had buried, below its floor-boards, 10–12000 dead bodies. Despite its prominence in Walker's campaign, this chapter is the first modern attempt to disentangle the Enon narrative. With the scandalous practices attributed to it, Enon was wholly untypical of Baptist Churches in its treatment of the dead. Yet all Baptist churches, because their children were not baptised, suffered from the Anglican discipline which forbad the burial of the unbaptised in consecrated churchyards. Thus Baptists, like Quakers and certain ethnic minority congregations, had normally to provide burial space for their own members. The context of inter-Church rivalry over the provision and control of (limited) burial space and their need, especially for voluntary and Dissenting churches in the towns, for burial fee income, made most Church authorities resistant to change. The extreme case of Enon Chapel illustrates the combination of ecclesiastical and secular pressures which, under the impulse of sanitary and social reform, led to the secularisation of burial space in mid-century Victorian Britain.

Julie Rugg provides a third perspective on burial reform with her discussion of private cemetery companies, 113 of which were formed between 1820 and 1853. She reconstructs, from company documents and the provincial press, the ethos and the achievements of an enterprise which, she argues, was in the vanguard of reform movements. Few cemetery companies operated strictly for profit: the joint-stock format chosen for private cemeteries reflected its far wider use in urban improvement in the early half of the century. Not all private cemetery companies were successful. Those that were represented two major concerns: a revived Protestant Nonconformity coupled, later, with a concern for public health.

Rugg thus challenges two assumptions. First, while Père Lachaise cemetery has often been assumed to have had the greatest influence upon English cemetery reforms, Rugg shows that there was no consensus on the attraction of Père Lachaise until the 1830s. By this time, Nonconformist-led companies had already been established to seek burial rights on a par with the Established Church. Thus Manchester preceded Paris. Second, Rugg challenges the role of Edwin Chadwick, the author of the Report *Interment in Towns* (1843). She shows not only that Chadwick was acting in a context where the need for burial reform on public health grounds had already been accepted, but that, in pressing for government action, Chadwick was concerned to belittle the earlier achievements of the private companies. Finally, Rugg emphasises that it was the companies, not Chadwick, who provided the successful model for the operation of the burials legislation of the 1850s. The provision of local authority cemeteries – as the eventual successors to parish churchyards – continued the tradition of a community response to a local though universal need.

Glennys Howarth takes up the theme of the commercialisation of death in an examination of the development of the funeral industry, whose origins were earlier discussed by Julian Litten. She analyses the subsequent development of the trade, in particular the shifts from executor-power to undertaker control in funeral arrangements. The role of religious ritual and the importance of the clergy at funerals had been truncated by the Reformation. The desire to express individual loss at death provided all sorts of entrepreneurial response, besides that of undertakers, but the latter, having first seized the initiative in establishing, applying and costing the code of funeral ostentation, maintained it as urbanisation advanced, exploiting the new needs raised, for example, by body-snatching fears and the travel arrangements necessitated by the new cemeteries. For Howarth, two critical stages in the reform of the undertaking industry were the early 1900s with a growing middle-class reaction against the parade of grief and funeral expense; and the Second World War, after which the search for simplicity in funerals spread to all classes, represented most sharply by the popularity of cremation. Significant twentieth-century developments are discussed: one such is the growth of trade associations like the British Undertakers

Association (1905) which was an attempt to protect the industry from allied trades, like carriage-masters. This was connected with rising professional aspirations, whereby less competent entrepreneurs were excluded and the ethos of other professionals, successively religious then medical, was adopted. New technology meanwhile offered new and profitable techniques, which indicate the key to funeral directors' current control: taking custody of the corpse.

In writing of the earliest Hindu cremations in Britain, Stephen White draws attention to the legal problems created by the increasing involvement of the state in the disposal of the dead, coupled with the legalisation of cremation. Local government responsibilities increased after the burials legislation of the 1850s, national government's with the rise of cremation agitation from 1874. The concern for public health was the major argument of pioneer cremationists. The Home Office became involved with cremation legislation when early criticism of cremation focused on its capacity for destroying criminal evidence. White's discussion of Hindu cremations illuminates the increasing role of law in the disposal of the dead by drawing attention to anomalies where the Home Office was prepared to dispense with specific legal requirements. The wider background to his analysis is the effects of the exigencies of war, politics and religion upon funerals. A first section discusses the arrangements for the cremation of Hindu soldiers killed on the Western Front. A second section concentrates on the Hindu funeral arrangements for members of the newly appointed Nepalese legation in London, involving complex negotiations both between the Nepalese and the Foreign, Home and India Offices and also the Cremation Society, now increasingly influential. The implications of the narrative and its resolution hint at the problems over the disposal of the dead after 1945. These issues include facilities for non-Christian death rituals in an era of a state-provided Health Service coupled with significant non-Christian immigration; the development of regulations for cremation as a mode of disposal now promoted by the state; and as a result of both these factors, the increased role and authority of medical personnel in death and disposal.

The enhanced roles of national and local government and the medical profession, along with the development of a multi-ethnic society, point at the increasingly marginalised role of the Christian religion in English death rituals. Secularisation is a theme common to the last three chapters and is first analysed in Alan Wilkinson's comparison of changing English attitudes to death in the two World Wars. Wilkinson explores the question, how was a democracy twice persuaded to accept death and bereavement in wartime upon such a vast scale? In the First World War, soldiers and their families drew upon a number of theodicies, including the Christian teaching about redemption through sacrifice (whose principal media were the Churches and Sunday Schools), the classical tradition (whose medium was the largely public school-educated officer class) as well as superstition, fatalism and humour. Traditional Christian doctrines of Hell and judgement underwent transition. War memorials, whereon the Classical/secular tradition challenged the Christian/religious, provide a sub-theme of the chapter and illustrate the political advantages to public authorities in interpreting death. Second World War writings illustrate different perceptions of death, with military conscription, in a war long anticipated and with heavy civilian losses. The ideological basis of the war against Nazi tyranny remained highly durable. There was therefore less need of Christian interpretations. Interwar secularisation also reduced resorts to spiritualism and to superstition. Nevertheless, a major responsibility of religion remains, to enable mortals both to cope with death and to interpret it.

Christine King analyses responses to one specific post-1945 death. Elvis Presley was the symbol of popular culture for a young American generation twice distanced from death: with no direct experience of (civilian) death in their parents' (foreign) war and with the enhanced (postwar) life-chances associated with greater health care and affluence. The sudden and early death of a cultural icon threatened the self-confidence of a generation, which resorted to a range of rituals of commemoration and bereavement, drawn from within and beyond the ethos of a Protestant society. These activities were not only spontaneous but also the result of marketing strategies by the entertainment industry. The scale of public mourning exceeded that accorded to President Kennedy. Paradoxically, whilst popular interest in the narrative of Presley's death helps interpret his death, the reluctance to accept these accounts symbolise its denial. In a longer perspective, one might add that this provides a second paradox. The capitalist market actually thrives on human mortality, because mortality, in limiting the time and opportunities for acquiring valued possessions, actually enforces a prioritisation of values. In enforcing choice, it promotes purchase. Meanwhile, in the Presley case, the entertainment market utilises a vision of immortality to exploit the purchasing instinct which normal mortality already encourages. The chapter provides examples of a range of religious and non-religious strategies for coping with sudden and early death, in a western world whose history and civilisation have not only distanced the generations but have shifted the prospect of death from junior to senior citizens.

There is, of course, a far longer pre-history behind contemporary attitudes to death. In the final chapter, Lindsay Prior analyses European statistical and medical developments that contributed to the de-mystification of the fact – and the probability – of death. The study of successive scientific representations of death has changed its image. Whilst death is every human's lot, its event was formerly conceived as random, unpredictable. Whilst all would die, anyone could die and at any time. Each seemed as likely to capitulate as the next: the image of dice.

Gambling first encouraged the discernment of the statistical laws of probability. De Moivre soon glimpsed, in a society still prone to believe in various forms of Providence and superstition, the secularising tendencies of this science. Studies of probability and mortality moved hand-in-hand: in the nineteenth century life tables were developed, especially by William Farr. These now calculated the life-expectancies of whole populations and of groups within them. The increasingly precise techniques for computing the probability, say, of surviving from one year to the next represent for Prior an 'actuarial vision of death'. Increasingly, life and death were no longer seen as a gamble. The insurance industry, for example, benefited from the growing realisation that death could be planned for rationally.

Yet this very rationality is not without bias. Farr himself was a miasmatist, an interpretation succeeded by the germ theory of disease. Whatever forms of classification were successively adopted to account for the cause of death, the role of human anatomy therein remained constant. Bertillon's nosology has remained the basis of classification for 100 years, steadily supplemented by such extra-anatomical factors as age, class and occupation. Yet these standardised classifications increasingly determine the facts they interpret. The classification of causes of death is culturally formed: the medical certificate, for example, upon which deaths are recorded, is completed according to sets of rules about what is, or is not, an acceptable cause of death. The classification of 'violent death' has also seen periodic readjustment (Prior, 1989). The medical standardisation of causes of death, Prior claims, helps to generate an illusion that death can be controlled. Death is caused not by 'old age' but by disease and is, therefore and theoretically, controllable. Simple individual precautions, like diets and exercise – without smoking – can ensure that the hitherto inevitable hour is itself postponed. These are the strictures of a cash-strapped National Health Service in a peacetime democracy.

Death knows less stable regimes, even today. Its universality will always bear a specific cultural face. Its ability to utter the last word will always need prior interpretation. We shall never be able, in this life, to post ourselves behind the candle which casts our shadow. Our ultimate glimpse of the face of death forbids any time for observations. Our knowledge of death must be constructed by its reflection in the faces of those other observers, whose time has not yet come.

REFERENCES

P. Ariès, *Western Attitudes Towards Death: from the Middle Ages to the Present*, (London: Marion Boyars, 1974).

P. Ariès, 'The Reversal of Death: Changes in Attitudes Towards Death in Western Societies', in D. E. Stannard (ed.), *op. cit.*, (1975).

P. Ariès, *The Hour of our Death*, (Harmondsworth: Penguin, 1981).

P. Ariès, transl. J. Lloyd, *Images of Man and Death*, (Cambridge, Mass.: Harvard University Press, 1985).

L. Barrow, *Independent Spirits: Spiritualism and English Plebeians, 1850–1910*, (London: Routledge & Kegan Paul, 1986).

S. Bassett, *Death in Towns*, (London: Leicester University Press, 1993).

Z. Bauman, *Modernity and the Holocaust*, (Cambridge: Polity, 1989).

G. Bennett, *Traditions of Belief*, (Harmondsworth: Penguin, 1987).

M. Bloch, 'Descent and Sources of Contradiction in Representations of Women and Kinship', in M. Bloch (ed.), *Ritual, History and Power*, (London: The Athlone Press, 1989).

M. Bloch and J. Parry (eds), *Death and the Regeneration of Life*, (Cambridge: Cambridge University Press, 1982).

A. Borg, *War Memorials*, (London: Leo Cooper, 1991).

J. Bowker, *The Meanings of Death*, (Cambridge: Cambridge University Press, 1991).

C. Brooks, *Mortal Remains*, (Exeter: Wheaton, 1989).

P. Brown, *The Cult of the Saints: Its Rise and Function in Latin Christianity*, (Chicago: University of Chicago Press, 1981).

D. Cannadine and S. Price, *Rituals of Royalty: Power and Ceremonial in Traditional Societies*, (Cambridge: Cambridge University Press, 1987).

E. Chadwick, 'A Supplementary Report on the Results of an Enquiry into the Practice of Interment in Towns' (*PP*, 1843)

F. Chalk and K. Jonassohn, *The History and Sociology of Genocide*, (New Haven: Yale University Press, 1990).

V. G. Childe, 'Directional Changes in Funerary Practices During 50 000 Years', *Man*, nos. 3–4, Jan–Feb 1945, pp. 13–19.

D. Clark (ed.), *The Future for Palliative Care: Issues of policy and practice*, (Buckingham: Open University Press, 1993a).

D. Clark (ed.), *The Sociology of Death*, (Oxford: Blackwell, 1993b).

D. Cohn-Sherbok and C. Lewis, *Beyond Death*, (Basingstoke: Macmillan, 1995).

H. Colvin, *Architecture and the After-Life*, (New Haven: Yale University Press, 1991).

J. S. Curl, *A Celebration of Death*, (London: Constable, 1980. Revised edition: London: Batsford, 1993).

L. M. Danforth, *The Death Rituals of Rural Greece*, (Princeton, N.J.: Princeton University Press, 1982).

J. Davies, *Ritual and Remembrance: Responses to Death in Human Societies*, (Sheffield: Sheffield Academic Press Ltd, 1994).

E. Duffy, *The Stripping of the Altars*, paperback edn (New Haven and London: Yale University Press, 1992).

N. Elias, *The Loneliness of the Dying*, (Oxford: Blackwell, 1985).

T. S. Eliot, *Murder in the Cathedral*, (London: Faber and Faber, various editions).

H. R. Ellis, *The Road to Hel*, (Cambridge: Cambridge University Press, 1943).

R. J. Evans, *Death in Hamburg: Society and Politics in the Cholera Years 1830–1910*, (Oxford: Oxford University Press, 1987).

R. J. Evans, *Rituals of Retribution: Capital Punishment in German History, 1600–1987*, (Oxford: Oxford University Press, 1996).

D. Field, *Nursing the Dying*, (London: Routledge/Tavistock, 1989).

D. Field, J. Hockey and N. Small (eds) *Death, Gender and Ethnicity*, (London: Routledge, 1996).

R. C. Finucane, *Miracles and Pilgrims*, (London: Dent, 1977).

P. Fussell, *The Great War and Modern Memory*, (Oxford: Oxford University Press, 1975).

P. Fussell, *Wartime; Understanding and Behaviour in the Second World War*, (Oxford: Oxford University Press, 1989).

M. Gilbert, *The Holocaust: The Jewish Tragedy*, (London: Collins, 1986).

C. Gittings, *Death, Burial and the Individual in Early Modern England*, (London: Croom Helm, 1984).

B. Glaser and A. Strauss, *Awareness of Dying*, (Chicago: Aldine, 1965).

B. Glaser and A. Strauss, *Time for Dying*, (Chicago: Aldine, 1968).

J. le Goff, *The Birth of Purgatory*, (London: Scolar, 1984).

J. Goody, 'Death and Social Control Among the LoDagaa', *Man,* vol. LIX (August 1959) pp. 134–8.

J. Goody, *Death, property and the ancestors. A study of the mortuary customs of the LoDagaa of West Africa,* (Stanford: Stanford University Press, 1962).

J. Goody, 'Death and the Interpretation of Culture: A Bibliographic Overview', in D. E. Stannard (ed.), *op. cit.*, (1975).

G. Gorer, 'The Pornography of Death', *Encounter*, 5 Oct. 1955, pp. 49–53.

J. Hick, *Death and Eternal Life*, (Glasgow: Collins, 1976).

J. Hockey, *Experiences of Death,* (Edinburgh: Edinburgh University Press, 1990).

R. Houlbrooke (ed.) *Death, Ritual and Bereavement*, (London: Routledge, 1989).

G. Howarth and P. C. Jupp (eds) *Contemporary Issues in the Sociology of Death, Dying and Disposal*, (Basingstoke: Macmillan, 1996).

R. Huntington and P. Metcalf, *Celebrations of Death: The Anthropology of Mortuary Ritual,* (Cambridge: Cambridge University Press, 1987).

P. C. Jupp, *The Development of Cremation in England 1820–1990: a sociological analysis,* (University of London, unpublished PhD thesis, 1993).

D. I. Kertzer, *Sacrificed for Honor,* (Boston, Mass.: Beacon Press, 1993).

T. A. Kselman, *Death and the Afterlife in Modern France*, (Princeton, N. J.: Princeton University Press, 1993).

W. Lessing, *Pictures at an Execution*, (Cambridge, Mass.: Harvard University Press, 1994).

L. McCray Beier, 'The Good Death in Seventeenth-Century England', in R. Houlbrooke (ed.), *op. cit.*, (1989).

P. Marris, *Loss and Change: Reports of the Institute of Community Studies*, (London: Routledge & Kegan Paul, 1974).

R. Mitchison, *British Population Changes Since 1860,* (London: Macmillan, 1977).

H. Morgenthau, 'Death in the Nuclear Age', in N. A. Scott Jr (ed.) *The Modern Vision of Death*, (Richmond, Va.: John Knox Press, 1967).

R. Nicol, *At the End of the Road*, (St Leonard's, N.S.W.: Allen & Unwin, 1994).

J. P. Parry, *Death in Banaras*, (Cambridge: Cambridge University Press, 1994).

R. Porter, 'Death and the Doctors in Georgian England', in R. Houlbrooke (ed.) *op. cit.*, (1989).

H. Potter, *Hanging in Judgement*, (London: SCM Press Ltd, 1993).

L. Prior, *The Social Organization of Death*, (Basingstoke: Macmillan, 1989).

R. Richardson, *Death, Dissection and the Destitute,* (London: Routledge & Kegan Paul, 1987).

L. Rose, *Massacre of the Innocents*, (London: Routledge & Kegan Paul, 1986).

G. Rowell, *Hell and the Victorians*, (Oxford: Oxford University Press, 1974).

G. Rowell, *The Liturgy of Christian Burial*, (London: Alcuin Club/S.P.C.K., 1977).

E. Shorter, *The Making of the Modern Family*, (London: Collins, 1976).

D. C. Sloane, *The Last Great Necessity: Cemeteries in American History*, (Baltimore: Johns Hopkins University Press, 1991).

D. E. Stannard (ed.) *Death in America*, (Pennsylvania: University of Pennsylvania Press, 1975).

D. Sudnow, *Passing on: The Social Organization of Dying*, (Englewood Cliffs, N. J.: Prentice-Hall, 1967).

L. Taylor, *Mourning Dress: A Costume and Social History*, (London: George Allen & Unwin, 1982).

P. Vitebsky, *Dialogues with the Dead: The discussion of mortality among the Sora of eastern India*, (Cambridge: Cambridge University Press, 1993).

D. P. Walker, *The Decline of Hell. Seventeenth-Century Discussions of Eternal Torment*, (London: Routledge & Kegan Paul, 1964).

T. Walter, *The Eclipse of Eternity: A Sociology of the Afterlife*, (Basingstoke: Macmillan, 1996).

J. L. Watson, 'Of Flesh and Bones: the Management of Death Pollution in Cantonese Society', in M. Bloch and J. Parry (eds) *op. cit.*, (1982).

A. Wilkinson, *The Church of England in the First World War*, (London: S.P.C.K., 1978).

M. Young, *The Metronomic Society: natural rhythms and human society*, (London: Thames and Hudson, 1988).

1   Expressions of Loss in Early Seventeenth-Century England

Clare Gittings

The early decades of the seventeenth century saw a revolution in funeral practices among the English aristocracy. The elaborate panoply of the heraldic funeral, controlled and orchestrated by members of the College of Arms, was replaced by speedy, torchlit burial by night, organised by the deceased's family. The word 'revolution' is not too strong here. Heraldic funerals had been established for about 150 years and were sanctioned by royal command. Yet, in a brief space of time, the heralds lost their hold over this major ritual among the greatest people in the land (Gittings, 1984).

Roy Strong, describing artistic development in England during the same era, also traces a revolution – 'a revolution in the sense of vision' (1969, p. 55). From this period come some of the most striking expressions of bereavement and loss in painting, sculpture, poetry and music ever produced in this country. The compartmentalisation of modern scholarship has tended to isolate each of these within its own subject discipline. However, to the bereaved patron, the commissioning of a painting, a tomb and an elegy, together with the deceased's funeral, were all part of the same process of mourning. This chapter will therefore examine the connections between these different expressions of loss, concentrating on a few examples each well-known within its own field, and explore common factors which influenced them.

When the Elizabethan ambassador Sir Henry Unton died in 1596 his widow Dorothy was involved with a whole range of different memorials to him, beginning with his funeral. A book of Latin verses in his memory was published by Oxford University and a tomb was erected over his grave with both inscription and sculpture. A picture was painted showing the story of his life and John Dowland composed a work entitled *Sir Henry Umpton's Funeral*. This chapter will examine each of these memorials to Sir Henry Unton and will then compare them with a memorial of a similar type from the early seventeenth century. It would be possible to find Elizabethan-style memorials similar to Unton's still being commissioned well into the seventeenth century, yet none of the seventeenth-century examples to be described here could have occurred during the sixteenth century. A very real change was happening.

THE CONTEXT OF CHANGE

The most immediately striking feature of such a comparison is the expression of sorrow in the early seventeenth-century examples where human grief was now openly displayed. The tenor of commemoration changed from a display of the deceased's position in the social hierarchy to a focus on the impact of loss on the bereaved. Status gave way to personal relationships as the prime area of expression.

This process has been ascribed to an increasing sense of individualism (Ariès, 1981; Gittings, 1984). This notion has aroused intense historical debate, considerable opposition and a degree of misunderstanding (Houlbrooke, 1989; Stone, 1977). It is possible to argue that an increasing sense of individualism can be traced in western history without saying that people in the past, or indeed in the many other areas of the world today with a less individualistic philosophy, are incapable of feeling with such intensity. Research suggests that emotions such as grief are basic human characteristics and vary little among different cultures (Stroebe and Stroebe, 1989). However, the way emotions are, or are not, expressed is very clearly culturally determined. So is the amount of comfort and assistance provided to the bereaved to work through their feelings – comfort coming both from human structures and from the religious or philosophical framework within which the bereavement occurs. These structures and frameworks, the culturally-mediated relationships between human beings themselves and between them and their gods, can certainly change to give greater prominence to the individual rather than to the wider group (Bloch and Parry, 1982). As such they affect the entire spectrum of human organisation and belief – religious, economic, social, sexual and so on. The fundamental causes of shifts in such underlying beliefs and structures will stimulate anthropological and historical debate for years. However, for the present, this chapter assumes that a growing emphasis on the unique individual can be found in early modern England, that this created increasing problems when that individual died, and that this helps explain changes in how the dead were commemorated.

Before examining these memorials in detail, three significant and interrelated strands in the background to the period should be considered. The first, which lies behind this chapter, and most of the chapters in this book, is the impact of the Protestant Reformation on attitudes to death. The second, especially for the purposes of this chapter, is the immediate politics of the time, the succession of James I to the throne of England following Elizabeth's death. The third, the cult of melancholy, relates to art forms in all media at this time and has a clear link with death.

The Protestant Reformation brought about a radical alteration in attitudes towards the dead, initially at the theological level through the abolition of the doctrine of Purgatory, and more gradually, thanks to the efforts of the Reformed clergy, among the population at large (Duffy, 1992; Gittings, 1984). It has recently been suggested that 'There is a case for saying that *the* defining doctrine of late medieval Catholicism was Purgatory' (Duffy, 1992, p. 8). Belief in Purgatory maintained strong links between the living and the dead, the prayers of the living shortening the torments of the deceased. It gave both a lifeline to the dying and a sense of purpose to the bereaved, who could still assist the deceased even after death. Eamon Duffy writes:

> the cult of the dead, so central in the pieties of every late medieval Catholic, was also in an important and often overlooked sense a cult of the living, a way of articulating convictions about the extent and ordering of the human community, and hence of what it was to be human. (1992, p. 8)

At the Reformation all this was swept away. The causes of the Protestant Reformation are too extensive to be examined in this chapter. However, it is worth recalling Ariès' conviction that exponents of the new spirituality 'exploit, rather than create, the tendencies of their times' (1981, p. 314). The underlying shift of emphasis from society to individual, indicated above, was accompanied by a similar shift of emphasis from the next world to this one, often described by the term humanism.

The effects of the Protestant Reformation on attitudes to death are well summarised by Keith Thomas:

> Protestant doctrine meant that each generation could be indifferent to the spiritual fate of its predecessor. Every individual was now to keep his own balance-sheet, and a man could no longer atone for his sins by the prayers of his descendants. This implied an altogether more atomistic conception of the relationship in which members of society stood to each other ... As a modern French historian puts it, 'Life ceased to look to death for its perspective.' (1978, p. 721, quoting Febvre, L., *Au Cœur religieux du XVIe siècle*, Paris, 1957, p. 58).

The Calvinist doctrine of predestination added a further element of uncertainty. Calvin wrote 'we must leave to God alone the knowledge of his church, whose foundation is his secret election' (Calvin, 1960, vol. 2, p. 1013). Neither the dying nor the bereaved could know whether a particular individual was among the elect, or was damned for eternity.

What the effects of these doctrinal changes actually felt like to an Anglican living in early seventeenth-century England may be gleaned from Sir Thomas Browne, in his *Religio Medici*:

> [I] have often wished it had been consonant to truth, and not offensive to my religion... [to be allowed] the prayer for the dead; whereunto I was

inclined from some charitable inducements, whereby I could scarce contain my prayers for a friend at the ringing of a bell, or behold his corpse without an orison for his soul. (1937, p. 9)

Browne's critic, Sir Kenelm Digby, certainly agreed with these sentiments. He had been driven back to Roman Catholicism by his desire to pray for his wife's soul, in so doing having to relinquish all hopes of public office, for which conformity with the Church of England was essential.

The death of Elizabeth I and the succession of James had a considerable impact on expressions of loss among the English aristocracy, particularly concerning funeral rituals. Elizabeth I kept strict control over the burial practices of the nobility and became, if anything, even more zealous as she aged. Heraldic funerals were a display of power, intended to reinforce the social hierarchy. In a sense they were performed almost to deny that a death had occurred at all; the whole emphasis was on continuity and on the undiminished strength of the aristocracy, despite the demise of one of its members. In reinforcing this hierarchic view Elizabeth was underlining her own position at the apex of the social order (Gittings, 1984).

James I, coming from Scotland, did not have the same grasp of the controlling mechanisms of English society. It is significant that some of the earliest deviations from heraldic burial were brought about by Scottish courtiers who had accompanied James to England. In 1616 John Chamberlain described how a Scottish courtier 'was solemnly buried in the night at Westminster with better than 200 torches, the Duke of Lenox... and all the grand Scottish men accompanying him' (1939, vol. I, p. 623).

The Scottish courtiers could also in part be blamed for the rapid deterioration of the tone of court life under the new king, so different from that of Elizabeth I's reign. Ultimately, however, the responsibility rested with James himself, whose uncouth and corrupt behaviour caused revulsion and despondency among the more cultivated and sensitive of the English aristocracy (Ashton, 1969).

In the arts, too, quite dramatic differences can be seen between the reigns of Elizabeth and James, and parallels made with their differing political outlooks. The Elizabethan period, especially in painting and sculpture, was characterised by insularity from the rest of Europe and by emphasis on symbolism and pattern rather than on naturalism. During James's reign, in broad terms, this insularity was eroded, in both politics and art, with naturalism coming to the fore, culminating, under Charles I, in the paintings of Van Dyck.

However, while this general alteration certainly did occur, the actual change of monarch was of lesser significance to the arts as the trend was well underway during the last decade of the old Queen's reign. Roy Strong described this as 'the collapse of the cut-out pasteboard Elizabethan world' and – in poetry as well as in art – cites neoplatonism as a prime cause of 'the artistic revolution of the [15]90s' (1969, pp. 52, 55). He adds: 'People who sit for their portraits in the 1590s are beginning to want to see themselves depicted less as symbols and more as vehicles of human emotion and feeling' (Strong, 1969, p. 36).

This new emphasis on psychology leads to the third significant influence on expressions of loss in this period – the development of the cult of melancholy. This occurred in England at exactly the same time as Strong's 'artistic revolution'. Again, one of the main influences on the development of this cult was neoplatonism, in particular the work of the Florentine, Marsilio Ficino, which led to a revision in the basic understanding of human psychology at this period (Strong, 1969).

Melancholy was one of the four humours which were believed to make up the human personality. It would be natural for anyone bereaved to be melancholy, but in some people the humour dominated so that they were fundamentally melancholic by temperament; Hamlet is the best literary example. Melancholia could also be an illness (MacDonald, 1981), but that lies outside the scope of this chapter. In astrological terms, melancholy was associated with Saturn; both underwent a revaluation in the early modern period. In medieval, Galenic philosophy, melancholy had been highly undesirable. However, at the Renaissance, the Aristotelian view was revived which associated melancholy with intellectual excellence, and so the cult of melancholy was born. It reached England from Italy, particularly through the travels of young English gentlemen on the sixteenth- and seventeenth-century equivalent of the grand tour (Babb, 1951; Harrison, 1929; Knights, 1937; Strong, 1969; Yates, 1979).

A number of aspects of the period from the late 1580s to the first stirrings of the Civil War created the mood for melancholy. One was undoubtedly the problem of death resulting from Reformation theology; for the generations born after the first flush of enthusiasm for Protestantism, the uncertainties could become overwhelming. The uncertainties of the next world were compounded by uncertainties in this world – insufficient posts were available for the many young gentlemen seeking preferment, especially for those of an academic disposition. Renaissance humanism, with its greater focus on present life rather than the hereafter, highlighted the differences between ideal and actual existence; this disparity became even more marked during the sordid excesses of James I's reign. All this was fertile ground for the cult of melancholy to flourish; Robert Burton was its principal English apologist.

In his *Anatomy of Melancholy*, published in 1621, Burton expounded the new creed: 'Melancholy men of all others are the most witty... [they are] excellent philosophers, poets, prophets etc.' (Strong, 1969, p. 352). Sir

Thomas Overbury, writing ten years earlier, described the appropriate setting for melancholy: the melancholic will 'seldom be found without the shade of some grove in what bottom a river dwells' (Harrison, 1929, p. 69). Shakespeare, in *Love's Labours Lost*, advises how the melancholic should dress: 'with your hat penthouse-like o'er the shop of your eyes, with your arms crossed on your thin belly, like a rabbit on a spit' (Act 3, Scene I). Hamlet, in Ophelia's description, displays the sartorial dishevelment which also denotes melancholy. In literature and painting, especially the more intimate art of miniature painting, can be found melancholics just as these writers describe, while in music their sadness is made audible. However, melancholy was not merely an artistic creation; real people suffered from it, too.

A number of factors predisposed people towards melancholy, one, of course, being bereavement. Melancholy was associated with love in real life, as well as in art. Foreign travel, especially to Italy, was another contributing factor, as was intellectual endeavour. A rather different impetus towards melancholy came from political disenchantment and concern over one's status, sufferers being called 'malcontents'. Often their disillusionment arose from having unorthodox religious views tending towards the extremes of Protestantism or Roman Catholicism, effectively excluding them from political life.

How far the various expressions of loss described in this chapter were the products of melancholic artists and patrons will be discussed later. Even some of the memorials to Sir Henry Unton have elements of melancholy; indeed Dowland's *Sir Henry Umpton's Funeral* has a melancholy practically unparalleled in music. The Unton memorial picture, while in general far from melancholic in tone, contains one representation of Unton lying on the ground beside his tomb, without his ruff, holding scrolls, now damaged, which read 'Oh living gods ... to die ... poor wretch ... am I.' The characteristics of melancholy would explain this otherwise rather puzzling section of the painting.[1]

FUNERAL RITUALS

The funeral of Sir Henry Unton is recorded both in documents in the College of Arms and in the Unton memorial picture (Strong, 1965). Both sources emphasise the central role of the heralds; in the picture, their tabards of the arms of Elizabeth I stand out dramatically from the black-clad mourners, showing most forcefully the source of all aristocratic power. The funeral was an elaborate affair, not least because, dying while on a diplomatic mission in France, Unton had first to be:

> brought over to London, and from thence he was worshipfully accompanied and carried in a coach to Wadley ... and in the parish church there buried

on Thursday the 8th day of July 1596, with a Baron's hearse, and in the degree of a Baron, because he died Ambassador Leger for France. (Strong, 1965, p. 65)

It is ironic that Unton reached his social apogee only after his death. Dorothy, his widow, clearly placed high importance on his funeral as it occupies a substantial area of the picture recording his life story. Being a woman, she would not have had a role at the burial; her husband was followed to his grave by seven barons and a wealth of heraldry, stressing that the power of the aristocracy was unweakened by his death. The heraldic funeral displayed continuity, not loss, and was concerned with the social standing, not the affective relationships, of the deceased (Gittings, 1984).

The outward forms of Dorothy's mourning were suitably proper, as a friend described:

She has very well beautified her sorrow with all the ornaments of an honourable widow. Her black velvet bed, her Cyprus veil, her voice tuned with a mournful accent, and her cupboard ... adorned with prayer-books and epitaphs do make her chamber look like the house of sorrow. (Strong, 1965, p. 71)

In contrast, when the Duke of Richmond and Lenox died in 1624 his widow, Frances, was far less restrained:

His lady takes it extreme passionately, cut off her hair that day with divers other demonstrations of extraordinary grief ... [his] loss she takes so impatiently and with so much show of passion that many odd and idle tales are daily reported or invented of her ... (Chamberlain, 1939, vol. II, pp. 545 and 551)

However, the Duchess persisted in her grief for 15 years, having her portrait painted in mourning, wearing a heart-shaped miniature of her husband. In her will she declared: 'With the loss of my Lord all earthly joys ended with me, and I ever computed his funeral day my burial' (Gittings, 1984, p. 193).

The Duchess's own funeral contrasts strongly with that of Sir Henry Unton, some 40 years earlier. By 1639, night funerals were well-established. Attempts by the College of Arms to stamp them out, even though backed by royal command, had proved futile. Frances herself willed:

that I may be speedily buried and not opened for so my sweet Lord out of his tender love commanded me that I should not be opened. I may be presently put up in bran, and in lead before I am fully cold. (Gittings, 1984, p. 190)

Frances continued in her will: 'Let them wind me up again in those sheets ... wherein my Lord and I first slept that night when we were married', again stressing the importance of affective relationships in her funeral preparations. Her burial itself was to be held on the first night a clear 24 hours after her death. She avoided the social coercion which often marked heraldic funerals by directing it should be 'without ... any great persons to be invited but if they come of their own good will let them be respectively and dutifully used' (Gittings, 1984, p. 191). She certainly was not trying to save money by having a night funeral. Two hundred poor people attended her interment in Westminster Abbey, each given a mourning gown that was 'not too short' and carrying a torch. In all, the funeral and associated gifts to charity, together with keeping her household in mourning for three or four weeks, cost £2000. By choosing to be buried by night Frances was able to exercise far more control over her interment than if it had been left to the heralds, and could manipulate the ritual to reflect personal feelings rather than just status.

On Henry Unton's death a volume of memorial verses in Latin, collected by his chaplain Robert Wright, was published by Oxford University (1596). Previously, only Sir Philip Sidney had received this honour, the more heroic nature of Sidney's death making the writers' task somewhat easier. The Unton verses are of little literary merit (Strong, 1965); their tone can be gathered from a translation of the title: 'Funeral elegies composed by the Fellows of Oxford University in mourning and regret for the precious memory of the noble and distinguished knight, Lord Henry Unton, twice royal ambassador to France, where lately it was his fate to die.'

COMMEMORATION

Verse of a very different quality was produced 15 years later by John Donne on the death of Elizabeth Drury, the 15-year-old daughter of Donne's patron Sir Robert Drury. Donne had never actually met Elizabeth when she died in 1610, but wrote some of his finest verse in her memory, particularly the *Second Anniversary* (Bald, 1986; Carey, 1981). The poems inspired by her death inhabit a completely different mental world from the Unton elegies. Her death, in *The First Anniversary*, brings about the disintegration of heaven, of the world and of the whole fabric of society, leaving individuals isolated without any structure, for which Donne employs the metaphor of the phoenix:

> 'Tis all in pieces, all coherence gone,
> All just supply and all relation:
> Prince, subject, father, son, are things forgot,
> For every man alone thinks he hath got
> To be a phoenix, and that then can be
> None of that kind, of which he is, but he ...
>
> (Donne, 1933, p. 214)

Choosing to convey the impact of a young girl's death through the imagery of the annihilation of the hierarchic world-order, not surprisingly, brought protests of extravagance. Jonson called the *Anniversaries* 'profane and full of blasphemies', adding that, if written about the Virgin Mary, 'it had been something' (Cary, 1981, p. 102). Most criticism centred on Elizabeth Drury's low social status. Donne was himself anxious that another patron, Lucy, Countess of Bedford, would feel slighted, and began a poem of apology:

> First I confess I have to other lent
> Your stock ...
> (Bald, 1986, p. 251)

Interestingly, no surviving criticism questions the central notion that the entire universe could be shattered by one individual's death, although this notion has worried twentieth-century critics immensely (Carey, 1981). Donne's imagery found contemporary favour with Joseph Hall, later Bishop of Norwich, who himself believed that 'the world groweth old' (Bald, 1986, p. 243). The world-view of the *Anniversaries* is very different from the self-perpetuating hierarchy enshrined in the heraldic funeral.

Henry Unton's monument in Faringdon Church is now incomplete, having suffered during the Civil War (Strong, 1965). However, its inscription has survived and records, in Latin, Unton's main achievements – his knighthood, his ambassadorship and so on. Typical of many Elizabethan inscriptions, it reveals only Unton's public face.

In the early seventeenth century a new type of inscription began to appear on monuments. This example comes from the tomb of Lord Tanfield, died 1625, at Burford, Oxfordshire, composed by his wife:

> Here shadows lie
> Whilst earth is sad;
> Still hopes to die
> To him she had.
>
> In bliss is he
> Whom I loved best;
> Thrice happy she
> With him to rest.
>
> So shall I be
> With him I loved;
> And he with me,
> And both us blessed.

> Love made me poet,
> And this I writ
> My heart did do it,
> And not my wit.
> (Gittings, 1984, p. 201)

She adds that she herself erected 'this monument of his virtues and her sorrows'.

The emergence of this type of inscription, recording the private, affective face of the deceased, is not necessarily evidence of a greater depth of feeling between husbands and wives, yet it reveals that it had become acceptable to express those feelings publicly on a church monument. The change is at the societal level, rather than the individual, but leads to the commemoration of the dead with greater individuality.

The figure of his widow Dorothy is, with the inscription, the only part of Unton's tomb to survive. Taken with the memorial picture, they give some idea of how the monument would have looked on its completion in 1606. It was typical of many Jacobean monuments, Sir Henry lying stiffly in armour with his hand under his cheek – in Webster's words, 'as if [he]... died of the toothache' (Gittings, 1984, p. 202) – and Dorothy kneeling.

Sixteen years later the same type of composition was commissioned from Epiphanius Evesham, 'that most exquisite artist', by the widow of Christopher Roper, Lord Teynham, at Lynsted, Kent. While employing the same elements – the recumbent man and the kneeling widow – Evesham's tomb has a totally different feel:

> He is completely relaxed and resigned looking with open eyes slightly outwards. Her noble face, strained with the effort of keeping back her grief, is framed by the backward-sweeping look of her widow's hood – and one can't take one's eyes from it. (Newman, 1983, p. 378)

Brian Kemp, outlining the development of English tombs, cites this as the supreme example of a new trend in monuments which 'emphasised ... more intimately the sense of grief and loss occasioned by the death of a member of the family, especially the distress felt by the surviving spouse' (1980, p. 105). It is the complete antithesis of earlier monuments commemorating the public achievements of the deceased. Here the personal is given prominence and the message is one of loss, not continuity.

The Unton memorial picture is a unique survival; there is nothing which can compare with its complexity, giving, as it does, a pictorial survey of the whole of his life. However, the section portraying Unton's death in France does have parallels in the seventeenth century, the finest example being Van

Dyck's picture of Lady Venetia Digby on her deathbed (Gittings, 1995). The Unton picture is schematic rather than naturalistic; the unknown artist is painting scenes he has been told about rather than witnessed. In the death scene Unton is shown in bed, but still alive. The French king's doctor is taking his pulse, an honour to Unton but ultimately to no avail; bowls of blood testify to further medical ministrations. A servant weeps while others wait and pray; death, a skeleton with dart and hourglass, hovers nearby.

The circumstances surrounding Venetia Digby's deathbed portrait are recorded in the letters of her husband, Sir Kenelm Digby. She died suddenly in her sleep in 1633, leaving her husband devastated. Digby wrote of the portrait:

> It is the master-piece of all the excellent ones that ever Sir Anthony Van Dyck made, who drew her the second day after she was dead; ... and hath altered or added nothing about it, excepting only a rose lying upon the hem of the sheet, whose leaves [petals] being pulled from the stalk in the full beauty of it, and seeming to wither apace, even whilst you look upon it, is a fit emblem to express the state her body then was in ... One could not distinguish whether it were of a sleeping or of a dead body;...it had the advantage to deceive one in judging whether it were a picture or not. (Gabrieli, 1957, p. 246)

Sir Kenelm Digby lamented that the portrait 'is the only constant companion I now have.' He recorded how, when it was first delivered:

> her old servant brought in ... [the] picture and set it down before me, going immediately out again without speaking one word; which I perceived his tears that ran trickling down his cheeks would not permit him to do. (Gabrieli, 1957, p. 246)

Although as much as two thirds of the Unton memorial picture concerns his death and burial, its tone is completely different from the Digby portrait. Unton's death and burial are acknowledgements of his worldly honour, symbolised by the personification of fame who descends from the heavens with a trumpet and his well-earned wreath of laurels. The Digby deathbed has none of this triumphalism; it is darker, sadder and far more moving.

By far the finest of all the memorials to Unton is Dowland's music; indeed, it is among Dowland's best works. It forms one of the *Lachrimae* published in 1604 and the opening four falling notes could be interpreted as falling tears, in the dolorous key of G minor; it was not actually composed for the funeral itself, however, as Dowland was abroad in 1596 (Poulton, 1982). Much seventeenth-century music still awaits appreciation but it is hard to imagine that *Sir Henry Umpton's Funeral* would be easily surpassed. The memorials to Sir Henry Unton previously discussed in this chapter were in the older Elizabethan tradition. However, in commissioning this work from John Dowland, Dorothy Unton can be considered among the innovative patrons who wished to create memorials stressing loss.

CONCLUSION

How do these various expressions of loss relate to the cult of melancholy? One way to approach this problem is to ask whether the people who were commissioning and creating these memorials were themselves melancholics, or how far their lives contained the factors, outlined earlier, predisposing people to melancholy. The exact relationship between artist and patron is far from clear, but all these patrons at the very least approved the finished memorials. The role of women, and especially widows, is of particular interest; afforded less social significance, it was possible for them more easily to present themselves or to be represented in unusual and innovative ways.[2] Several of the women involved with these memorials were extremely assertive individuals; both the Duchess of Richmond and Lenox and Lady Tanfield were fearsome to their tenants, while Dorothy Unton drew up a marriage settlement aggressively in her own favour, of which her second husband rapidly fell foul (*D.N.B.*, Tanfield; Stone, 1965; Strong, 1965). It is perhaps not surprising that their memorial commissions are equally distinctive.

Several of the people discussed in this chapter were recognisable melancholics. Biographers of both Dowland and Donne describe them as melancholic; indeed Donne had himself painted in a large black hat as a melancholy lover (Cary, 1981; Poulton, 1982). Some of the others clearly went through melancholic phases – Frances, Duchess of Richmond and Lenox, in her prolonged mourning, or Sir Kenelm Digby who, for two years after Venetia's death:

> retired into Gresham College at London, where he diverted himself with chemistry and the professors' good conversation. He wore there a long mourning cloak, a high crowned hat, his beard unshorn, looked like a hermit, as signs of sorrow for his beloved wife ... (Aubrey, 1898, vol. I, pp. 226–7)

The different factors predisposing towards melancholy may be found, to differing degrees, in the lives of the people looked at in this chapter. While the key figures discussed here were of high status – even the sculptor Evesham was a gentleman's son (Esdaile, 1981) – many had worries about either their own status or that of their spouse. Before becoming a duchess, Frances Stuart had been married off to a wine merchant, a severe dent to her pride (Stone, 1965). Tradition has it that Lady Tanfield was furious that her husband was not buried in Westminster Abbey. Lord Teynham's father had paid James I £10000 for his baroncy, which even in a reign noted for blatant corruption, occasioned hostile comment (Stone, 1965). Donne's patron Robert Drury never fulfilled his lifelong ambition to become a diplomat, a role for which his quick temper made him highly unsuitable (Bald, 1986).

Several of the people associated with these memorials suffered penalties for being Roman Catholic. John Dowland was born and died a Protestant, but for some years embraced Catholicism; after his rejection by Elizabeth I as a court musician he wrote: 'My religion was my hindrance, whereupon my mind being troubled, I desired to get beyond the seas' (Grove, *Dict. Mus.*, Dowland). Lord and Lady Teynham were life-long Catholics, which excluded him from high office; Evesham, who made tombs for other recusant families incorporating Catholic imagery, may well have been a convert to Catholicism (Esdaile, 1981). Donne's career would have been impossible if he had remained a Catholic; only Van Dyck, being a foreigner, escaped the usual adversity associated with Catholicism. Kenelm Digby's father was executed as a Gunpowder Plot conspirator; Digby himself, after a brief spell as an Anglican, reverted to Catholicism. The degree of religious ambivalence shown by these people is interesting, hovering between Protestantism and Catholicism with their two very different doctrines of death. Digby's letters reveal that it was the desire to pray for Venetia's soul after her death which prompted his reconversion (Gabrieli, 1957).

Foreign travel and links with abroad played a substantial part in many of these people's lives. Dowland, Evesham and Van Dyck all worked abroad for several years. Donne and his patron Drury made a foreign tour together while Digby travelled widely. Both Digby and the Teynhams had female relatives in Catholic convents on the continent (Esdaile, 1981). Additionally Donne and Digby engaged in considerable intellectual activity; incidentally, both concluded that the world was decaying (Bald, 1986; Gabrieli, 1957).

As has been suggested, it can be dangerous to make value-judgements about the quality of couples' relationships in the past. However no one reading the letters of Digby or Donne would deny the depth of feeling revealed; likewise Lady Tanfield's lines, the mourning of the Duchess of Richmond and Lenox, and Dorothy Unton's forebodings about a second marriage all suggest strong feelings, if sometimes tinged with *egotism à deux*. It is also clear that a number of these relationships were afflicted with the anxiety of having no heir, denying these people the traditional form of replacement after death in a hierarchical society. Both Drury's children died young, the Untons and the Duchess were childless while the Tanfields just had one daughter.

From these examples it would seem that the lives of the creators and commissioners of some of the most striking expressions of loss in this period were coloured by clusters of factors, whether political, religious or emotional, that predisposed them towards melancholy. It could well be argued that these same factors led them to create funerals, tombs and other works of art which reflected irrevocable loss and change when an individual died, rather than the unchanging, hierarchic replaceability of one person by another. In so doing, they were making visible a major revolution in attitudes towards life and death.

NOTES

1   C. Phythian-Adams, Leicester University (personal communication).
2   A. White, Temple Newsam House, Leeds (personal communication).

REFERENCES

P. Ariès, *The Hour of Our Death*, trans. H. Weaver (London: Allen Lane, 1981).

R. Ashton, *James I by his Contemporaries*, (London: Hutchinson, 1969).

J. Aubrey, *Brief Lives*, ed. A. Clark, 2 vols. (Oxford, 1898).

L. Babb, *The Elizabethan Malady: a study of melancholia in English Literature 1580 –1642*, (East Lansing, Mich., 1951).

R. C. Bald, *John Donne a Life*, paperback edn. (Oxford: Clarendon Press, 1986).

M. Bloch and J. Parry, *Death and the Regeneration of Life*, (Cambridge: Cambridge University Press, 1982).

T. Browne, *Religio Medici and Other Writings*, Everyman edn. (London: J. M. Dent & Sons, 1937).

J. Calvin, *Institutes of the Christian Religion*, ed. J. T. McNeill (Philadelphia: Westminster Press, 1960), vol. 2.

J. Carey, *John Donne: Life, Mind and Art*, (London: Faber, 1981).

J. Chamberlain, *The Letters of John Chamberlain*, ed. N.E.M. McClure, 2 vols. (Philadelphia, 1939).

D.N.B. (Dictionary of National Biography).

J. Donne, *The Poems of John Donne*, ed. H.J.C. Grierson (London: Oxford University Press, 1933).

E. Duffy, *The Stripping of the Altars: Traditional Religion in England c. 1400 – c. 1580*, paperback edn. (New Haven and London: Yale University Press, 1992).

E. Esdaile, ' "A Most Exquisite Artist" the work of Epiphanius Evesham', *Country Life*, vol. 169, no. 4373 (1981) 1970–73.

V. Gabrieli, *Sir Kenelm Digby, Un Inglese Italianato*, (Rome, 1957).

C. Gittings, *Death, Burial and the Individual in Early Modern England*, (London: Croom Helm, 1984).

C. Gittings, 'Venetia's Death and Kenelm's Mourning', in A. Sumner (ed.), *Death, Passion and Politics*, (London: Dulwich Picture Gallery, 1995).

G. B. Harrison, 'An Essay on Elizabethan Melancholy', in N. Breton, *Melancholike Humours,* (London, 1929).

R. Houlbrooke (ed.) *Death, Ritual and Bereavement*, (London: Routledge, 1989).

B. Kemp, *English Church Monuments*, (London: Batsford, 1980).

L. C. Knights, *Drama and Society in the Age of Jonson*, (London: Chatto and Windus, 1937).

M. MacDonald, *Mystical Bedlam: Madness, Anxiety and Healing in Seventeenth-Century England,* (Cambridge: Cambridge University Press, 1981).

J. Newman, *The Buildings of England: North East and East Kent*, (Harmondsworth: Penguin, 1983).

D. Poulton, *John Dowland*, (London: Faber, 1982).

L. Stone, *The Crisis of the Aristocracy*, (London: Oxford University Press, 1965).

L. Stone, *The Family, Sex and Marriage in England 1500–1800*, (London: Oxford University Press, 1977).

W. Stroebe and M. Stroebe, *Bereavement and Health: The psychological and physical consequences of partner loss*, paperback edn. (Cambridge: Cambridge University Press, 1989).

R. Strong, 'Sir Henry Unton and his Portrait: An Elizabethan Memorial Picture and its History', *Archaeologia*, XCIX (1965) 53–76.

R. Strong, *The English Icon: Elizabethan and Jacobean Portraiture*, (London: Paul Mellon Foundation for British Art, 1969).

K. V. Thomas, *Religion and the Decline of Magic: studies in popular beliefs in sixteenth- and seventeenth-century England*, paperback edn. (Harmondsworth: Penguin, 1978).

R. Wright (ed.) *Funebria Nobilissima ad Praestantissimi Equjitis D. Henrici Untoni*, (Oxford, 1596).

F. Yates, *The Occult Philosophy in the Elizabethan Age*, (London: Routledge & Kegan Paul, 1979).

2 'A Kind of Lawful Adultery': English Attitudes to the Remarriage of Widows, 1550–1800

Stephen Collins

This chapter is about widows, and about attitudes to their remarriage which prevailed in England from the mid sixteenth century until the end of the eighteenth. I shall start by describing the almost universal opposition to the remarriage of widows, and then move on to offer some tentative explanations for it.

An initial flavour may be had from the case of Hesther Piozzi, formerly Mrs Thrale, a prominent blue-stocking, and a close friend and subsequent biographer of Samuel Johnson. In 1784, Mrs Thrale, a widow of some years' standing, married Gabriel Piozzi. She thereby became one of the subjects of a late eighteenth-century book called *The Female Jockey Club*, a scurrilous and unpleasant work about a number of contemporary women to whom the anonymous author had taken exception. Of Mrs Piozzi and her marriage, he has this to say:

> rich and jolly – little more than forty, with warm passions, which the parturition of a dozen children had not been able to subdue. ... [She] falled in love ... yet it were barbarous to deny a blooming widow the right of pleasing herself in an affair, where female happiness is so intimately connected ... who had been so long accustomed to hymeneal enjoyments, that she knew not how to submit to a solitary life of celibacy. (Anon., 1794)

My reason for unearthing this distasteful pamphlet is not because it has any literary merit, but as an example of the way in which a widow's remarriage was still being viciously criticised at the very end of the eighteenth century. A similar disapproval, with similar thinking behind it, had made up the dominant view of the matter for the previous three centuries, and this disapproval is the theme of this chapter. In describing and analysing it, I shall draw on two main bodies of material. The first is the extensive didactic and polemical literature on marriage that existed in the form of advice on the subject, and of discussion, often frivolous, of the institution of marriage itself. Secondly, I shall refer to imaginative literature, not, obviously, as evidence of how people actually lived, but to illustrate the climate of opinion with which this chapter is concerned – and it must be stressed that it is this climate of thought that is my subject, not the real lives of real widows, many of whom remarried despite the often repugnant rhetoric with which the matter was discussed, and the fears that lay behind the rhetoric.

A widow who contemplated the disapproval and ridicule of her potential marriage might have asked herself why nothing comparable seemed to exist for the remarriage of widowers. Occasional writers on the subject did raise the point that what was sauce for the goose was sauce for the gander (Anon., 1683; Anon., 1706), but such evenhandedness was rare, and throughout the period it was overwhelmingly the remarriage of women that was at issue. This is not altogether surprising in a society which not only tolerated significantly different standards of sexual behaviour for men and for women, but which embodied legal and conventional discrimination against women in terms of property and opportunity. All that follows must be understood in the context of the prevailing double standard which so disfigured the moral life of the period.

There was nothing illegal about remarriage in either ecclesiastical or civil law. Legality was not, however, the same thing as approval: a character in an early seventeenth-century play describes 'widows' marriages, as being but a kind of lawful adultery, like usury permitted by the law, not approved' (Chapman, *c*. 1605/1975, pp. 49f.). Although Christian tradition allowed remarriage, it is probably true to say that it was unenthusiastic. Jesus said nothing of substance on the subject, but St Paul insisted that both marriage and remarriage were permissible. St Paul's opinion was hardly a ringing endorsement of either, for he made clear that celibacy was on the whole to be preferred, concluding his advice with the grim epigram 'It is better to marry than to burn' – and there is, by the way, little discrimination between men and women in his comments (1 Corinthians 7: 9). A reference to 'widows that are widows indeed' (1 Timothy 5: 11) appears to associate remarriage with younger widows who have 'begun to wax wanton against Christ', but seems to be more about the potential usefulness of widows in the early church than advice about daily life. The Fathers of the Church, notably St Augustine and St Jerome, were cool about remarriage, though this has to be put in the context of a celebration of celibacy, and an assumption that marriage was not something in which the spiritual élite, endowed with the gift of continence, would engage (Augustine, 1952; Kelly, 1975).

Such ambivalence survived well into the nineteenth century. Significant defences of remarriage were few and far between (Whatley, 1619): there is a particularly magisterial support for the remarriage of widows in a sermon by John Donne (1956), but most writers on the subject began by making clear that remarriage was legally and scripturally acceptable, and then got down to setting out their scorn and disapproval. Though the theological and civil aspects of widows marrying were scarcely an issue, there was a high measure of agreement that it would be better if they did not. The argument is presented in two ways.

First, there was a highly idealised image of widowhood. With the death of her husband, a woman lost the best part of herself, and had completed the purpose for which she had been made. But God's will had been done, and all that remained was to embrace the limited opportunities now available to a woman deprived of a man's guiding hand, and to await her own dissolution with uncomplaining patience. The virtuous widow by her behaviour continued to honour her husband, and she kept his memory alive by constantly rehearsing his merits far more effectively than brass or stone or gilded monument. She lived as a chaste matron, caring for her children both for themselves and because they were her husband's, and, freed from the cares of marriage, was able to devote her new leisure to piety and charity (Vives, 1541; Heywood, 1657; Kenrick, 1701).

Such was the ideal. It was not, though, perhaps the most enticing of prospects, and it was backed up by the second broad approach to remarriage: a ruthless criticism of widows who chose to disregard the ideal by remarrying. Their behaviour was treated with heartless cynicism, and made the subject of a series of jokes and canards that crop up regularly both in imaginative literature and in polemical writing – and the subject is hardly ever dealt with in terms of rational argument. It is possible to divide this material up according to whether it was primarily addressed to men, aimed at discouraging them from marrying widows, or at women, urging them to remain single. To start with the supposed disadvantage for men, a widow was depicted as a very poor substitute for a spinster; so, for example, when Dr Johnson was told of the marriage of a friend, he snorted 'He has done a very foolish thing, Sir; he has married a widow, when he might have had a maid' (Boswell, 1906, I, p. 360).

A large part of the appeal of spinsters was that they were expected to be sexually inexperienced. Throughout the period it was taken more or less for granted that a virgin was to be preferred to a widow as a marriage partner. There were two main reasons given for this. The first was that a wife who had not previously been married was in no position to compare her husband – to his detriment – with anyone else. A constant theme in the advice not to marry widows, for example, played on men's incipient sexual insecurities, and implied a guarantee that any inadequacy in bed would be hidden from a woman who had no experience against which to judge her husband's sexual performance (Fielding, 1965, p. 330). Not only sexually, but in all areas of domestic life a widow was placed to make odious comparisons, and would be forever pointing out the inferiority of her present husband compared with his predecessor, who was a better worker, provider, manager, and, in a text of 1652, more considerate in that he farted in bed more decorously. The general advice, regularly repeated, was that anyone wishing to avoid such comparisons should marry only a widow whose husband had been hanged, but even then might be better advised to find a spinster (Vives, 1541; Anon., 1652; Seymar, 1673; Anon., 1747b; *Spectator*, 1965 p. 518; W., E., 1718).

Secondly, a virgin was presumed to be more sexually disciplined than a widow. By preserving her chastity, she had demonstrated a self-control that gave promise of marital fidelity. A frequent and wearisome charge against women was their supposed sexual voraciousness. This was not only liable to erupt in adultery, but in the foisting of children on to a cuckold who was not their father and whose estate they inherited, in a blow at the very basis of the social order. A widow was particularly suspect, for by even contemplating remarriage she was demonstrating a level of sexual appetite that boded ill for marital faithfulness. The argument was that marriage unlocked a woman's sexuality, and that men were hard put to it to contain it: a widow 'the fontinel of whose desires hath been opened by the former permissions of the marriage bed' (Taylor, 1650/1863) showed by her readiness to remarry that she was going to be particularly hard to contain, and that adultery and a brood of doubtful children were to be expected.

Apart from not being virgins, widows had other disadvantages for the man in search of a wife. One was that they were persistently assumed to be old. Clearly many will have been nothing of the sort, but their almost invariable depiction as old and toothless was a routine part of the disparagement of widows. Another disadvantage concerned children. If they had none, they might be sterile, which was a major drawback (Richardson, 1750); if they were past child-bearing age, what business had they marrying when they were unable to fulfil the main purpose of marriage (Defoe, 1727)? If they did have children, these at best would cost the earth to feed and at worst would be predatory monsters: 'The man who marries a woman with four children marries five thieves' was a proverb approvingly quoted by authors throughout the period (Vives, c. 1550; Seymar, 1673; Ward, c. 1720; Anon., 1755).

Widows, then, were depicted as old, sexually out of control, liable to make humiliating comparisons, and as either sterile or encumbered with costly or dishonest children: hardly the sort of companion a judicious man would choose. These disadvantages might become less significant if the widow were rich, but even then her attractions might still be illusory:

> Is it a rich widow you would marry, you are forever ruined; she'll not only make away all beforehand to her children, but continue as long as she lives to furnish them out of your estate. (Anon., 1755)

A similarly unsavoury and coercive body of images was commonplace in writing addressed to widows by way of discouragement to remarriage. Again, sex dominated the argument – and to reduce the question of remarriage to the issue of sex is wilfully perverse in some of these writers who often show great depths of understanding of personal relationships, and who were well aware that marriage involved a lot more than coition. Yet with a notable lack of generosity, the many reasons for marrying, such as the human characteristic of companionability, the potential pleasure in an often harsh world, and the practical and economic conveniences, were disregarded. The supposed sexual indiscipline of widows was given as their sole motive (Davies, 1975, pp. 171ff.; *Tatler*, 1987; *Spectator*, 1965; Miller, 1734). In Chapman's play *The Widow's Tears*, a virtuous widow committed to the ideal of perpetual mourning for her husband changes her mind within the space of half a dozen lines on the news that her suitor, who up until then she had scornfully rejected, was capable of satisfying nine women in a night (Chapman, *c*. 1605/1975). The same joke crops up with monotonous regularity throughout the period.

The implication was that a widow who remarried was admitting something about her sexual needs that no woman of proper modesty would want the world to know:

> Marry? they are most luxurious
> Will wed twice. ...
> Their livers are more spotted
> Than Laban's sheep
> > (Webster, 1972, p. 186)

She was not just immodest but ridiculous, and remarrying widows were regularly portrayed as ludicrous old women frantically copulating with younger men whose interest in them was purely commercial; typically these were younger sons looking for a meal ticket and using their wife's wealth to support a mistress and the rest of the lifestyle of a rake. One particularly unpleasant example of the genre suggests that elderly widows might be pleasured to death by their young husbands who 'entertain their old wives ... as they bewitch them even to their latter gasp' as December mates with May in a farcical dance of death (Whetstone, 1582, Sixth Day).

A remarrying widow was betraying not just her immodesty, but other moral shortcomings. Her affection to her first husband must have been superficial or feigned to be forgotten so soon, showing personal coldness; and her grief at the death of her first husband must have been fictitious, her tears induced by an onion in her sleeve, revealing a devious and insincere nature; and even considering a replacement showed fickleness and disloyalty (Swan, 1635). Perhaps most importantly of all, a remarrying widow demonstrated her moral irresponsibility by putting her children at risk from a stepfather.

The self-serving and harsh stepmother was a commonplace of the period, but stepfathers by contrast were generally ignored or treated with much more respect. In discussion of the remarriage of widows, however, the wicked stepfather takes his place alongside his female counterpart. The routine allegation against stepmothers was that they sought the disinheritance of the children of the first marriage in favour of those of the second, and the alleged disadvantage of a stepfather was of a piece with this, though it was concerned less with his ill-treatment of the children than his freedom with their prospective wealth (Anon., 1714; *Spectator*, 1965; Fleetwood, 1705). Women were usually less well-placed to disinherit their children, so stepfathers were accused of squandering the property laboriously accumulated by their predecessor for the benefit of his children. Stepfathers could do this because widows were so driven by lust that they would seize on the most unsuitable husband, careless of the welfare and future prospects of their children, and refuse him nothing, so urgent was their lubricity.

Having described the clamour against remarrying widows, and the idealised role prescribed for them as a sort of animated gravestone, I shall now attempt an explanation. There are two distinct problems here. The first is to make sense of something that has now largely passed from our consciousness. Modern western societies have no problem with remarriage – though individual families may – and indeed, the hostility is likely to seem to a modern reader to be not just obsolete but wrong-headed, for a common attitude is to hold prolonged and excessive grief to be pathological. Secondly, part of the problem in explaining the disparagement of remarrying widows is to understand its persistence through three centuries of dramatic changes in English society and in its intellectual and moral basis. These centuries saw major alterations in what was written about marriage and the family – though not necessarily in what happened in practice. Yet through all this the same essential attitude to widowhood persisted, and people – men – were saying very much the same things in 1800 as in 1550. We have, therefore, to account not just for what was said about remarrying widows, but for its persistence.

Perhaps not surprisingly, no single, all-embracing theory seems able to explain the persistent disparagement of remarrying widows, so instead of trying to construct one, I shall briefly explore five interconnected themes that are to be found with varying emphasis in all the material so far summarised. These are misogyny, the social order, personal choice in marriage, sex and money. These themes together may help us to understand the ideas and habits of thought behind a hostility towards remarriage that has now largely passed out of our consciousness.

MISOGYNY

Misogynist polemic abounded in the period, and a stock item in such writing was an account of what women were supposed to do to their husbands. Many of the attacks on remarriage are merely extensions of this ridicule of marriage in general. Widows, in this view of things, are the apotheosis of all that is supposed to be bad about women: 'Widows ... are the sum of the seven deadly sins, the friends of Satan, and the gates of hell' (Ward, *c*. 1720, pp. 70f.). Distasteful as such rhetoric is to modern sensibilities, these rancorous polemics need to be put in context, for they may have been more of a commercial exercise reflecting a ready market than attempts to say anything serious. Certainly the writers of these squibs made little virtue of originality, and there is a highly repetitious quality in what passes for argument in this kind of writing. The scheming, avaricious, over-sexed widow is therefore, at least in part, a routine comic figure, on a par with the cuckold, an easy joke for an unsophisticated audience to recognise and respond with sniggers.

But this in itself brings us to a paradox, for this misogynist literature was countered by numerous pamphlets and broadsheets countering the sneers of the 'women-haters'. In some of these the same opposition to remarriage is to be found, only this time used to defend women by giving instances of widows who had remained faithful to their husbands' memories and adopted the posture of idealised widowhood. The argument, in other words, is about whether women are capable of being continent widows, not about whether such continence is legitimate or appropriate (Heywood, 1657; Gerbier, 1651; Newstead, 1620). The misogynist tradition had it that women were too highly-sexed and too unreliable to be virtuous widows, the defenders of women said that they were fully capable of living the life of a permanent widow; but neither side challenged the ideal itself.

THE SOCIAL ORDER

Misogyny is an important contributory component of the second theme. This is the set of questions about the whole social order that remarriage supposedly raised, hinted at by Charles Carlton in his discussion of widowhood in the English renaissance (Carlton, 1978). Throughout the period, English society was highly ordered. This order was based not only on inequalities of wealth, but was set about with theoretical and moral justifications of a metaphysical nature. The force of these justifications was clearly weakening towards the end of the period, but until well into the eighteenth century there persisted a belief that the social order was a mirror of the universe created by God, with its hierarchies of angels and archangels, stretching down through humans to the animal world. Civil society reflected this order, with the monarch at the apex of the innumerable gradations of society, and families in turn replicated these gradations, with the father at their head and the lines of authority flowing from him. Women were subordinate to men, sons to their parents, sisters to their brothers, younger to older, in a coherent and pleasing model that claimed divine authorisation as well as efficiency for its rationale.

This vision of society gave distinctive connotations to remarriage; for the coherence of such a view of society was severely threatened by the uncomfortable fact of death. It was no doubt the source of a pious frisson to realise that sceptre and crown will tumble down, and that Death lays his icy hand on kings; but Death the leveller was an uncomfortable citizen in a hierarchical society, for he called in question the structure of authority by picking off, sooner or later, all the nodal points of power. To thwart the egalitarian tendencies of death required a system of orderly succession, with authority passed by well-established rules down the generations. Since authority depended to a large extent on the ownership of wealth, the maintenance of an ordered society depended also on the coherent transmission of property from one generation to the next, usually to the eldest son. A major function of marriage was to consolidate and secure the patrimony, so marriage was also a bulwark against the economic threat of death.

In practice, of course, the world was a messier place. Wives might be technically subordinate, but they could dominate their husbands by their intelligence, by force of personality or greater determination, by their sexual blandishments, sometimes by violence. Such behaviour did not fit the hierarchical model, which was probably never adequate for the task of explaining and articulating social values and relationships in the real world, or of managing the conceptual and emotional needs of many of society's members. The elegant simplicity of the model with its tidy hierarchies of duty and power was not at its best when trying to account for significant minorities like widows – nor, for that matter with bastards, orphans, younger sons and stepchildren (Collins, 1991, 1992, 1995; Fleetwood, 1705; R., C., 1598; Anon., 1747a). Moreover, the notion of order in its purest form was becoming obsolete even by the end of the sixteenth century and both its defence and the vilification of people who were seen to be undermining it became increasingly the province of conservative commentators seeing the old order suborned, and tetchily wishing to put the clock back, while the derision towards remarrying widows outlived this kind of social thinking.

FREEDOM OF CHOICE IN MARRIAGE

Such perturbation in the ordered scheme of things brings me to the third theme, that of freedom of choice, which stems from these issues of authority. Widows and widowers were at the very least untidy in an orderly scheme of things. A widow, in particular, hung around, a relic of the power of a previous generation, her own authority ambiguous in relation to the new patriarch who was also her son. In very grand estates she could be installed in a dower house with her own household and authority over it, but in less prosperous families the problem could not be removed from view in this way. When it came to remarriage, the lack of authority over a widow was potentially alarming to an age which embodied the profound belief that women were not to be trusted with business of any importance. Some authors (Perkins, 1609) recommended that parental consent should be sought for remarriage, but the suggestion sits uneasily in the theory of authority to which it refers, for control of a woman did not revert to her parents when her husband died, and there is little doubt that widows were outside normal conventions of authority, and were often in a position to please themselves: 'I have been a widow these ten years; nobody to control me: and I am said not to bear control. ... And I know I could not be in the least accountable for any of my ways' says a fictional widow refusing a marriage proposal (Richardson, 1748/1965).

WOMEN'S SEXUALITY

Such freedom was alarming, for it brought into play concerns about the destabilising effects of women's sexuality in an ordered society (Defoe, 1727). This is my fourth theme. There was a widespread and no doubt sometimes justified fear that sex was able to threaten the lineaments of society and in particular the intergenerational maintenance of the social order. Unwise marriages, contracted out of sexual desire rather than prudence, could wreak havoc with the whole system, and remarriage was potentially even more subversive, for it opened the possibility that children of one union could be disinherited in favour of those of subsequent marriages, or have their patrimony squandered by their parent's new spouse (Newnham, 1590; Collins, 1991, 1992, 1995). As well as the understandable concern this possibility caused children glumly watching their prospects disappear before their eyes, there was the more abstract sense already described of that remarriage striking potentially at the very roots of civil society by threatening the divinely authorised system of primogeniture and the passage of wealth and power down the generations. This helps us to understand the persistent emphasis on sex in the rhetorical treatment of remarriage; for sex is at the heart of the socially destabilising potential supposed to belong to widows. Their sexual over-excitement – and this brings us back to misogyny – caused them to remarry when they were widowed, and, almost inevitably it seemed, to marry unsuitably, to choose gold-diggers, social inferiors, younger men, or just poor substitutes for their first husband – all instances of women's normally imbecile judgement made worse by lust. This leads to my final theme, that of wealth.

WEALTH

Women's lechery was supposed to lead them to connive with their new husbands in dissipating their children's birthright; their guile and greed made them use their sexual charms to persuade their husbands to eschew the socially and morally correct course and disinherit children of previous marriages in favour of those of the new one, thereby upsetting the rights of inheritance proper to an orderly society. There is, obviously, an inconsistency here, as well as a strong but largely neglected argument against the remarriage of widowers. If men, who had at least theoretically greater power in such matters than women, failed to put their collective foot down, and so prevent this damage to the social order, they surely were the more culpable. The defence against such a charge is typical of the callow quality of much of the argument: it is that men were beguiled by their wives' sexual temptations; so the blame is shifted to women, in exactly the way that Adam blamed Eve in only his third recorded remark, 'The woman ... gave me of the tree, and I did eat' (Genesis 3:12).

The relative strength of these five themes varied throughout the period. Misogyny was fairly consistent. The question of wealth and inheritance remained important throughout the period, though the thinking behind the question changed: until perhaps the mid seventeenth century, inheritance had a significance as a reflection and mainstay of the social order that had lost much of its force by the end of the eighteenth century. Problems of inheritance caused by remarriage should in theory have fallen away as the eighteenth century wore on; for the development of marriage settlements in the seventeenth and early eighteenth centuries clarified who had disposal over what, and removed the scope of individuals in the chain of inheritance to behave in ways that jeopardised the expectations of their heirs, so the material basis at least of the opposition to a widow's remarriage was on the wane by the end of the eighteenth century (Bonfield, 1983).

The strength of the objection to remarriage stemming from a hierarchical sense of society was also very much greater in the sixteenth century than in the eighteenth when the metaphysical basis of the social order had largely disappeared. All these changes were, however, a matter of emphasis, but when we come to the place of sexuality in the argument, we encounter a fundamental shift in the basis of the argument. The immoderate sexual appetite of widows is constant, but its significance changes. Early in the period, the concern was with the alleged social destabilisation of this sexuality. This slowly gave way to two different concerns, that of modesty and of the wish to deny sexuality in an idealised version of femininity. Although the eighteenth century was in many respects very open about sex, an increasing protectiveness towards women's modesty developed to a point more often associated with Victorianism. Eighteenth-century disapproval of remarriage lost the early straightforward derision of women's sexual appetites, and acquired instead a wish to spare them the unpleasantness of a second marriage. The argument went that a woman might have to put up with sex with one husband in order to fulfil her destiny as wife and mother, but a respectable woman would not dream of enduring it again, though she might need to be reminded of how distasteful it all was. An unusually frank argument of the mid century illustrates the point:

> For I believe no woman who ever entered the pale of matrimony with sprightly hopes about her, found the possession (sex only considered) equal to her expectations. The maid may hope, may fancy much, in the commerce between the sexes, from her meditating on the heightened scenes which pernicious novels, and idle romances, the poison of females minds, abound with. But the widow knows 'tis all freemasonry, all empty hope, flashy, foolish, unworthy, unpermanent, and, but for the law of nature, despicable. (Richardson, 1750, p. 206)

All societies of any level of complexity acquire some form of regulation of sexual relationships. In England during the sixteenth to eighteenth centuries, the disapproval of the remarriage of widows seems a clear case of such regulation. It operated through ridicule and pious exhortation to discourage a supposed potential threat to established social institutions. Throughout the period covered in this chapter, there was a strong and persistent belief that marriage was for all its difficulties a major source of consolation in a world which for many people had few pleasures. Widows had lost this consolation, yet had to defy strongly articulated disapproval if they sought to replace it by remarriage. Behind the disapproval was a combination of misogyny, a clinging to a traditional and well-understood hierarchical model of society, a foreboding of what remarriage might do to the economic aspects of the model, an uncertainty brought on by widows' freedom to please themselves, and above all a fear of women's sexuality and its supposedly subversive potential. The disapproval of remarriage was often brutal, usually anti-human, and it is therefore gratifying that it was so frequently ignored. One woman who did ignore the disapproval and sought what happiness she could in remarriage is commemorated with a disapproval that we can glimpse two centuries later in an extremely cross epitaph in the parish church of Lowestoft in Suffolk which records her defiance:

> In memory of Charles Ward who died May 1770, aged 63 years; a dutiful son, a loving brother and an affectionate husband. N.B. This stone was not erected by Susan his wife. She erected a stone to John Salter, her second husband, forgetting the affection of Charles Ward, her first husband.

The idealised role of the virtuous widow was embraced with some enthusiasm 90 years later by Queen Victoria, and served to prolong the sombre attitudes to widowhood of earlier centuries. At the same time 'though her exaggerated behaviour may have done much to discredit the beliefs and attitudes described in this chapter. In the century since her death, widowhood has steadily shed the social and economic connotations illustrated here. The Great War was particularly important in accelerating the growth of more amiable attitudes to bereaved women; and changing attitudes towards sexuality, greater life expectancy, and greater equitability between men and women in terms of wealth have all combined to render obsolete much of the prejudice and sheer unpleasantness on the subject of remarriage that prevailed in the past. Some threat to the economic expectations of children caused by a parent's remarriage still exists (Collins, 1988), but for the most part the ideas dealt with in this chapter have passed into history: reminders of the ways in which societies struggled to integrate our last necessity into their particular scheme of things.

REFERENCES

The place of publication or printing is London unless otherwise indicated.

Anon. (1652) *A Juniper Lecture. With the Description of all sorts of Women, Good and Bad. From the Modest to the Madest &c.*

Anon. (1683) *Fifteen Real Comforts of Matrimony &c.*

Anon. (1706) *Rare and Good News for Wives in City and Country or, a Pleasant Vindication of the Married Women &c.*

Anon. (1714) *The Ladies' Library &c.*

Anon. (1747a) *The New Whole Duty of Man &c.*

Anon. (1747b) *The Young Gentleman and Lady Instructed &c.*

Anon. (1755) *Reflections upon Matrimony, and the Women of this Country &c.*

Anon. (1794) *The Female Jockey Club, or a Sketch of the Manners of the Age &c.* Fourth edition.

St Augustine, 'The Excellence of Widowhood', in *Treatises on Various Subjects*, The Fathers of the Church vol. 14 (Washington, DC: Catholic University of America Press, 1952).

L. Bonfield, *Marriage Settlements, 1601–1740*, (Cambridge: Cambridge University Press, 1983).

J. Boswell, *The Life of Samuel Johnson*, (Dent, 1906).

R. C(awdrey?), *A Godly Form of Household Government &c.*, (1598).

C. Carlton, 'The widow's tale' *Albion*, 10 (1978), pp. 118–29.

G. Chapman, (*c.* 1605) *The Widow's Tears*, edited by Akihiro Yamada (Methuen, 1975).

S. Collins, *Step-parents and their Children*, (Souvenir Press, 1988).

S. Collins, 'British Stepfamily Relationships, 1500–1800', *Journal of Family History*, 16, 4 (1991), pp. 331–44.

S. Collins, (1992) *Stepparents in the English renaissance*, International Conference on the History of the Family, Ottawa, May 1992.

S. Collins, (1995) '"Against Reason, nature and order": stepparents in the English renaissance', in R. Phillips (ed.), *The History of Marriage and the Family in Western Society*, (Toronto: Canadian Scholars' Press, 1995).

J. Davies, in R. Kruger (ed.), *The Poems of Sir John Davies*, (Oxford: The Clarendon Press, 1975).

D. Defoe, (1727) *Conjugal Lewdness; or, Matromonial Whoredom. A Treatise Concerning the Use and Abuse of the Marriage Bed*, A facsimile reproduction with an introduction by Maximillian A. Novak (Gainesville, Florida: Scholars' Facsimiles and Reprints, 1967).

J. Donne, in E. R. Simpson and G. R. Potter (eds), *The Sermons of John Donne*, (Berkeley and Los Angeles: University of California Press, 1956).

H. Fielding, *Joseph Andrews and Shamela*, (Methuen & Co. Ltd, 1965).

W. Fleetwood, *The Relative Duties of Parents and Children &c.*, (1705).

C. Gerbier, *Elogium Heroinum: or the Praise of Worthy Women*, (1651).

T. Heywood, *The General History of Women &c.*, (1657).

J.N.D. Kelly, *Jerome: his Life, Writing and Controversies*, (Duckworth, 1975).

W. Kenrick, *The Whole Duty of Woman: or a Guide to the Female Sex. From the Age of Sixteen to Sixty &c.*, Written by a Lady (Third Edition, 1701).

J. Miller, *The Mother-in-Law &c.*, (Dublin, 1734).

J. Newnham, *Newmans [sic] Nightcrowe. A Bird that Breedeth Brawles in Many Families and Households*, (1590).

C. Newstead, *An apology for Women: or, Women's Defence*, (1620).

W. Perkins, translated by T. Pickering, *Christian Economy: or, a Short Survey of the Right Manner of Erecting and Ordering a Family*, (1609).

S. Richardson, *Letters to and for Particular Friends, on the Most Important Occasions &c.*, (Fourth Edition, 1750).

S. Richardson, *Clarissa: or, the History of a Young Lady*, (Dent, 1965).

W. Seymar, *Conjugium Conjurgiam &c.*, (1673).

The Spectator, edited by Donald F. Bond (Oxford: The Clarendon Press, 1965).

J. Swan, *Speculum Mundi, or, a Glass Representing the Face of the World,* (Cambridge, 1635).

The Tatler, edited by Donald F. Bond (Oxford: The Clarendon Press, 1987).

J. Taylor (1650), *The Rules and Exercises of Holy Living,* (Oxford: John Henry and James Parker, 1863).

L. Vives, *A Very Fruitful and Pleasant Book Called the Instruction of a Christian Woman, &c.,* (1541).

L. Vives, *The Office and Duty of a Husband &c.,* (c.1550).

E.W., *The Whole Pleasures of Matrimony &c.,* (1718).

E. Ward, *Female Policy Detected &c.,* (c.1720).

J. Webster, *The Duchess of Malfi,* I, ii, 221ff.; in *Three Plays* (Harmondsworth: Penguin Books, 1972).

G. Whetstone, *An Heptameron of Civil Discourse &c.,* (1582).

W. Whatley, *A Bride-Bush: or, a Direction for Married Persons, &c.,* (1619).

3 The Funeral Trade in Hanoverian England 1714–1760

Julian Litten

A Swiss observer, N. Misson, provides significant evidence for the early development of the undertaking industry in London (Misson, 1719). He described the registration of deaths, the dressing of the corpse, the etiquette of 'viewing', the street procession and the church service. His minute details suggest he attended the funeral of a 'person of quality', that is, of middle- or upper middle-class status.

First, Misson tells us, the death was notified to the parish minister who in turn was responsible for ascertaining the cause of death from those who laid-out the body. Ministers filed a 'certificate' with the parish clerk whose duty it was to publish a record of deaths and their estimated cause. In the City of London such returns were made to the Company of Parish Clerks who produced monthly 'Bills of Mortality' covering all the city churches (Ditchfield, 1907, p. 123). As the majority of the certificates were completed by 'good women' with no medical experience whatsoever, the reliability of the cause of death is highly questionable.

Shrouds were generally white in colour and came in 'different Sorts of Fineness', obviously an allusion to linen and silk, and were to be had 'ready made..., for People of every Age and Sex'. Chin-cloths, caps, stockings and even gloves were available at equally competitive prices (Litten, 1991, pp. 57–84). The use of the woollen shroud was introduced by the 1678 Act for Burying in Woollen, an attempt 'for lessening the importation of Linnen from beyond the Seas, and the encouragement for the Woollen and Paper Manufacturers of the Kingdome' (30 Car.ii. c.3 and 36 Ejusdem c.i.). The penalty for not complying with these terms was £5, shared equally between the 'informer' and the poor. This penalty proved no deterrent for the wealthy. Hannah Deane of High Ongar, Essex, took account of the £5 fine in drawing up her Will in 1784: 'And I do hereby Order and direct that [the] sum of Ten pound shall be paid to the person who shall...see me Inclosed and laid in my Coffin in Linnen and shall give Information and Oath wheereby the Poor of the parish Will be intitled to the sum of fifty shilling'.[1]

The time lapse between death and funeral was about three or four days. The open coffin, resting on low trestles, was placed in the main reception room of the house of the deceased 'which Time they allow', according to Misson, 'as well to give the dead Person the Opportunity of Coming to Life

48

again... as to prepare Mourning'. The fear of premature burial was a chilling thought, increased by the unreliability in ascertaining the cause of death. It was only when the funeral was about to set off that the coffin was nailed up.

Unlike today, the refreshments for guests preceded the funeral. Misson records that it was 'usual to present the guests with something to drink, either a red or white wine, boil'd with Sugar and Cinnamon, or some such Liquor'. A trade card issued in about 1725 by the Greenwich confectioner Richard Innocent, in the manner of contemporary funeral invitations, depicts a house scene with a palled coffin on trestles surrounded by cloaked mourners amongst which are passing a young man offering glasses of wine from an earthenware jug and a young woman with a tray of sweetmeats.[2]

Palls were available in varying sizes for children's and adults' coffins, and in different quality of material dependent upon the social status of the deceased. At the lower end of the scale were black baize palls with a white woollen hem. At the top of the scale was black Utrecht or Geneose velvet, lined and hemmed in white silk, large enough to throw over the shouldered coffin and reach down to the ground. Occasionally six friends of the deceased were invited to support the hem of the pall – three each side – to stop it from trailing in the dust. These came to be known as 'pall bearers'. To guard against any hideous accident, the front of the pall was gathered up on top of the coffin to allow the two bearers at the front to see.[3]

The complexity of the funeral witnessed by Misson is supported by his account of the street procession. This left the house preceded by two beadles with silver-topped staves, the parish minister and the clerk. Next came the palled coffin on the bearers' shoulders with the attendant pall-bearers and then 'all the Guests two and two (making up) the rest of the procession'. The size of the procession and the number of parish officers suggests a London funeral, which is shown by a likeness of a funeral ticket designed in about 1720 by Hogarth for the Westminster undertaker, Humphrey Drew. Preceded by two cassocked beadles, their staves swathed in black crepe, the coffin approaches the steps of St Paul's, Covent Garden, with the clerk in front of the minister followed by the palled coffin with its pall-bearers and the black-cloaked mourners, two by two, bringing up the rear.[4]

Sir, You are desired to accompany the Corps of Mr James Hart, (late one of the Gentlemen of his Majesty's Chappel-Royal) from Founders-Hall in Lothbury to Westminster-Abbey on Thursday the 15th May, 1718, by Three of the Clock in the Afternoon precisely. N.B. The Corpse will be mov'd by five at farthest being to be interr'ed by Daylight, and several Persons to return in the Country.[5]

The organisation of the early Hanoverian funeral of the type performed for James Hart was both complex and complicated. From the invitation card issued by an anonymous funeral furnisher, we learn that Hart was a Lay Clerk at the Chapel Royal, St James' Palace, a Liveryman of the Worshipful Company of Founders and, as a consequence, a Freeman of the City of London. The burial in Westminster Abbey affirms he was a man of some social standing. The invitee – almost certainly male, as funeral invitations were either not sent to women or, if they were, none survive – was asked to present himself at Founders Hall by 3.00 p.m. so that the cortège might leave promptly at 5.00 p.m. to ensure burial by daylight as a number of the mourners had come in from the country and were anxious to begin their return journey before darkness. The two-hour interval was provided for the pre-burial refreshments.

The nocturnal funeral made its appearance at the beginning of the seventeenth century and lasted, in some regions, until the middle of the eighteenth. They were primarily performed for the lesser nobility and armigerous members of the landed gentry and upper middle classes, and owed their innovation to an increasing backlash against the funeral control of the College of Arms, the accoutrements of which – including the number of mourners and the heraldic devices – were supplied against a sliding scale related to the rank or social status of the deceased. In truth these heraldic funerals were becoming too expensive and, whilst a family might have been able to afford the necessary public honour provided by the College of Arms for the holder of the title, they would have been straitened if required to repeat the performance for the deceased's widow and children.

The nocturnal funeral was not popular with the College of Arms, but the funeral furnisher was only too willing to be associated with the private mourning of the upper middle classes and to show how well he could emulate the pageantry formerly provided by the College of Arms. Clare Gittings argues that 'it was a desire to emphasise private loss in the ritual, rather than any public display of strength, which led to the fashion for burial by night'(Gittings, 1984, p. 197). T.T. Merchant confirmed the popularity of the nocturnal funeral and added: 'Since the method of these undertakers have got a footing, persons of ordinary rank may, for the value of fifty pounds, make as great a figure, as the nobility or gentry did formerly with the expense of more than five hundred pounds...the gaiety and splendour both of the nobility and gentry is hereby very much eclipsed so that not many of them do exceed the show of the common people' (Merchant, 1698, pp. 6–7).

Fees for attendants at a nocturnal funeral were graduated according to the hour – five shillings at 9.00 p.m., ten shillings at 10.00 p.m. and £1 at midnight – and as many as 30 men could be employed and as much as 56 lb of candles (Jackson, 1977, p. 76). These candles, especially the 'linkes'

– three thick wax tapers twisted at the stem and then branching out – could be expensive. Ten shillings reward was offered for convictions of theft in 1713:

> Riots and Robberies. Committed in and about Stepney Church Yard, at a Funeral Solemnity, on Wednesday the 23rd September, and whereas many Persons, who being appointed to attend the same Funeral with white Wax lights of considerable Value, were assaulted in a most violent manner, and the said Wax lights taken from them. (Davey, 1889, p. 110)

The elaborate trade card of 'Richard Chandler, Armes-painter and Undertaker at St Lukes Head in Kill Lane in Shrewsbury' issued in about 1718,[6] provides an insight into the range of items then available from the quality funeral furnisher, for undertaking funerals such as James Hart's. Chandler advised that he 'Compleatly Furnishes Funeralls, with Coffin, burying Suit, Pall, Hanging, Silver'd Sconces and Candlesticks, Cloakes, Hatbands, Scarves, Flambeaux, Linkes, Torches, Ticketts &c and performed after ye same manner as by ye Undertakers of London, at Reasonable Rates.' In the background of the trade card, two funeral processions are shown, one a horse-drawn heraldic funeral, the other a foot funeral of a person of quality.

Was Chandles correct to say that his funerals were 'performed after ye same manner as by ye Undertakers of London'? A crude woodcut trade card of about 1720 issued by 'Eleazer Malory Joiner at the Coffin in Whitehall, near Red Lion Street end', a funeral furnishing repositor, advertised that he[7] 'maketh Coffins, Shrouds, letteth Palls, Cloaks and Furnishings with all things necessary for funerals, at Reasonable rates, Also Appraiseth and Buyeth all sorts of Household Goods.' Here, then, was a competent joiner making and dressing coffins and whose wife, one presumes, made shrouds, owning a complete set of funeral furnishings – pall, feathers, flambeaux, linkes, gloves, hatbands, and so on – all available on hire, willing to make a little extra money on the side by house clearance. A good and honest tradesman, no doubt; but not able to provide for the performance of a quality funeral.

For Chandles's London parallel one had to look to funeral furnishers such as 'Robert Green, Coffin Maker & Undertaker at the Four Coffins St Margaret's Hill, Southwark' whose rococo trade card of 1753 (Heal, 1925, pl. xcvii) – its border dripping with banners, a pennon, a bannerol, two escutcheons, two targes and a brace of hatchments – advertised that he

> Sells and Lets all Manner of Furniture for Funerals, on Reasonable Terms, Viz., Velvet Palls, Hangings for Rooms, large Silver'd Candlesticks & Sconces, Tapers & Wax Lights, Heraldry, Feathers & Velvets, fine Cloth Coats & midling Do. Rich Silk Scarves, Allamode & Sarsnett Hatbands,

Italian Crape by the piece or Hatband, Black & White Favors, Cloth
Black or Grey, Bays, Flannel Do. Burying Crapes of all Sorts, fine Quilting
and Quilted Matrices the best Layc'd, Plain & Shammy Gloves, Kidd &
Lamb Do. &c. NB All Sorts of Plates and Handles for Coffins, in Brass,
Lead or Tin, likewise Nails of all Sorts, Coffins, Shrouds in all Sizes ready
made. Where the Country Chapman and others may be furnished in the
most Expedient Manner at the least Notice.

As a new and identifiable discipline, the undertaking trade appeared
during the last quarter of the seventeenth century in London. Before then,
the disposal of England's post-Reformation dead was left to such carpenters
and joiners as were willing to do so, with the funerals of persons of
consequence being performed by cabinet makers and those of rank by the
College of Arms. Undertakers rarely – if ever – advertised, for theirs was,
and remains, a trade governed by discretion; neither did they publish
testimonials from satisfied clients.

But the funeral furnishing warehousemen issued trade cards, and it is from
such items, and the illustrated funeral invitations and related mercantile
ephemera, that an overview of the trade can be established and a reconstruction
of their stock made together with a reliable indication of their connection
with other businesses, such as coach proprietors and livery stable owners.
The eighteenth-century trade cards varied in size from 100mm x 150mm to
200mm x 300mm in folio. Precisely how they were used is not generally
agreed upon (Heal, 1925, pp. 1–3) for, whilst some of these 'shopkeeper's
bills' – as they were known by eighteenth-century tradesmen – were
occasionally used as invoice sheets, those relating to the funeral furnishing
trade in public or private collections appear not to have been so utilised. As
the majority itemises services available from the funeral furnishing warehouses
to the small town and country undertaker – or more likely carpenter/
joiner/cabinet-maker – they would appear to have been used as early examples
of today's mail-shots. Trade cards were important forms of advertising
during the eighteenth century and a number of well-known artists were
commissioned to design them.[8]

The first recorded operative trading as an undertaker *per se* – and, indeed,
the earliest of a number of late seventeenth-century trade cards – was William
Boyce 'at ye Whight Hart & Coffin in ye Grate Ould Bayley Near Newgeat,
London'.[9] His trade card of about 1675 is a reproduction of the shop's sign
board: to the left, and hanging from a hook, an upholstered coffin above a
skull and crossbones, with the initials B.I.A. on the lid, with lid motifs of an
hourglass and a skull and crossbones, whilst to the right is the badge of Richard
II, a white hart couchant sporting a crown collar with a chain attached. The

accompanying legend reads: 'By Willm BOYCE Coffinsmaker at ye Whight Hart & Coffin in ye Grate Ould Bayley Near Newgeat London You May Be Furnished With all sorts & sizes of Coffins & Shrouds Ready Made And all other Conveniences Belonging to Funerals.'

Competing for the distinction of first undertaker is William Russell, an heraldic painter and coffin maker, also trading in London. Far more ingenious and innovative than Boyce, Russell entered into an agreement with the College of Arms in 1689 whereby, for an arranged fee, its members would attend certain funerals of persons of rank furnished by Russell. This was a shrewd move on his part for it meant that not only did he secure the blessing and guidance of the College, but also avoided their censure. However, as an heraldic painter, Russell was probably already known to the College and may well have once worked for them directly or received work on contract. Whatever the association, Russell's agreement with the College was an astute political ploy and must have been seen by him as an exceptional opening into the mysteries of the College's funeral practices.

For the College, it proved to be a disaster as their involvement in the literal performance of funerals soon declined, the embers being fanned into a brief blaze with the public obsequies for Queen Mary II in 1695. (She died in 1694.) It is in any case debatable whether the College of Arms could have survived usurpation from the private sector. Its lawsuits against an aggressive, rapid-growth competition from the private sector diminished once it was realised that it had literally priced itself out of the market and had little, if anything, extra to offer than could be provided by the well-equipped funeral furnisher, apart from traditional kudos. Furthermore, less importance was being attached to the need for a public display of the deceased's rank (Gittings, 1984, p. 197) as funerals were becoming more private affairs than 'public' (Houlbrooke, 1996). Nevertheless, the College of Arms remained in charge of the obsequies of royal personages until 1751 when a private funeral furnisher-cum-cabinet-maker, Mr Harcourt, supplied and organised the funeral of Frederick, Prince of Wales. Although this is the first recorded instance of a private funeral furnisher being used by the royal household it is possible, of course, that the public sector had been previously involved in some way at royal funerals, for it is unlikely that the College of Arms had their own in-house cabinet-makers and plumbers to supply coffins. Indeed, one is tempted to wonder whether, with his newly-found association with the College of Arms, William Russell was commissioned to supply and provide the coffin for Queen Mary II. There must have been many jealous eyes directed towards Russell, who, due to his association with the College of Arms, was able to attract such business within the environs of London. The partnership, though, was short-lived, for no heralds attended at the funeral of the Hon.

Thomas Howard, performed by William Russell at Ashtead, Surrey on 13 April 1702 (Jackson, 1977, p. 76).

Yet neither Boyce nor Russell enjoyed an absolute monopoly, for there were others in business at that time, such as William Grinley of Fleet Street whose trade card of about 1700 was advertising 'At ye lower corner of Fleetlane at ye Signe of ye Naked Boy & Coffin you may be Accomodated wth. all things for a Funeral as well ye meanest as thos of greater Ability upon Reasonable Terms more particularly Coffins Shrouds Palls Cloaks Sconces Stans Hangings for Roms Heraldry Hearse & Coaches wth. all other things not here mentioned',[10] and John Clarke of Jermyn Street, who was advertising from about 1725.

In the early years of the trade there were no written rules or code of practice; anyone could set themselves up as a coffin-maker or undertaker, and many did. The extant trade cards reveal that the furnishing of funerals in the early eighteenth century was, in the main, restricted to those already involved in the carpentry, joinery and cabinet-making and upholstery trades (Heal, 1953). Territorial boundaries seem to have been honoured, especially in London and the large conurbations, for funeral furnishers appear to have limited their operation to the parishes in which they were situated. Though many of the late eighteenth-century trade cards offered 'Funerals performed in all parts of Great Britain', it is doubtful that this offer was ever taken up. Fourteen trade cards issued by London undertakers during the period *c*.1680–*c*.1760 survive, and as none indicate any other craft-affiliation it could be assumed that they were able to make a living and furnish from stock all that went to provide for a funeral (Heal, 1957, pp. 45 and 174–5).

From surviving pattern books, bill headings and livery company registers, Southwark and Whitechapel appear as the two centres in London accommodating the funeral furnishing trading houses and manufactories during the eighteenth and early nineteenth centuries. Southwark specialised in the production of coffin furniture, that is, the metal fittings for coffins, such as depositum plates, lid motifs, handles and escutcheons. Whitechapel developed an expertise in the production and manufacture of coffins and fabric-covered outer cases. Both areas were close to the docks, with the majority of the iron foundries being sited in Southwark and the timber yards at Limehouse and Whitechapel. Moreover, Whitechapel bordered onto Spitalfields, the Huguenot centre for linen, velvet and silk weaving, particularly those items known as 'black stuff', the crêpe, Utrecht and Geneose velvets reserved for the exclusive use of the funeral furnishing trade. Yet whilst certain cabinet-makers and upholsterers occasionally furnished funerals, there is no evidence to show that iron founders did the same.

It seems, then, that the average undertaker was little more than a speculative carpenter or joiner who, either by direct contact with the metalworking trades, or via such funeral houses as Robert Green's, was able to buy-in all that was required to furnish a funeral. However, it was not unknown for upholsterers and drapers to run a funeral furnishing branch to their main business; whilst able to provide the soft furnishings such as coffin linings and coverings, shrouds, palls, gloves, cloaks, mourning hatbands, scarves and, possibly, feathers from their own stock in trade, they would have contracted-out for the provision of the coffin. There were a number of coffin makers around in London during the eighteenth century whose sole business was the provision of coffins to the trade.

The undertaker and funeral furnisher was able to offer a quality of choice to the mourner: hire or outright purchase of the gloves, mourning hatbands and scarves. The pall, cloaks, feathers and house/church drapery were usually hired as they would be of little or no use to the client after the funeral. None of Robert Green's private clients would have wanted to retain the large silvered candlesticks or sconces. In heraldic funerals, the armorials would have been of no use to the funeral furnisher: these would be treated as an outright purchase on the part of the client. Green's hire service enabled the less wealthy country undertaker to furnish a funeral in the London fashion if required to do so, passing on the hire cost, plus a small handling charge for his own services, to the client.

Whilst the possibility of hiring-in was a boon to the country undertaker, it would not have been cheap to set up in business as a funeral warehouseman as he would have needed at least four complete sets of funeral accoutrements to make a reasonable living. This stock would have included eight velvet palls (four adult size, four children's), 400 yards of black baize for room hangings, 24 silvered candlesticks, 48 sets of black osprey plumes, one gross scarves, 48 cloaks and one gross gloves of various quality and sizes, canvas and paints for heraldic achievements, two gross of assorted size candles, 100 yards of crêpe, one gross black and white rosettes, shrouds of varying sizes, coffin linings and miscellaneous grave clothes, coffin mattresses, roughly 168 coffins, sheet lead for lead coffin shells, one gross yards of velvet for coffin coverings and a multitude of copper, brass, lead and tin coffin furniture; all with, perhaps, a small stock of repoussé painted copper coronets and three-dimensional coronets of all degree for the funerals of the nobility. He may also have had to own four funeral carriages.

Assuming items to the value of £500 would need to be hired at, say, £50 to furnish the funeral of a member of the middle classes, the hiring undertaker would recoup this outlay by charging his client £100, with the funeral warehouse receiving the £50 hire charge and the undertaker making £50 profit for himself. Suitably maintained it would have been possible for a complete set of funeral accoutrements as outlined by Robert Green to last for 30 funerals before requiring replacement, earning for the warehouseman during that 'lifetime' a total of £1500. Thus if it cost £500 to buy-in a set of accoutrements and £500 to replace them the warehouseman was making £500 profit, a 100 per cent mark-up against expenditure. One could argue that the country undertaker was also making 100 per cent profit against the hire; yes, but it is doubtful that he would have been asked to provide funerals for persons of quality as often as the warehouseman. Items requiring replacement were more often than not disposed of within the trade, being acquired by the down-market undertakers, such as Oliver Twist's Mr Sowerberry, who carried out the funerals of the poorer classes of society.

Whilst most undertakers knew what to order from the warehouseman, few truly understood the symbolism of the artifacts. In 1843 Edwin Chadwick interviewed a London undertaker:

Chadwick: Are you aware that the array of funerals, commonly made by undertakers, is strictly the heraldic array of a baronial funeral, the two men who stand at the doors being supposed to be the two porters of the castle, with their staves, in black; the man who heads the procession, wearing a scarf, being a representative of a herald-at-arms; the man who carries the plume of feathers on his head being an esquire, who bears the shield and casque, with its plume of feathers; the pall-bearers, with batons in their hands, being representatives of knights-companions-at-arms; the men walking with wands being supposed to represent gentlemen-ushers, with their wands: are you aware that this is said to be the origin and type of the common array usually provided by those who undertake to perform funerals?

Undertaker: No, I am not aware of it.

Chadwick: It may be presumed that those who order funerals are equally unaware of the incongruity for which such expense is incurred?

Undertaker: Undoubtedly. (Chadwick, 1843, p. 267)

Chadwick's comments, albeit a century later, clarify why hire companies such as Robert Green's were required:

The number of persons whose sole business is that of undertaker, whose names are enumerated in the post-office directory for the year 1843 for the metropolis, is 275. It is stated that much larger numbers than are named in the Directory retain the insignia of undertakers in their shop-window, for the sake of the profits of one or two funerals a year. They merely transmit the orders to the furnishing undertakers, who supply materials and men. (Chadwick, *ibid.*, p. 51)

In the countryside, similar enterprise existed. In Essex, 'the smaller shops in villages, and some in towns too, produced insufficient income to support a family, so that the wife or daughter often managed them while the man followed another occupation. Where the latter did keep the shop, he might also be the local undertaker, as at Toppesfield, Great Clacton, Thorpe and Weeley' (Brown, 1969). The impression given is that anyone in woodworking – from chippie to cabinet-maker – would turn his hand to coffin-making at least, and perhaps funeral furnishing if the opportunity arose. Such were the dangers of a trade not protected by its own guild.

When the College of Arms hindered the grant of a new Charter to the Upholders Company in 1722, some of the London undertakers made an attempt to form their own livery company. A contemporary trade card, designed by George Bickham, for the United Company of Undertakers was produced in anticipation. It was an elaborate coxcombery: Youth and Age, represented as Bacchus and Clotho, sit on an oval cartouche flanked by Time and Eternity, whilst below is a pair of mourning cherubs, each resting on a child's coffin. The inscription reads: 'Funerals Performed To & from all parts of Great Britain; in ye Best, and most Reasonable Manner; By ye United Company of UNDERTAKERS; At their House, the Corner of Southampton Street Bloomsbury, in Holborn LONDON.'[11]

But was this no more than a co-operative of local tradesmen? Probably, for the United Company of Undertakers was never admitted at Guildhall, and their 'house' in Bloomsbury was none other than the business premises of Robert Legg Snr, upholder, appraiser and undertaker. Whatever ensued between the Worshipful Company of Upholders and Legg, the United Company of Undertakers did not receive livery status, though they did excite sufficient interest to merit a sarcastic caricature from William Hogarth entitled 'The Company of Undertakers', and with the motto *'Et Plurima Mortis Imago'* – 'The Very Image of Death'.

This engraving was erroneously published by Bertram Puckle in 1926 as the 'Sign of the now extinct "Company of Undertakers"' (Puckle, 1926, facing p. 128). Had he but read the caption then he would have quickly understood the lampoon:

Beareth Sable, an Urinal proper, between 12 Quack-Heads of the Second and 12 Cane Heads Or, Consultant. On a Chief Nebulae, Eermine, One Compleat Doctor isuant, checkie sustaining in his Right Hand a Baton of the Second. On his Dexter & Sinister sides two Demi-Doctors, isuant of the second, & two Cane Heads isuant of the third; The first having One

Eye conchant, towards the Dexter Side of the Escocheon; the Second Faced per pale proper & Gules, Guardant. With this Motto *Et Plurima Mortis Imago*.

Whilst Robert Legg Snr and his compatriots were enjoying a short-lived grandeur within the ill-fated United Company of Undertakers, the Upholders' Company continued to support those of their members who furnished funerals as part of their everyday trade. Though the list of admissions does not identify those freemen trading as coffin-makers or undertakers, it may have been that these occupations were known sidelines of upholders and mercers whom they did admit. By the mid 1730s the Upholders' Company saw fit to make available to their members blank funeral invitation tickets for overprinting, affiliation to the Company being shown by an inscription on the plate-mark beneath the main illustration, and reading 'Performed by the Company of Upholders at Exeter Change & at their Hall in Leaden Hall Street'.[12] This copper engraving, designed by A.N. Coypel and cut by Ja. Chereau, was an up-market plagiarism of the more stylised primitive original issued by the United Company of Undertakers. In front of a tall classical tomb, its centre panel left blank for overprinting, reclines a shrouded skeleton, representing Death, leaning forward to the viewer's right to prevent Youth from detaining Time, who is shown flying off to his next assignment. On the left, Age addresses her gaze towards Death, thereby distracting her from cutting the Thread of Life joining Eternity to Clotho, seen resting on a cloud to the upper left of the plate. The silent, bloodless war between the United Company of Undertakers and the Worshipful Company of Undertakers did not last: by 1748 the imprimatur had been dropped from the Undertakers' blank funeral invitations and the United Company of Undertakers disappeared.

Few illustrations survive of the interiors of funeral furnishing establishments of the eighteenth century. Trade cards tend to depict stylised street processions with the occasional spurious hatchments, targes and other heraldic devices. A proof engraving of a trade card of about 1730 exists of the St Paul's Churchyard upholsterer and cabinet-maker Christopher Gibson.[13] Gibson and his assistants are shown attending to two clients. To the left of the shop a gilder prepares an armchair, below two large hatchments and a brace of pall escutcheons. In the back of the shop, beyond the baulks of material and the cutting bench, are five more escutcheons. Judging from this display of funerary heraldry, funerals appear to have played an important part in Gibson's regular business.

Views of the exteriors of undertakers and funeral furnishing premises are equally rare. Perhaps the best-known image of a funeral furnisher's shop sign appears in Hogarth's engraving, *Gin Lane*, of a suspended coffin and a figure of Father Time. An engraving of 1737 by John Kip of St Clement Danes, Strand,[14] illustrates the shop front of a furnishing undertaker, with its window of 21 small panes within which are displayed five funeral hatchments bearing coats-of-arms of dubious authenticity. The addresses on the many extant trade cards and funeral invitation tickets indicate that the majority of coffin-makers and funeral furnishers was situated off the high street, discreet but not inaccessible. But this was not particularly important as house visits were more usual. The undertaker/funeral furnisher could thus glean at first hand the social status of his clientele and estimate the quality of their funeral.

The funeral trade had three distinct branches: coffin-making, undertaking and funeral furnishing. The coffin-maker made coffins. He might also have performed funerals, but not necessarily so. In the main he sold his coffins on, to undertakers and funeral furnishers. The undertaker, who might also be his own coffin-maker, performed funerals at the lower end of the social scale, much like Charles Dickens' Mr Sowerberry. The funeral furnisher bought-in coffins from the coffin-maker, dressed and upholstered them, and performed the funeral. A coffin-maker, then, could look up to a funeral furnisher whilst respecting the undertaker; an undertaker respected both the coffin-maker and the funeral furnisher, but might have looked down on the coffin-maker who performed funerals; the funeral furnisher needed the coffin-maker, and probably ignored the undertaker.

There was little interference from those ordering the funeral regarding the manner of its execution for it was the undertaker/funeral furnisher who decided on what was considered customary in any specific situation. He alone selected the coffin wood, the coffin furniture, the quality of the pall and the number of attendant mutes/bearers/pages. The standard instruction from the bereaved client was to 'provide that which is customary'; a pathetic comment, in which the trade's development of funeral etiquette for each rank in society was recognised and the client's control over the funeral cost surrendered. Occasionally the trade overstepped the mark and offered to the bereaved a funeral of a type that was above their station. Whilst this was tolerated, it would have put at risk the possibility of the bereaved giving future custom to the undertaker.

Undertaking had become a necessary, rather than a popular, trade. It provided a public service. Few undertakers expected, or got, much thanks for their pains. The Upholders' bid for guild status was blocked. Yet undertakers hardly merited the description in 1747:

> They are a set of men who live by death and never care to appear but at the End of Man's Life...their Business is to watch Death, and to furnish out the Funeral Solemnity, with as much pomp and feigned sorrow as the

Heirs or Successors of the Deceased chose to purchase: They are a hard-hearted Generation, and require more money than Brains to conduct their Business: I know no one Qualification peculiarly necessary to them, except that is a steady, demure and melancholy Countenance at Command: I do not know, that they take Apprentices in the Capacity as Undertakers, for they are generally Carpenters, or Herald-Painters besides; and they only employ, as Journeymen, a set of Men whom they have picked up, possessed of a sober Countenance, and a solemn Melancholy Face, whom they pay at so much a Jobb. (Cambell, 1747)

By the 1760s the English funeral had reached its zenith. In an age of quality and respectability the funeral furnisher was able to provide his clients with merchandise of the highest quality. The elaborate street processions and the sumptuously upholstered and decorated coffins depicted in the mid eighteenth-century funeral furnishers' trade cards and invitation tickets were not confections, as an inspection of examples of their surviving wares in the many private burial vaults beneath England's churches will prove.

NOTES

1   Chelmsford, Essex County Record Office. *Parish Records, High Ongar* D/AEW 39.
2   *c.* 1725 trade card issued by Richard Innocent, confectioner of Greenwich (Master and Fellows, Magdalen College, Cambridge). Litten, *op. cit.*, illus.81.
3   Funeral ticket for Humphrey Drew, undertaker of King Street, Westminster. By William Hogarth, *c.* 1720. Author's collection.
4   Funeral ticket of Humphrey Drew, *op. cit.*
5   Hon. Christopher Lennox-Boyd Collection.
6   Hon. Christopher Lennox-Boyd Collection.
7   British Museum, Department of Prints & Drawings. Heal 124.48.
8   A pen and ink wash design of 1746 by Hubert Gravelot for a funeral ticket is in the Metropolitan Museum of Art, New York, Prints & Drawings Department. This is the only known surviving English funeral ticket design of the eighteenth century.
9   British Museum, Department of Prints & Drawings. 37021–1.
10 Victoria and Albert Museum, London Department of Prints & Drawings. Unaccessioned item.
11 Hon. Christopher Lennox-Boyd Collection.
12 Hon. Christopher Lennox-Boyd Collection.
13 Victoria and Albert Museum, London Department of Prints and Drawings.
14 Private Collection, Cambridge.

REFERENCES

A. F. J. Brown, *Essex at Work 1700–1815*, (Chelmsford: Essex County Council, 1969).

R. Cambell, *The London Tradesman*, (London, 1747).

E. Chadwick, 'A Supplementary Report on the Results of a Special Inquiry into the Practice of Interment in Towns', (*PP*, 1843).

R. Davey, *A History of Mourning*, (London: Jay's, 1889).

P. H. Ditchfield, *The Parish Clerk*, (London: Methuen, 1907).

C. Gittings, *Death, Burial and the Individual in Early Modern England*, (Beckenham: Croom Helm, 1984).

A. Heal, *London Tradesmen's Cards of the XVIII Century*, (London: Batsford, 1925).

A. Heal, *The London Furniture Makers from the Restoration to the Victorian Era*, (London: Batsford, 1953).

A. Heal, *Sign Boards of Old London Shops*, (London: Batsford, 1957).

R. Houlbrooke, 'Public' and 'private' in the funnals of the later Stuart gentry: some Somerset examples', *Mortality*, vol. 1 No. 2 July 1996, pp. 163–176.

A. A. Jackson (ed.), *Ashtead: A Village Transformed*, (Leatherhead & District Local History Society, 1977).

J. W. S. Litten, *The English Way of Death*, (London: Robert Hale, 1991).

T. T. Merchant, 'Some General Considerations offered relating to our present trade...' (1698), cited in J. S. Burns, *The History of Parish Registers in England*, (London, 1862) pp. 109–10.

N. Misson, *Memoirs and Observations of His Travels over England*, trans. J. Ozell (London, 1719).

B. Puckle, *Funeral Customs*, (London: Werner Laurie, 1926).

4 Memento Mori: The Function and Meaning of Breton Ossuaries 1450–1750

Elizabeth Musgrave

> A very strange practice takes place in Brittany. The kin of the deceased unearth the dead after several years, when they believe that the soil will have absorbed all of the decomposed flesh. The recovered bones are then placed in a small building constructed... near to the church, the ossuary. Often, great zeal does not allow time for the complete defleshing of the corpse and shreds of putrefying flesh attract dogs which no-one cares to chase away. (Mérimée, 1836, pp. 164–5)

Visitors to western Brittany in the nineteenth century were impressed by three attributes of Breton culture: the Celtic language and traditions, Catholic piety and a remarkable veneration for the dead. A *départemental* administrator who toured Finistère in 1829–31, remarked 'nothing is more sacred... than the veneration given to the dead, than the religion of the tomb' (Badone, 1989, pp. 1–2).

The building patrimony and material culture of ecclesiastical sites still reflect these former characteristics; the west is rich in elaborate parish churches, calvaries, ossuaries (or charnel houses) and elaborate gateways into church precincts, the 'parish closes' for which Brittany is renowned. Church monuments, folklore and popular art are rich in emblematic material in which representations of death and hell abound.

Alain Croix has investigated the origins of the apparent cultural distinctiveness of Breton-speaking Brittany in the sixteenth and seventeenth centuries. He explains Catholic piety and the veneration of the dead as the product of the dissemination of Counter-Reformation ideals into the Breton countryside after 1600. To raise the level of spiritual awareness and to increase formal participation in the rites of the Catholic church, the Church promoted an existing cult of the dead. This proved so successful that Catholic adherence and the veneration of the departed remained important aspects of Breton culture until the twentieth century (Croix, 1981a, vol. II, ch. 18).

A dearth of written texts surviving from the Breton-speaking rural parishes makes any attempt to reconstruct popular piety and changing practice difficult. The peasantry left few records of their beliefs other than entries in the parish registers and occasional wills. Western Brittany is, however, rich in religious monuments and art. It is possible that the design, construction and iconography of religious buildings, together with information gathered from wills and printed religious works, might help to explain the origins of the Breton 'Culture of Death' and its changing importance in the community of the living. This study is an attempt to discuss some of these issues by considering the building and use of one particular monument, the ossuary or charnel house, found in and associated with other religious structures in western Brittany from the fifteenth century onwards. This chapter will examine the ways in which the design and function of ossuaries was influenced by religious belief and social context.

The construction of monumental ossuaries began in Brittany in the fifteenth century, primarily in association with secular religious foundations patronised by the ducal and other seigneurial families, such as the chapel at Saint-Jean-du-Doigt (Côtes d'Armor) founded by Duke Jean V in 1441. By the mid sixteenth century, ossuary building had become widespread in the parishes of western Brittany, in association with parish churches and important chapels: over one half of the surviving ossuary monuments were constructed between 1550 and 1600. After a period of slow but persistent monument construction in the first third of the seventeenth century, a second notable phase of ossuary building occurred between 1630 and 1680. After 1700 there was little new construction; of the ossuaries erected in the eighteenth century, some were second or third ossuaries for the same churchyard as at Plouneur-Trez, Finistère (F.) or the reconstruction of existing structures as at Châteaulin (F.).

Ossuaries were only one of an ensemble of religious monuments to be constructed in association with parish churches in early modern Brittany. The late fifteenth century onwards was a period of great rebuilding of religious monuments in the province. The material foundation was economic prosperity after the end of the Hundred Years' War, based on shipping between the Atlantic and Flemish ports, fishing on the banks of Newfoundland, grain exports, linen and canvas production. This increased revenue was used in part to finance the embellishment of religious sites through increased offerings, donations and levies on parishioners. At Guengat (F.) the parish church was rebuilt in the fifteenth century, with the addition of two further chapels in the sixteenth century. A triumphal gateway and walls enclosed the cemetery in the second half of the sixteenth century, which was further embellished by the erection of a calvary and an ossuary in 1577 (Pelletier, 1981, p. 78). At Argol (F.) the church was rebuilt in the mid sixteenth century, a calvary erected in 1617, a monumental gateway and walls enclosed the cemetery precinct in 1659 and an ossuary was added in 1665. By the mid seventeenth century, most western Breton parishes had some if not all the features of a monumental parish close. Breton beliefs in the afterlife had not, after all, suffered from a Protestant Reformation (see chapter 1).

Charnel houses were common throughout western Europe in the later Middle Ages. The ossuaries of Brittany are unusual for their distribution, density, form and longevity of function, in many cases continuing in use until the twentieth century. Firstly, permanent, monumental ossuaries constructed of stone are geographically dense in the Breton-speaking west and north of Brittany, the modern *départements* of Finistère, Côtes d'Armor and Morbihan. Almost every parish had its ossuary in the early modern period and more than 200 of these structures still survive. The high rate of survival in western Brittany contrasts with that of England where most ossuaries were cleared in the sixteenth and seventeenth centuries (Curl, 1980, p. 136). The greater number of structures built in western Brittany, their stone construction and the conservative attitude to cult sites – pre-Christian megaliths and springs and fountains, embellished with Christian iconography, were in use as religious sites throughout the Middle Ages and early modern period, for example – caused the conversion of ossuaries to other, secular, uses rather than their destruction after their original function had ceased. The survival of large numbers of ossuaries in western Brittany is also in contrast to the eastern half of the province, where most charnel houses were constructed of wood and subsequently demolished, so there is little surviving physical evidence of their construction and distribution.

A second distinctive feature of the ossuaries of western Brittany is their monumental construction. Built of durable materials, granite or schist with slate roofs, they were appropriate structures for the long-term storage of human remains in an appropriately dignified repository. Three types of ossuary were built in western Brittany. At their simplest, arcaded niches built into cemetery walls could be used as charnel houses, as at Laz (F.). The earliest and most persistent design was the 'attached' ossuary, constructed as a lean-to against the south wall of a church or chapel, between the south porch and the tower, abutting the nave, as at Lochrist, Morbihan (M.) and at Saint-Herbot (F.). From the mid sixteenth century, chapel-ossuaries appear, free-standing buildings at the west end of cemetery precincts, near to the church tower, with easterly-facing windows and doors: the ossuaries of Pleyben and Saint-Thégonnec (F.) are of this type. Chapel ossuaries might also house altars as at Sizun (F.) and at Ploudiry (F.), where the chapel built in 1639 had an ossuary at its south end and an altar and chapel at the north end, divided by the entrance door to the building. All three types of ossuary were open to the elements, to exhibit bones as well as to shelter them. Niche and attached ossuaries were arcaded, so that their contents were visible to visitors to the cemetery precinct. The windows of chapel ossuaries were left unglazed, for the same purpose. The visual display of human remains was central to the purpose of these monuments.

The iconography associated with ossuary buildings shared motifs with the rest of Catholic Europe: scenes recalling death, judgement and repentance. There were distinctive Celtic elements in the repertoire of symbols however and the decoration of western Breton ossuaries had a specific, pedagogic function. *Ankou*, in Breton tradition, is the personification of death in skeletal form who leads away the souls of the dead to the world beyond. He is represented in sculpture and relief on ossuary buildings. He is sometimes shrouded, armed with a spear or dart, and is often depicted opposite the angel of the resurrection as at Brasparts (F.) where *Ankou* appears with the motto 'Je vous tous tue' (I will kill all of you) and the angel responds with 'Levez-vous' (Rise up!). Motifs of skulls and bones are common: at La Martyre (F.) a man holds aloft a femur. At Landivisiau (F.) statues of the living in their finery contrast with the dry bones seen through the windows of the ossuary. The central message is clearly stated: whoever you are, death is inevitable. This prospect was intended to have a moralising effect, which also functioned to underpin the sanctions of the Church.

Inscriptions reinforced this simple message with theological prescriptions for the small numbers of literate élite in the countryside. At Saint-Thégonnec (F.) the dead speak to the living:

O sinners repent while you are alive because for we dead there is no more time. Pray for we dead because one day you will be as we are now. Go in peace!

At La Martyre, the parishioners are reminded,

Death, Judgement, Cold Hell. When men think of these they must tremble. Foolish is he who does not reflect that we will all die.

Statues of saints also appear on chapel ossuaries, to inform the living and to protect the dead, to remind the faithful that prayer and intercession can ameliorate the awful prospect of hell, if not the agonies of death itself. Death was inevitable, but there were practical measures that the living could take, through the mediation of the Church and its saints, to lessen the time a soul spent in the agonies of purgatory.

The ossuaries of western Brittany were repositories for the bones of the long dead displaced by subsequent inhumations. Charnel houses were constructed throughout Europe during the Middle Ages but their use declined after the sixteenth century. Medieval Christians were conservative in their use of burial sites; their desire for a resting place physically close to sacred sites where the living said their prayers, the chancel or altars of a church and to churchyard calvaries or crosses, meant that traditional burial grounds continued in use for hundreds of years, long after they were full. The bones of old interments were constantly disturbed by new inhumations. A charnel house provided a practical, dignified shelter for skulls and long bones to reside in until Resurrection Day, even if other bones were buried in a common pit.

Parish registers, records of diocesan visitations and letters between church officials show that Breton burial grounds were overcrowded in the sixteenth and seventeenth centuries. In 1617, the rector of Malestroit (M.) noted in the parish register that to inter Jean Menaud, it was necessary to empty three graves; in 1675, the diocesan visitor to Cordemais (Loire-Atlantique) was concerned about the quantity of bone found piled up in the cemetery and at the back of the church (Croix, 1981a, II, pp. 1100–1). The shortage of burial space was exacerbated in this period by population growth throughout the province. Croix estimates that the population of Brittany grew to two million people between 1480 and 1670, to become one of the most dense in France, at about 50 people per square km (Croix, 1981b, p. 127). The death rate of 50 to 80 individuals per year in most rural parishes put great pressure on existing burial space. Clerical attempts to extend the burial into the churchyard met with resistance: in 1653, the *curé* of Port-Louis (M.) noted that 'for some time, the majority of parishioners have shown great aversion to the burial of their relatives and friends in the cemetery' (Croix, 1985, sect. 21).

Shortage of space was greatest in the west of Brittany. The late fifteenth and sixteenth centuries saw changes in burial practice which exacerbated the shortage of available interment space within rural communities. The early modern period saw increased burial inside churches in western Brittany, unlike the rest of northern Europe; by 1600 inhumation inside the church, once the preserve of the clergy and nobility, was the norm for all but the poorest of rural adults. At Ménéac (M.) only 19 per cent of parish interments were made inside the church; by 1600 this had risen to 35 per cent and the incidence of church burial increased during the seventeenth century (Croix, 1985, sect. 21). This practice continued into the eighteenth century. At Plélan-le-Grand, Ille-et-Vilaine (I.V.) in 1720, 95 per cent of all adults aged 21 to 65 were buried inside the church; 89 per cent of burials in the churchyard were children and adolescents below the age of 20 (Lemaître, 1983, p. 253). The near-ubiquity of church burial in the west led to great overcrowding below the floor of the nave where the laity were interred. The small area of primary burial space for these communities, compared to cemetery-using parishes, and the greater population growth of the west, put great pressure on available resources. The Church's solution was simple. To accommodate demand, residence inside the church was limited in time, to between five and seven years. Periodic translations of bones from the church to the cemetery made room for the more recently departed.

Christian concerns for the sanctity of the dead, the need to preserve at least major skeletal remains for Resurrection Day and the close kinship of living parishioners with the departed under the nave, necessitated careful and solemn secondary disposal of the dead. The high incidence of ossuaries in the west of Brittany, where church burial was greatest, is thus linked to the practical need for a dignified and appropriate site for the secondary disposal of remains. In communities where physical proximity to sacred places was a source of spiritual salvation and comfort, the departed were still housed close to the holiest sites of altars, saints' statues and relics and to the prayers of the living. The ossuary itself was used as a commemorative site or chapel for prayers and masses. The monumental ossuary was thus an important feature of western Breton church-burying communities, for it allowed many of the faithful a period of time close to the sanctuary of the church and a secondary resting place in a structure which was the particular focus and site of prayer and ritual for the dead.

The function and significance of the monumental ossuaries in western Brittany went beyond the simple repository of human remains. If storage alone were required, a common grave in the cemetery, a wooden lean-to shelter against the church wall or the conversion of a room above the south porch would have sufficed as at Iffendic and Miniac-sous-Bécherel in eastern Brittany. Storage was not the sole purpose. The pedagogic iconography of symbols, inscriptions and the display of remains themselves; the association of ossuaries with a suite of refurbished religious monuments in a carefully enclosed space; the delineation and ritualisation of sacred and funerary space, are all indicators of spiritual as well as material changes in the circumstances of parish life during the early modern period.

Croix has interpreted the enclosure of parish church precincts and the greater ritualisation of the use of sacred space as a product of the impact of Counter-Reformation ideas on Breton Catholicism. Tridentine-inspired clergy worked to enhance the level of participation in, and understanding of, Catholic rites and doctrine in rural regions of Europe. The clergy sought to eliminate superstitious belief and improve moral behaviour, through careful teaching and the increased role of the priesthood in secular and religious life. Croix suggests that this was achieved in western Brittany by the adoption by the Church of a pre-existing cult of the dead. Increased use of the themes of death, judgement and repentance in preaching and teaching led to improvements in moral behaviour through constant reference to the 'Wages of Sin'. The construction of monuments in which the Church could conduct and control religious practice in rural areas was a physical manifestation of religious and cultural change in the countryside of western Brittany (Croix and Roudaut, 1984). Colvin suggests that the renewed insistence on personal mortality of Counter-Reformation Catholicism led to enhanced use of morbid iconography; in charnel houses where bones had previously been chaotically deposited, human remains were 'arranged with macabre skill as baroque tableaux of mortality' (Colvin, 1991, p. 225).

The chronology of the construction of parish closes and their iconographic embellishment shows, however, that the ideals of the post-Tridentine Church were only one, and a relatively late, influence on the rural parishes of western Brittany. By the late Middle Ages, the use of images of death in art and in speech were important in both informal, popular belief and formal religious theology. By the fifteenth century, the mental world of the rural Breton was coloured by the presence of the community of the dead, the *Anaon*, defined by Croix as a term used to describe the collective society of the souls of the departed (Croix, 1981a, vol. II, p. 1059). The worlds of the living and the dead were contiguous. This was a Manichean world in which Satan, *Ankou* and the departed intervened constantly in the affairs of the living. Elaborate precautions were taken to appease the dead and to avoid the malign influences they could invoke. Père Véjus's 'Vie de Michel Le Nobletz' (1666) describes folk practices current in the early seventeenth century, although with the disdain of the missionary; Le Nobletz witnessed the relatives of a dead person emptying out all the water stored in their house to prevent the soul of the deceased from drowning; on the eve of the feast of Saint John the Baptist, when fires were lit in all homes, stones were placed around the hearth so that departed relatives and ancestors might warm themselves in comfort (Delumeau, 1977, p. 163). These were clearly non-Christian customs coloured with Christian context and detail.

The informal beliefs and practices of the rural world had been conditioned, extended and rationalised by the doctrine and rituals of the late medieval Catholic Church. The spirituality of the fifteenth century emphasised the greater responsibility of the individual for his or her own salvation, through the medium of priestly intercession and prayer, together with meditation and good works. The principal images used to promote personal commitment were that of the suffering Christ, the inevitability of death and the horrors of purgatory and hell. The theological design was to prompt the sinner to repentance, prayer, Christian morality and good works. The practical results were an art, literature, spirituality and preaching in which the teachings of the Church seemed to have been reduced to a single image, that of the perishable nature of all things (Huizinga, 1949, p. 138).

From the thirteenth century, the preaching of mendicant friars, popular in Brittany as elsewhere in western Europe, had Sin, Death and Hell as its central themes. The verbal message was reinforced by visual images. The fifteenth-century *Danse Macabre* at Kernascléden (M.) and the three living and three dead on the wall of the chapel at Kermaria in Plouha (F.), the construction of monumental ossuaries with seigneurial chapels to display the wages of sin, all encapsulated the ultimate commonality of human experience as preached by the friars. The earliest books to be printed in Brittany such as *Loys des trespassez* (Laws of the Departed) (1485), *Buhez mal den* (The Life of Man) (1530) likewise reveal the centrality of death and eternal punishment in contemporary Catholic thought.

The complex interaction between sin and death, justification and good works, was understood in diverse ways in different communities. An important result of the interaction of informal beliefs about the closeness of the supernatural world with formal Church teachings about salvation through prayer and priestly intercession was the increased importance of ritual for the dead. A central function of the Catholic church was intercession for the dead. Chantry and Mass priests serviced their needs with prayers and ceremonies. Quéniart has suggested that confraternities devoted to Marian cults, widespread in the north and west of late medieval Brittany, were the rural equivalent of urban confraternities for the souls of the departed, where social and spiritual activities were organised to commemorate deceased members of the group (Quéniart, 1985, sect. 25). Duffy has argued that in late medieval England, religious gilds or confraternities existed in almost all villages as well as towns and that membership was available to the majority of the adult population. A central activity of gilds was funerary: members participated in the burial of their departed brethren and procured prayers and masses for the repose of their souls (Duffy, 1992, pp. 142–3). Peasants who could not individually afford to endow masses and obits could still share in the prayers of the community through the actions of the confraternity (Houlbrooke, 1989, p. 36).

The impulse to salvation through faith and good works is witnessed throughout the Breton countryside. In the Trégor, 46 parish churches and 60 chapels were rebuilt or refurbished between 1400 and 1500, in a diocese of 101 parishes (Minois, 1985a, sect. 20). Croix's study of wills shows that between the late fifteenth and the seventeenth centuries testators were concerned to secure prayers to help release them from purgatory. Bretons who left wills devoted most of their disposable wealth to post-mortem intercession; 80 per cent of pious donations went to found obits and masses, compared with 20 per cent for charitable works in the first third of the seventeenth century (Croix, 1993, p. 382). This increased to 87 per cent by the period 1661–68 (Croix, 1981a, vol. II, p. 1141). Prayer through the mediation of the Catholic priesthood was a means of individual salvation and of appeasing the collectivity of the dead who continually entered into the lives of the living. In fifteenth- and sixteenth-century Brittany there were no firm boundaries between official and popular belief in the rural world. There were simply more or less useful strategies for coping with death and the departed.

The late medieval emphasis on the centrality of death and judgement as a human experience led to an increased formalisation of the use of religious space in which the prayers of the living and the remains of the dead coexisted. Firstly, the religious centres of parishes were embellished to promote the teachings of the Church. Secondly, increased emphasis on lay prayer, meditation and reflection increased concern for the appropriate use of sacred monuments and space. Official ecclesiastical prescriptions concerning the use of religious sites and appropriate behaviour therein began in Brittany in the fifteenth century. In 1462, a synodal ruling of Tréguier ruled against the playing of games, mummeries and dancing in churches and cemeteries, and the holding of fairs and markets on holidays; in 1585, synodal statutes of Rennes condemned all those who dealt with enchantments, spells and the apparitions of spirits; also dances, drinking, banquets and games in churchyards (Pelletier, 1990, II, pp. 90, 99).

The rural world of western Brittany responded to the complex and eclectic mixture of popular belief, redemption theology and changing standards of behaviour at religious sites with a rebuilding programme beginning in the fifteenth century. Catholic and popular belief fused in the widespread monumentalisation of religious space, commissioned by the lay leaders of rural society. The refurbishment of parish precincts was a response to a growing acceptance of the need for decorum in the outward ritual expressions of religious sentiment, at all social levels. It perhaps also shows a desire to delimit the zone of the dead, to contain them physically, away from the outside world of the living. Churches were enlarged, calvaries were built as focal points for preaching and so that living and dead Christians might be close to the image of the Crucified Christ. Churchyards were enclosed by high walls with monumental gateways clearly to define the sacred space of God which was also the zone of the dead. The importance of sacred sites is further shown by the increased frequency of church burial. Finally, ossuaries were built to house the bones of the dead in dignity and to act as sites for prayers. These strategies both incorporated the dead into the social space of living worshippers but also kept them apart within it.

There is some evidence in the disposal practices of western Brittany to support Ariès' suggestion that in the later Middle Ages, there was increased awareness of individual identity and a corresponding decline in the importance of the community, but in the realm of the living rather than in the disposal of the dead (Ariès, 1977). The late medieval and Counter-Reformation church urged individual action and repentance on Christians rather than mere participation in communal, collective church rites. Ariès suggests that this was expressed in death with individualised burial and commemoration. But in western Brittany, an individual's burial site remained intact only for a short period of time. Badone suggests that the identity of the individual disintegrated as the flesh decayed. Hertz observed that in traditional Indonesian societies, the dead were 'stored' until their flesh had decayed; only then were they buried with full funerary rites and admitted to the company of their ancestors (Hertz, 1960, p. 35). In the ossuary, the individual's bones mingled with those of the collective dead (Badone, 1989, p. 135). The living individual, responsible before God for his or her own actions, joined a community of the dead, whose individual identities disappeared with the advance of time. The living community was responsible for the collectivity of the dead, which was not seen in personalised terms. Changing attitudes to the individual in death only came later in western Brittany, in the late eighteenth and nineteenth centuries, when a more individualistic treatment of the departed began; after translation to the ossuary, skulls were kept apart from other bones, in boxes labelled with their names.

Intimacy with the other world and a vision of an afterlife dominated by hell created for Croix 'un terrain idéal pour la pastorale de la mort' which he sees as an even more marked feature of church teaching after 1640 (Croix, 1993, p. 391). The period after 1630 saw a systematic attempt to improve pastoral care and the quality of religious life in the rural parishes of Brittany, especially in the west. Synodal decrees on pastoral care and moral behaviour of the laity were more systematically enforced by parish visitations. Increased admissions to the regular clergy in the towns of Brittany produced missionaries eager to work amongst the poor and in the countryside. The Jesuit Maunoir led 439 missions to the Léon, Cornouaille and the Trégor between 1640 and 1683, while the Lazarists were one among several orders who were active in the north and east of Brittany between 1645 and 1700. Seminaries to train parish priests were founded in each diocese. By the early eighteenth century the standards of education and commitment of the Breton parish clergy was greatly enhanced.

There is no doubt that in the late seventeenth century religious observance and church attendance increased in rural Brittany. There were numerous manifestations of greater lay participation in the rural Church. The decades between 1620 and 1660 saw a rapid foundation of new confraternities in country parishes. The new Confraternity of the Rosary, another Marian confraternity, associated by Quéniart with intercession for the departed of the community, rapidly spread; 40 per cent of the parishes of the diocese of Vannes, over 60 per cent of those of Saint-Brieuc and 85 of the 101 parishes of Tréguier, adopted the cult (Quéniart, 1985, sect. 25; Minois, 1985b, sect. 26). A second phase of monumental building associated with parish churches occurred, particularly in the Léon, Cornouaille and the Trégor, where much missionary activity was concentrated. The great parish closes of Pleyben,

Guimiliau and Saint-Thégonnec (F.) date largely to the mid seventeenth century. The heightened fervour of rural Christians shown by these indicators was not the result of clerically-inspired changes in religion and popular culture as suggested by Delumeau, Croix and others. They were traditional responses to new spiritual ardour.

The apparent success of the post-Tridentine Church in enhancing rural participation in formal religious activities has been explained by its adoption of popular visions of death and hell as a central theme of teaching. The Church substituted its own rites for traditional practices to appease the dead; the role of the parish priest as intermediary between the community of the living and that of the dead was augmented. The missionaries and seminary-trained priests certainly used images of death and hell in their preaching, art and theatre to promote morality and repentance. When Le Nobletz left the Île de Batz after a mission in 1611, he gave the parishioners a skull as a souvenir of his sermons, to remind them of the serious purpose and inevitable end of their lives (Lascaux, 1983, p. 30). The building of high walls and ossuaries in parishes which lacked closes was encouraged, to emphasise and control entry to the domain of the dead. Religious practice was focused more closely on parish institutions with the promotion of local saints' cults and that of the faithful departed of the parish.

But the success of the Counter-Reformation Church in western Brittany did not lie in the novelty of its message. The visual and mental images of death and judgement were a constant theme in the teaching of the Church and the popular culture of the Bretons from at least the fifteenth century. Attachment to local parish structures was already strong in Brittany. Investment in parish monuments and the popularity of regional saints such as Yvi and local cults of Saint Anne are notable from the late Middle Ages. At the beginning of the seventeenth century, testators requested an average of 500 masses for their souls, with the nobility demanding an average of 1500, a pious action again strongly rooted in local religious structures although the large numbers of masses requested reflects the high social status of the testators, 72 per cent of whom were nobles, clerics, professional groups and merchants (Croix, 1993, p. 384; Croix 1981a, vol. II, p. 1142).

The novelty of Counter-Reformation Catholicism lay not in its themes and principles but its more systematic and organised teaching in the Breton countryside through preaching, Masses, greater use of the sacraments and schools, and the new institutions of catechism and individual confession. The use of better-trained agents, seminary-trained parish priests and professional missionaries gave new impetus and meaning to the old themes. As Houlbrooke states, 'Despite the influence of the new currents which flowed through the post-Tridentine church, the most vigorous forms of 'Baroque' piety had their roots in the Middle Ages' (Houlbrooke, 1989, p. 36).

The Catholic reformers did not sweep away old beliefs and practices, replacing them with a new image of death and repentance. They adapted their message to the culture of the rural world, which received and interpreted the teachings of the Church on its own terms. In western Brittany, the building of ossuaries and parish precincts, the iconography of death and its representation in art and literature, stories and theatre, shows that an eclectic mixture of official theology and popular belief about the dead pervaded rural religious life. The dead remained present in the world of the living; they walked at night and entered into houses. The Catholic church in all periods encouraged participation by offering means of pacifying and commemorating the dead, through prayer and ritual. The construction of ossuaries and parish closes was a result of fusion of theological message and popular desire to pacify the dead. The monuments were understood in different ways by different sections of the community. They remain a physical manifestation of the accommodation of élite and popular belief; their longevity shows the durability of the traditions of the rural world, to which new religious movements had to adapt if they were to have any success.

Parish building slowed in the late seventeenth century, as economic prosperity in Brittany declined and the fiscal demands of the Bourbon kings increased. An edict of the king's council of 1695, confirmed by the *Parlement* of Brittany in 1702, forbade new parish constructions if their necessity were not recognised by the provincial administration (Pelletier, 1981, p. 15). In the eighteenth century, parish building projects had to be approved by the royal intendant, whose concern was that funds should not be diverted from royal taxes to church building. From the mid eighteenth century, the use of parish monuments also began to change, again sanctioned and enforced by the secular élite of the province. Church burial and the use of ossuaries slowly declined. Salvation through the benevolence of God rather than through fear of hell gradually gained acceptance. Vovelle and Chaunu found changes in the provisions of wills and a decline in observance in Provence and Paris respectively, which they explain by dechristianisation in this period (Vovelle, 1973; Chaunu, 1978). New ideas of hygiene and fears of the danger of the vapours of decay led to prohibitions on church inhumations (McManners, 1981, pp. 233, 306). The growth of Romantic sentimentalism, its rejection of the Baroque image of the horrors of death and the increasing focus of families on their private lives and property, altered attitudes to collective ritual and communal burial (McManners, 1981, p. 445).

After a terrible epidemic of scarlet fever in Rennes in 1719, the *Parlement* of Brittany forbade church burial. This was strongly resisted in the countryside and largely ignored. But the attack was renewed with another edict of 1749 and after 1755 parishes began to comply (Danigo, 1980, p. 123). The movement for cemetery reform was extended throughout the kingdom in 1776 by a royal decree which ordered the removal of burial grounds to the outskirts of towns; reformers in cities such as Angers proposed to adopt the edict by opening large *extra muros* cemeteries franchised to commercial companies (McManners, 1960, 1981; Kselman, 1993, p. 167). Before 1789, cemetery reform was slow to permeate the countryside but from the mid eighteenth century ossuaries began slowly to go out of use, in towns before the countryside and in the east of Brittany before the west. The Revolutionary period accelerated these changes. In 1827, the ossuary of Pleyben was converted into a school and then into a *mairie*. There was occasional, local opposition to such moves: when the authorities of the town of Quiberon tried to close the ossuary in 1848, the townsfolk rioted.

In the twentieth century, economic and commercial considerations have caused cemeteries to be relocated to the outskirts of villages and the conversion of churchyards to car parks. In 1981, Croix estimated that the number of functioning ossuaries had declined from 22 in 1961 to 8 in 1979 (Croix, 1981a, II, 919–21). The grand constructions of the dead are now frequented as tourist attractions and promoted as quaint relics of a distinct, Celtic past.

REFERENCES

P. Ariès, *L'homme devant la mort*, (Paris, 1977).
E. Badone, *The Appointed Hour: Death, world view and social change in Brittany*, (Berkeley, 1989).
P. Chaunu, *La mort à Paris (16è, 17è, 18è siècles)*, (Paris, 1978).
H. Colvin, *Architecture and the After-Life*, (New Haven and London: Yale, 1991).
A. Croix, *La Bretagne aux 16è et 17è siècles. La vie-la mort-la foi*, 2 vols., (Paris, 1981a).
A. Croix, 'Un culture originale: la vie, la mort, la foi au Bretagne aux 16è et 17è siècles', *L'Information Historique*, 43 (1981b), pp. 123–9.
A. Croix, 'Les lieux de sépulture', in A. Croix (ed.), *Les Bretons et Dieu. Atlas d'histoire réligieuse 1300–1800*, (Rennes, 1985), section 21.
A. Croix, *L'âge d'or de la Bretagne 1532–1675*, (Rennes: Ouest-France, 1993).
A. Croix and F. Roudaut, *Les Bretons, la mort et Dieu de 1600 à nos jours*, (Paris: Messidor, 1984).
J. S. Curl, *A Celebration of Death*, (London: Constable, 1980).
J. Danigo, *Eglises et Chapelles du Canton de Cléguérec*, (U.M.I.V.E.M., 1980).
J. Delumeau, *Catholicism between Luther and Voltaire*, (London, 1977).
E. Duffy, *The Stripping of the Altars. Traditional Religion in England 1400–1580*, (New Haven and London: Yale, 1992).
R. Hertz, *Death and the Right Hand*, (London: Cohen and West, 1960).

R. Houlbrooke, 'Death, Church and Family in England between the late Fifteenth and early Eighteenth centuries', in R. Houlbrooke (ed.), *Death, Ritual and Bereavement,* (London: Routledge, 1989).

J. Huizinga, *The Waning of the Middle Ages*, (1924, New York: St. Martin's Press, 1949).

T. A. Kselman, *Death and the Afterlife in Modern France*, (Princeton: Princeton University Press, 1993).

M. Lascaux, *Légendes et Traditions de la Mort en Bretagne*, (Châteaulin: J.O.S., 1983).

A. J. Lemaître, 'Espace sacré et territoire vital au XVIIIè siècle', *Annales de Bretagne*, 90 (1983) 249–59.

J. McManners, *French Ecclesiastical Society under the Ancien Régime: A study of Angers in the Eighteenth Century*, (Manchester: The University Press, 1960).

J. McManners, *Death and the Enlightenment*, (Oxford: Clarendon, 1981).

P. Mérimée, *Notes d'un voyage dans l'Ouest de la France*, (Paris, 1836).

G. Minois (1985a), 'Églises et chapelles en chantier: l'exemple du Trégor au 15è siècle', in A. Croix (ed.), *op. cit.* (Rennes, 1985) section 20.

G. Minois (1985b), 'Les confréries pieuses: l'exemple du Trégor', in A. Croix (ed.), *op. cit.* (Rennes, 1985) section 26.

Y. Pelletier, *Les Enclos Paroissiaux*, (Rennes: Ouest-France, 1981).

Y. Pelletier (ed.), *Histoire Générale de la Bretagne et les Bretons*, 2 vols. (Paris, 1990).

J. Quéniart, 'Le réseau des confréries pieuses', in A. Croix (ed.), *op. cit.* (Rennes, 1985) section 25.

M. Vovelle, *Piété baroque et déchristianisation en Provence au 18è siècle*, (Paris, 1973).

5 The Green Ground
John Pinfold

The 'Green Ground' was the popular name for an irregularly shaped piece of land in the parish of St Clement Dane's.[1] It was for centuries the location of a graveyard which became notorious for its insanitary conditions and the numerous abuses which took place within it. As an extreme, but not necessarily untypical, example of inner-city graveyards, it featured prominently in campaigns by reformers in the early nineteenth century to close down the insanitary and overcrowded metropolitan graveyards.

In the sixteenth century this area of London was still open land. A map of 1592 shows that the area was covered by fields and gardens. In the south-east corner of the site was the Grange belonging to Lincoln's Inn (from which the present-day Grange Court derives its name), whilst to the west, running parallel to Clement's Lane was an open sewer which led directly and insalubriously to St Clement's well, the parish's principal supply of drinking water. This sewer was bridged at the corner of Portugal Street and Clement's Lane by the Lord Treasurer's Bridge. It almost certainly follows the same course as the sewer which today runs under the car park and part of the basement of the Lionel Robbins Building which presently houses the British Library of Political and Economic Science of the London School of Economics.

This irregular space of land was purchased for use as a graveyard in 1638 as is shown by a commission for a rate to wall it in, granted to the parish of St Clement Dane's by Dr Juxon, the Bishop of London. One corner was to be occupied by the parish poor house. The graveyard is clearly marked on two maps of 1658, the first drawn by Hollar and the second by Faithorne and Newcourt. These show that at that time Portugal Street (or Portugal Row as it was usually called then) was still only half built. Nevertheless the population of the area was growing steadily. A rudimentary housing census carried out in the parish in 1636–37 gives an indication of the increasing pressure of population when it reports that over the previous seven years 17 houses had been divided into tenements.

The population was set to expand even more rapidly in the years following the Restoration, and especially so after the Great Plague and the Great Fire which had given added impetus to the move westwards which had already begun. Between 1620 and 1656, 183 new houses were built in the parish, but between 1656 and 1677 another 253 were added. Development along the north side of the graveyard took place in 1674 after Bishop Henchman had given his permission for shops and houses to be built there. With the poor house and the Grange Inn on the east side and St Clement's Lane to the west, this effectively meant that the graveyard was totally surrounded by buildings, and access to it soon became possible only through a dingy passageway which Dickens memorably described 200 years later in *Bleak House* as 'a reeking tunnel of a court [which] gives access to the iron gate – with every villainy of life in action close on death and every poisonous element of death in action close on life' (Dickens, 1853).

In the late seventeenth century, however, this area was far from being the slum it later became. Indeed, Portugal Street was very fashionable during the Restoration period; the name indicates that it was at one time the home of the Portuguese ambassador. The rate books of St Clement Dane's reveal that in 1668 its inhabitants included Lady Arden, Sir Charles Waldegrave, Lady Fitzharding, Lady Diana Curzon, Lord Cardigan, Lady Wentworth, Lady Coventry, Judge Weld and Lady Davenant. No doubt many of them were attracted to the locality by the famous Duke's Theatre which stood on the north side of the street, opposite the burying ground and 'the handsome house for the poor', on the site now occupied by the Royal College of Surgeons. Wilmot, Earl of Rochester, the Restoration wit, lived for a time next door to this theatre. The theatre also appears in Pepys' diary, and, at a slightly later period, it saw the premières of some of Congreve's plays and of Gay's *Beggars Opera*.

Despite all these famous people living in the neighbourhood, however, it seems as though none of them was buried in the Portugal Street burying ground which, right from the start, appears to have been primarily the last resting place of the poor and the destitute of the district. Many of the wealthier inhabitants of the neighbourhood no doubt owned country estates and chose to be buried there; it is also possible that those that were buried within the parish were buried in the church itself. The only person of any note that I have been able to establish as having been buried there was Joe Miller, famous in the eighteenth century and indeed through to the middle of the nineteenth century as the inspiration of *Joe Miller's Jest Book*. Joe Miller died in 1738 aged 54. He was best known in his own day as a comic actor, particularly in some of Congreve's plays, and also as a compiler of other men's jokes and witticisms. In fact the *Jest Book* was not published until after his death and was probably written by John Mottley. This book was a bestseller in its day; it went through three editions in the first year, and then another seven in the following seven years. Almost everyone will have come across the reference to it, probably without realising what it means, in Dickens' *Christmas Carol*, for when the reformed Scrooge, at the end of the book, sends the goose round to the Cratchit family he declares that this will be a jest better than any of Joe Miller's.

An interesting snapshot of the state of the graveyards in the mid eighteenth century is provided by a survey of St Clement Dane's carried out by the Company of Parish Clerks in 1732. This, as quoted by Diprose, reported that:

> In the upper churchyard are three schools, one for seventy boys, who are taught reading, writing and arithmetic by the master, who is allowed £40 per annum, and coals and candles. The boys are also interested in the mathematics, and are taught to sing by masters who are paid for teaching them. In the second school are forty girls, under a mistress, who teaches them to sew, read, knit &c, and she has £20 per annum, besides coals and candles. These girls have also a singing master to teach them; and both boys and girls are clothed in blue. The third school is the Horn-book school, where thirty children are taught by the mistress.
>
> In the upper churchyard there are also six Almshouses with six rooms, and twelve poor women in each house who are allowed 2s. per week; and in the lower churchyard are five rooms for poor women, each of whom has 2s.6d. per week; they have also coals at Christmas, if they can make interest to get them. (Diprose, 1868, pp. 42–3)

The Almshouse had its own burial ground, at the south-west end of St Clement's Lane.

The impression given is that of a well-ordered and stable community, more like that one would expect to find in the countryside than in the heart of a thriving and rapidly expanding metropolis. The same survey lists the number of houses in the parish as 1750.

The impression is only partly correct, however, for throughout the eighteenth century, as the death rate fell, London was becoming increasingly overcrowded. Moreover, the population of St Clement Dane's was changing socially as the wealthy and the fashionable continued their migration towards the new West End. The rate books of the parish record this change as names of gentry and obviously professional people disappear; at the same time one increasingly finds annotations, made no doubt by the rate collectors, recording that individuals 'can't pay' or 'won't pay'. By the middle of the century the houses in St Clement's Lane had declined into beggars' lodging houses. No doubt these were like those described by Saunders Welch in a letter to the Duke of Newcastle in 1753:

> old ruinous houses which the occupiers fill up with straw and flock beds, which they nightly let out for twopence for a single person or threepence for a couple... Four or five beds are often in one room, and what with the nastiness of these wretches and their numbers such an inconceivable

stench has arose from them that I have been hardly able to bear it the little time that my duty required me to stay. Spiritous liquors afford means of intoxication... and the houses are open all night to entertain rogues and receive plunder. (S. Welch, 1758)

There are also eighteenth-century reports of houses in the parish falling down, rather as Mrs Clennan's was to do in Dickens' *Little Dorrit*. On occasions this would cause loss of life, with the bodies being carried into the poor house for laying out and then being interred in the paupers' pit in the burial ground.

In 1770 the poor house in the corner of the graveyard became incorporated as a workhouse. It also became increasingly overcrowded as the numbers of the poor grew. We can get a good idea of what the workhouse was like at this time from the details given in the Parliamentary Report on the Laws which concern the Relief and Settlement of the Poor (1776). This reveals that the building was of brick (which cost 23 shillings per thousand – unfortunately the report does not tell us how many bricks were used) and stone, and consisted of 30 apartments, exclusive of the offices. Its capacity was 300, suggesting that there were ten people to a room, and the available figures suggest that it was full or almost full for most of the time. At Midsummer 1773 the number of occupants was 285; this rose to 297 at Christmas. The pattern was the same the following year when there were 290 inmates at Midsummer and a capacity 300 at Christmas. At all times a very high proportion of the inmates, usually around 30 per cent, were children under eight years old. Odd as it may seem today, this actually represented an improvement for prior to this time St Clement's was notorious for continuing the old practice of putting out destitute or orphan children to nurse. This sounds more humane than confining them to an institution, but was not so in practice. Jonas Hanway, writing in 1766, tells of how, during a period of nine months, 23 children had been entrusted to a Mrs Poole; two of these had been discharged, three were still alive and *eighteen* had died after being in her care for about one month (Hanway, 1766).

As in all workhouses, those who were capable of it were put to work. At Portugal Street this consisted of 'making slop work and carding wool for mops, and the infant poor in spinning ditto'. This work brought in £82.7.0d in 1773 and £222.14.0d the following year. The staff was headed by the master and the matron who were paid £30 and £20 a year respectively. There was also a baker and brewer, paid £20, and a 'master of mop work' who was paid £25. The workhouse was no doubt a harsh regime and deaths were frequent. Forty-eight inmates, of whom 11 were children died in 1773; in 1774 the number almost doubled to 83, 16 of them children. Throughout this period,

the 'Green Ground' and St Clement Dane's Churchyard absorbed the vast
majority of the corpses in the parish.

Given the state of the Portugal Street burying ground, it is not surprising
that it should have attracted the attention of George Walker during the course
of his campaign for the closure of the pestilential inner-city graveyards in
London. Walker was a surgeon who lived locally in Drury Lane and who
thus clearly had first-hand knowledge of the appalling condition of the
graveyard. He also had studied in Paris and had come to the conclusion that
the French system of establishing large cemeteries outside the city boundaries
was infinitely preferable to the welter of crowded and insanitary inner-city
graveyards which could be found in London. He was convinced that the smell
emanating from these overcrowded graveyards was poisonous and could ruin
the health of those who had to live nearby. The miasmic theory of disease
held sway until successfully challenged by the germ theory after the fourth
cholera epidemic. The 'Green Ground' in Portugal Street provided him with
a great deal of evidence to support his case and his account of the burying
ground in his book *Gatherings from graveyards* provides a graphic description
of how it appeared in 1839.

Walker reported that the soil of the burying ground was saturated with
human putrescence. Graves were shallow and were often left open, so that
human bones could be seen lying on the surface. One reason for this was
that the grave-diggers re-used the coffin wood, and every day large heaps
of this could be seen waiting for removal at the corners of the graveyard.
The nails and tin plates were also removed and re-used or sold.

This desecration of the graves did not escape the notice of passers-by. Walker
quoted the following letter from *The Times* of 25 June 1838:

Sir, Passing along Portugal Street on Saturday evening, about ten minutes
before seven, I was much shocked at seeing two men employed in carrying
baskets of human bones from the corner of the ground next the old watch-
house (where there was a tarpaulin hung over the rails to prevent their being
seen, and where they appeared to be heaped up in a mound), to the back
of the ground through a small gate...why is this desecration? Sir, – I feel
more particularly than many might do, as I have seen twelve of my nearest
and dearest relatives consigned to the grave in that ground; and I felt that,
perhaps, I might at the moment be viewing, in the basket of skulls which
passed before me, those of my own family thus brutally exhumed. At all
events, for the sake of the community at large, it should be inquired into.

J.M.

For those who had to live in the area the effluvia from the burying ground was almost equally offensive. The smell was so bad that the inhabitants of Clement's Lane were compelled to keep their windows closed, and the walls of the houses which backed onto the graveyard were frequently seen 'reeking with fluid'.

It was to Walker's way of thinking, therefore, hardly surprising that fever was so prevalent in the neighbourhood. He tells of one occasion in early 1839 when he was called upon to attend a poor man who lived at 33, Clement's Lane, and who was 'fast merging into that low form of fever of which this locality has furnished so many examples'. On looking into the 'Green Ground', through a window of this man's room, Walker noticed a grave open within a few feet of the house. The sick man told him that:

> that grave is just made for a poor fellow who died in this house, in the room above me; *he* died of typhus fever, from which his wife has just recovered, – *they have kept him twelve days*, and now they are going to put him under my nose, by way of warning to me. (Walker, 1839, p. 152)

Up until about 1820, Walker reported, the poor were buried in a vault underneath an area of the graveyard known as the 'pauper's promenade'. Trap doors covered the entrance to the vault, in the centre of which was a large chimney or shaft which released foul gases into the atmosphere; the smell was 'disgustingly offensive', and was frequently intolerable during hot weather. For pauper burials inferior coffins, made of 'slight deal three-quarter stuff', were used. These soon crumbled away or were destroyed by being packed tightly on top of one another. As the coffins broke up, the bodies began to fall out of them, and had to be pushed back in as tightly as possible to make space for new arrivals. On one occasion when this happened three guineas were found in one of the broken coffins; it is likely that they had been stolen and hidden there by the nurse from the workhouse, who had then not been able to retrieve it before the burial took place.

The exact location of the paupers' vault is not known, but it very likely adjoined the workhouse in the north-east corner of the site. In 1839 this was finally closed down, as Walker explained:

> The workhouse, at the north-eastern extremity of this ground, has, within the last few weeks been disused; and the building, it appears, is about to be converted into an hospital, for the reception of patients, belonging to the Medical and Surgical department of King's College. (Walker, 1839, p. 153)

But although the workhouse became a hospital nothing else changed. The buildings remained the same, and, more importantly, the graveyard remained open and subject to the same practices which had taken place there 'beyond the memory of man'. It is surprising that, in the early years, this did not seem to bother the hospital authorities unduly. Nevertheless, Walker continued his campaign to have the burying ground closed and the bodies reinterred elsewhere.

The Portugal Street burying ground figured prominently in the evidence given to the 1842 Parliamentary Select Committee on Improvement of the Health of Towns. Bartholomew Lyons, a grave-digger, was asked whether he had ever worked at the Portugal Street graveyard. His answers show how overcrowded it had become:

> No; I would not work in the place on any account.
>
> Why not? – Because it bore such a bad character.
>
> What do you mean by a bad character? – For cutting up the coffins; they do not bury the dead there above two feet deep, or hardly that.
>
> Do you mean that it was reckoned particularly unhealthy to dig graves there? – I should not like to dig in a place unless I could get what is regularly allowed by law, five feet; five feet is what I am obliged to dig.
>
> You mean that the graves were not sufficiently deep? -Yes.
>
> If they go down five feet, that you consider legal? – Yes, that is regular.
>
> But in this Portugal-street graveyard they have not that practice? – No, they cannot do it by all accounts.
>
> Is it the custom ever to dig through coffins in that graveyard? – By all account they cannot dig a grave at all without digging through coffins.
>
> Do you speak here from your own knowledge and observation? – I only go by what they tell me, and I have seen the graves there where I could put my arm against the bottom.
>
> (*PP*, 1842, QQ. 1109–18)

It is interesting to compare this with Charles Dickens' fictional account of the burying ground in *Bleak House*, when Jo the crossing sweeper says that Nemo's body is 'among them piles of bones, and close to that there kitchin winder! They put him in wery nigh the top. They were obliged to stamp upon it to git it in. I could unkiver it for you with my broom if the gate was open'.

Another grave-digger, John Eyles, gave evidence of the nauseous gases which were given off from the 'Green Ground': 'I have seen the ground smoke and reek on a summer's morning; about five o'clock you will see it smoke the same as if there had been hot water poured down' (*PP*, 1842, Q. 1207). He added that graves were often left open four or five days, and, on being asked whether this practice caused a smell to come up replied simply and no doubt with considerable feeling: 'It does' (*PP*, 1842, Q. 1210).

One of the members of the Select Committee, Peter Ainsworth, MP, corroborated this account with a description of his own visit to Portugal Street. Like so many others, he was struck by the strong smell, and felt that this was prejudicial to the health of the local inhabitants. He also pointed to the small size of the graveyard, and to the fact that it was situated in the middle of a very densely-populated neighbourhood. Ainsworth noticed a hole in the ground and was told that this had been bored into a coffin to allow the gases to escape. The combination of all these factors led him to the conclusion that the state of the graveyard was a major cause of disease in the parish (*PP*, 1842, Q. 1308).

It is clear from some of the evidence to the Select Committee that this condition of the graveyard was far from new, and that it had been both overcrowded and a health hazard for many years before. George Thomas White, a barrister, gave evidence as follows:

> I wish to state that with reference to the burying-ground in Portugal-street, in the year 1819... I resided in Lincoln's-inn-fields, and I daily went down from Lincoln's-inn-fields, the north side of them, along Portugal-street, and passed that burying-ground, and whilst graves were being dug there; I was constantly annoyed by the stench of the ground.
>
> Have you any knowledge of the ground later than 23 years ago? – Yes, I have very often passed it since that.
>
> With the same result? – When there have been graves opened I have smelt the same offensive odour. (*PP*, 1842, QQ. 2506–8)

One small piece of evidence given by George Walker throws a particularly gruesome light on the overcrowded nature of the old graveyard. Describing an interview he had had with the Bishop of London on the subject, he stated:

> I mentioned to him the circumstances of shocking desecrations having been perpetrated in my neighbourhood, and that while in Paris I read in a London newspaper that his lordship had been present at an interment in the city, and had seen 13 sculls thrown up; he said, 'Yes, it was so.' I told his lordship that they were thrown up wholesale in my neighbourhood; that I was informed that upwards of 500 sculls had been thrown up in one day and deposited in another part of the grave-yard, and that the grave-digger had amused himself by chalking the number on the wall. (*PP*, 1842, Q. 2072)

Walker, and many of the other witnesses, were particularly concerned at the proximity of King's College Hospital to all this, but, strangely enough, some of the medical witnesses seemed very unconcerned. Consider the evidence of Dr Robert Bentley Todd, Fellow of the Royal College of Physicians and of the Royal Society:

> I can state to the Committee that no inconvenience [to the hospital] has been felt from the contiguity of the grave-yard. (*PP*, 1842, Q. 2408)

The Committee pressed him on the point:

> Are you able to state...that no case of fever has been aggravated, so far as you can trace the result, by the contiguity of the grave-yard and the effluvium thence arising? – I feel quite satisfied that no case has been aggravated from its being in that hospital; it is remarkably well ventilated.
>
> It has been stated to this Committee that the exhalation of the effluvium from grave-yards furnishes one of the most powerful causes of disease and mortality in this metropolis. As a medical practitioner, and a physician, of considerable experience, are you able to state to the Committee any opinion upon that subject? – I think that some very erroneous opinions have been put forward on that question.
>
> Have you never heard any of complaints as to the unpleasantness of the effluvium arising from that burial-ground? – Not in our building.
>
> At no period of the year? – When the hospital was first opened I heard some vague complaints, but I apprehend that was more arising from fancy, arising from persons resident in the hospital, than anything else.
>
> What was the nature of those complaints? – They complained of smells which they perceived in the lower part of the building; for the last year and a half I have not heard of any such complaints.
>
> Have you any knowledge of the state of health in the houses immediately adjoining? – I should say little or none.
>
> ...As a medical man, you have no objection to the state of King's College Hospital? – No objection. (*PP*, 1842, QQ. 2412–3, 2437–41)

Opposition to George Walker's campaign came both from other clergy and from other doctors. Dr Todd's lofty complacency is perhaps more easily understandable when it is remembered that the hospital had only recently been established on the site, that it was well-ventilated, and, above all, that it was a very great improvement on the workhouse it had replaced. The workhouse, despite being described as a 'remarkably healthy' one, frequently contained as many as 500 inmates (this figure is particularly striking when compared with the capacity of 300 given for the same building in 1776), whereas the hospital, on the same site and to begin with using the same building, did not admit more than 120. It is also worth recalling that, whilst the Medical Committee of the Hospital disagreed with much of the detail of the submissions by Walker and others, they did accept the general principle that graveyards should not be sited in the middle of densely populated towns. In a letter of 21 June 1841, submitted as evidence to the Select Committee, they stated that:

> They quite agree with Mr. Walker that the metropolitan grave-yards are, in general, too small for districts so densely peopled as those in which they are situate, and that, in consequence, graves are often prematurely disturbed; this gives rise to revolting scenes, such as Mr. Walker describes, and renders the grave-yards a great public nuisance. (*PP*, 1842, p. 496)

Despite the great amount of evidence that was presented to the committee, little progress on achieving the closure of the metropolitan graveyards was made at this time. The reasons for this are fairly clear. First, there was considerable clerical opposition to Walker's campaign. The Bishop of London, for example, told Walker that he had lived next to Bishopsgate graveyard without any ill effects, to which Walker retorted that the Bishop's lodging was no doubt greatly superior to most other people's. More seriously, many of the inner-city churches needed the income from burials in order to maintain the clergymen's stipends and pay for church expenses; vestries, beadles, parish clerks and sextons all also made money from their involvement in funerals and burials. Income from burial fees was even more important for some of the (voluntary) Nonconformist churches, as is illustrated by the extreme case of Enon Chapel, which was situated close to the 'Green Ground', and which is discussed in the sixth chapter of this volume. Furthermore, the parishes were largely independent of central control in these matters and could safely ignore instructions from above if they wished. It is also clear from the evidence that many of the medical authorities were supremely complacent about the health hazards created by graveyards such as Portugal Street; that local government bodies, under the control of vested interests and anxious to keep rates low, proved unwilling to act; and that, of course, many of the local inhabitants, having lived with the nuisance all their lives, did not even think about it: the graveyard had always been there and no doubt always would be. It took a committed outsider like Walker to point up the abuses and set the campaign for their remedy in motion.

Walker's cause had a powerful ally in Edwin Chadwick whose report on *Interment in towns* (1843) widened the argument into the whole area of urban mortality and the arrangements made for death and burial among the working classes. Chadwick argued that the existing situation was unacceptable on both medical and moral grounds, and that comprehensive remedies were needed as a matter of urgency. Given the scale of the problem, it was the state which needed to become involved and to provide solutions on a national level.

However, despite the support of a number of members of parliament, such as William Mackinnon, Robert Slaney and Anthony Ashley-Cooper (later Earl of Shaftesbury), it proved impossible to pass any significant legislation at this time. In 1842 Mackinnon introduced a bill which would have abolished intramural burial in London and given vestries the power to establish new cemeteries outside the city. This bill was later withdrawn, partly in response to criticism from Chadwick that it did not go far enough, partly because the government promised to bring forward a bill of its own. This then became conveniently forgotten as parliamentary and government interest moved on to other larger issues, such as the Repeal of the Corn Laws, the agitation for Free Trade, and the upturn in the economy from 1842, which contributed to the second phase of private cemetery building, which is covered in the seventh chapter of this volume.

Nothing daunted by this apparent failure, Walker continued his campaign, using such bodies as the National Philanthropic Association and the National Society for the Abolition of Burials in Towns as a platform. He also attempted to stimulate local opinion on the issue, and in this he had some success. On 12 August 1848, for example, he addressed a public meeting of local inhabitants at which he said that:

> it had been stated by eminent French Physicians that Cholera was caused there by the practice that prevailed, of *burying* their dead only a few inches under the surface of the earth. He was quite sure that not only *Typhus Fever*, but *Measles, Small pox*, and other diseases were caused by the contiguity of *GRAVEYARDS*.....he felt that the *Public Health* would never be secure, until they prevented the DEAD from being buried *under the noses of the living*. (National Philanthropic Association, 1850, p. 71)

Walker's reference to cholera in his speech is significant, for it was the great cholera epidemic of 1848 which was to lead to the closure of Portugal Street as it was to the closure of so many other inner-city burial grounds. As R.J. Morris has pointed out, cholera funerals were particularly horrible, with rushed burials, coffins containing lime and shrouds dipped in coal tar (Morris, 1976). Even the most complacent local inhabitants feared the sight of them. This fear was important in changing the climate of opinion, but perhaps even more important was the fact that the cholera epidemic proved conclusively, at least as far as the vast majority of people, and especially those in the medical profession, was concerned, that there really was a connection between the disease and the state of public hygiene and sanitation. The cholera revival helped stimulate the first Public Health Act of 1848.

The first measure to tackle the burial problem was the 1849 Act To Amend the Nuisances Removal and Diseases Prevention Act. This empowered the General Board of Health to inquire into the state of burial grounds and where necessary to prohibit interments; churchwardens were to be encouraged to agree that parishioners could be buried outside the parish where further burials would constitute a health hazard. The National Philanthropic Association reported the effects of this Act as follows:

> This Act, as if providentially, has been most opportune with regard to the pestilence lately prevailing so extensively throughout the Metropolis; and if cholera have had no other beneficial result, it certainly has been the means of shutting up some of those monstrous foci of infection, – the London grave yards. – The labours of this Association, – even when joined to the powerful appeals of Mr. George Alfred Walker, and the researches of Parliamentary Committees, were almost futile, when opposed to the interests of the parochial clergy and the apathy of a population, already sickening with disease; – until the appalling fact became public that London was burying 3000 human carcases within itself, week after week! and that, by far the greater proportion were interred in golgothas already too crowded, – hemmed in by dwelling houses, – open to its streets, courts and alleys, – and surrounding its churches and chapels!!. The Council has much satisfaction in recording that within the last month, the General Board of Health, – in order to stem the tide of cholera which threatened to slay its tens of thousands per week, instead of its present number of victims, – (that is if intramural interment had been continued) – has ordered [a large number] of burying grounds to be shut up. (National Philanthropic Association, 1850, p. 80)

In practice, however, this legislation failed in much of its purpose, many of the old corrupt practices continuing to exist. Certain burial grounds, temporarily closed, re-opened for funerals. This led to the Metropolitan Interments Act 1850, which forbade any further burials in London's inner-city graveyards. It also provided compensation for the loss of burial fees to the Anglican clergy whose graveyards had been closed, and to the parochial vestries, clerks and sextons, thereby neutralising one of the main sources of opposition to change. Further legislation came in 1852 with the Act to amend the laws concerning the Burial of the Dead in the Metropolis. This gave the Privy Council the power to prohibit further interment in any place of burial in the metropolis if such action was necessary for the protection of public health.

These measures signalled the end for the 'Green Ground'. In the immediately succeeding years, the bodies were removed to one of the large new out of town cemeteries, and King's College Hospital tore down the old workhouse building to replace it by a fine new hospital building which occupied the majority of the site. This was opened in 1855 and received a laudatory welcome from Charles Dickens in *Household Words*. The hospital moved out of the centre of London in the early years of this century, and the site was then acquired by W.H. Smith & Son in 1913. Smith's pulled down the hospital building and replaced it with 'Strand House' which was completed in 1916; and it is this building, converted to house the British Library of Political and Economic Science in 1978, which occupies the site today.

The significance of the story of the 'Green Ground' is that it provides an outstanding example of many of the issues the early Victorian reformers were confronting, and of the necessity of government intervention in burial reform. Only government action could overwhelm the resistance to reform from Churches, chapels, parish undertakers and private cemetery owners. As the population expanded and as urban areas, especially in London, became more overcrowded, questions of public health, of the forms and effectiveness of local administration, and, more generally, of the whole condition of the poor became ever more urgent. The appalling state of the 'Green Ground', and other similar burying grounds, showed only too clearly that the existing arrangements, however appropriate they may have been in the past, were no longer acceptable. In *Bleak House* Dickens used the graveyard as a powerful symbol of decay and corruption, and it is perhaps appropriate to close this account with Esther Summerson's description of her approach to the graveyard which forms the climax of the hunt for her mother, Lady Dedlock:

> At last we stood under a dark and miserable covered way, where one lamp stood burning over an iron gate and where the morning faintly struggled in. Beyond it was a burial ground – a dreadful spot in which the night was very slowly stirring, but where I could dimly see heaps of dishonoured graves and stones, hemmed in by filthy houses, with a few dull lights in their windows, and on whose walls a thick humidity broke out like a disease. (Dickens, 1853)

Thanks to the efforts of Walker, Chadwick and their associates the 'Green Ground' was already history by the time Dickens wrote those words. The public accommodated itself rapidly to the new local authority cemeteries. Much remained to be done, but at least the 'Green Ground' had played its part in contributing to the process of much-needed reform.

NOTE

1   For a general overview of the development of the Clement's Lane area, see, for example, Brooks (1989), George (1951), Heckethorn (1896), Holmes (1896), *Survey of London Vol. III* (1912) and Walford (*c.* 1875).

REFERENCES

C. Brooks, *Mortal remains: the history and present state of the Victorian and Edwardian cemetery*, (Exeter: Wheaton, 1989).

E. Chadwick, *Report on the sanitary condition of the labouring population of Great Britain: a supplementary report on the results of a special inquiry into the practice of interment in towns*, (London: 1843).

C. Dickens, *Bleak House*, (London: 1853).

J. Diprose, *Some account of the Parish of Saint Clement Danes, past and present*, 2 vols. (London: Diprose and Bateman, 1868–76).

D. George, *London life in the eighteenth century*, 3rd ed. (London: Kegan Paul, 1951).

J. Hanway, *An earnest appeal for mercy to the children of the poor*, (London: 1766).

C. W. Heckethorn, *Lincoln's Inn Fields and the localities adjacent: their historical and topographical associations*, (London: Elliot Stock, 1896).

Mrs B. Holmes, *The London burial grounds: notes on their history from the earliest times to the present day*, (London: T. Fisher Unwin, 1896).

Household Words, 15 December, 1855.

R. J. Morris, *Cholera 1832: the social response to an epidemic*, (London: Croom Helm, 1976).

National Philanthropic Association, *Sanatory progress: being the fifth report of the National Philanthropic Association*, (London: Hatchard & Son, 1850).

Rate books of the parish of St. Clement Dane's. [mss].

'Reports from Committees on the Laws which concern the Relief and Settlement of the Poor, [1775–1788]'. *Reports from Committees of the House of Commons, 1715–1803*, IX, 239ff.

Select Committee on Improvement of the Health of Towns. 'Report...together with the minutes of evidence; Effect of interment of bodies in towns', 'British Parliamentary Papers' (*PP*), 1842, X, 349–618.

Survey of London. Volume III. The parish of St. Giles-in-the-Fields. Part 1. Lincoln's Inn Fields, (London: London County Council, 1912).

E. Walford, *Old and new London: a narrative of its people and places. Volume 3. Westminster and the western suburbs*, (London: Cassell, Petter & Galpin, *c.* 1875).

G. Walker, *Gatherings from graveyards, particularly those of London*, (London: Longman, 1839).

S. Welch, *Proposal to render effectual a plan to remove the nuisance of common prostitutes from the streets of this Metropolis*, (London: 1758).

6   Enon Chapel: No Way for the Dead[1]
Peter C. Jupp

Students of Victorian Church History often receive their first glimpse of Enon
Chapel in Sir Owen Chadwick's distinguished *The Victorian Church* (1966).
Chadwick describes the difficulties encountered by the Church when, as a
long-established rural organisation, it needed to adapt its procedures, personnel
and resources to operate successfully within a rapidly growing urban
environment. The Established Church had allowed metropolitan growth to
flourish without a serious policy either of church or of church-yard extension.
In this context Enon Chapel is instanced:

> The cemetery illustrates how the life of the country needed converting into
> the life of the city...The church was the home of the dead as well as the
> living. The countryman passed the graves of his father and grandfather
> on his way to worship God...A few prudent parishes...bought extra
> land...And still the old churchyards continued in use. Hideous stories
> were told: how the floor of the Enon Street Baptist chapel off the Strand
> was bare planks dividing the congregation from mounds of skeletons
> beneath...how some of the bones from Enon Street helped to make the streets
> by Waterloo Bridge. (Chadwick, 1966, p. 326)

This chapter has a double aim. It offers a first attempt to unravel the Enon
narrative and sets it in its context as an extreme example of the competitive
resort to which Churches might go when the tradition of inter-Church rivalry
coincided with a crisis in the provision of burial space (Manning, 1952;
Mackintosh, 1972). The resolution of this crisis involved the loss by the English
Churches of their monopoly on the provision of burial space, after a period
of over one thousand years (Jupp, 1993). This provision was then entrusted
to local government authorities who have wrestled with their inherited
responsibility until the present.

'Enon Street' never existed. While the geographer will search the London
atlas for it in vain, yet he will find Enon in the New Testament:

> John [the Baptist] was baptizing at Enon near Salim, because there was
> much water there: and people came and were baptized. (John 3:23 A.V.)

Enon is thus a fitting name for a Baptist Chapel. Enon Chapel was situated
in Clement's Lane or, more fully, St Clement's Lane. It connects the Strand
with Portugal Street. John Pinfold introduced the neighbourhood in the

previous chapter. He revealed that Enon's nearest 'much water' was the Essex Street sewer that ran underneath the Chapel.[2]

Enon Chapel became the newest burial place in this neighbourhood. There were eight others within 600 yards: St Clement Dane's churchyard, the Almshouse ground in Clements Lane, Drury Lane, Tavistock Street, St Mary-le-Strand, Savoy Chapel, St Paul's Covent Garden and the Green Ground (less than 100 yards away). The immediate area was 'one of the most filthy places which can be found anywhere; here is Enon burying ground on one side, and this in Portugal-street on the other, and the stinking market in the centre' (*PP*, 1842, Q. 291).

Improvements had not been unknown. In the 1790s Pickett Place had been built north of St Clement Dane's; it was demolished in the 1870s. In 1828 King's College was established adjacent to St Mary-le-Strand. The new King's College Hospital leased the parish workhouse vacated in 1839. The poor health of the inhabitants may be illustrated by the Hospital's initial report: 47 000 out-patients were treated in the first 21 months, 1840–1 (Hearnshaw, 1929, pp. 143–5).

Enon Chapel opened as a Baptist Chapel on 16 April 1822 (Walker, 1847, p. 15)[3]. The Baptists were independents: that is, each chapel was responsible for its own affairs, calling (and dismissing) its own minister, and raising its own income. One condition of membership of the Church was traditionally by immersion in water upon confession of faith as a believer. That each Baptist congregation contained a core of convinced adult volunteers was one great part of its strength. Another was the Baptist allegiance to traditional Protestant principles. The Higher Criticism of the Bible had not then affected the centrality of literal Scripture interpretation as one Dissenting source of authority, nor had the foundation of the Baptist Union (1812) made sufficient headway to raise the quality of local leadership by nationally encouraged standards.

Enon was unusual to have originated with both a minister and a building. Normally, a Baptist congregation originated with a group of (Baptist) Christians who ran their own affairs until they could afford a minister. Most new Nonconformist Churches of that era began as a congregation gathering in a domestic dwelling and seeking permanent accommodation when they were more numerous and sufficiently funded. This development had been encouraged by 'The Little Toleration Act' of 1812 which ended the registration of Nonconformist chapels.

In July 1821 the Surveyor for the Commissioner of Sewers reported that new houses were being built in Clement's Lane. Building had commenced over the main line of the Essex Street sewer, where other houses had fallen down during stonework repairs on the sewer (perhaps during the rebuilding of the sewer in August 1820). The Committee of Works took the unusual step of giving notice to the 'party building such house' that he should face any consequences of choosing such a site.[4] Enon Chapel was built by John Evans of 19, High Street, St Giles. On 4 January 1822 the Surveyor reported that Evans was, without leave from the Commissioners, erecting a chapel over the sewer in the Sawyer's Yard in Clement's Lane. Evans was summoned to appear before the committee on 18 February. There is no record that he complied.[5]

On 16 April 1822, Mr W. Howse (variously, House) became the minister at Enon. He sought immediately to raise a congregation to fill and finance it. He and his wife took up residence next door, presumably in rented lodgings. Evidence was later adduced suggesting that Howse had built the chapel himself as a speculation (*PP*, 1842, QQ. 167–8) but the exact situation is not yet clear. The upper storey of the chapel was used for worship and, later, for the education of the young in a Sunday School (three sessions every Sunday). The lower storey was used, from October onwards, to bury the dead.

Enon was not unusual in seeking to raise its income by burying the dead. Vault burial had been a lucrative source of church income since the mid seventeenth century. Its frequent practice in London had been encouraged by the Fifty New Churches for London Act 1711 (Litten, 1991, p. 221). Vault burial in crowded cities was almost a necessity. St Clement Dane's provides the nearest example. Whilst its churchyard measured 12 779 square feet, its vaults contained 13 916 cubic feet. Fees followed the traditional pattern: in the 1840s, the vault (nearest the altar) cost £6 12s 4d (Diprose, 1868, p. 80). Burial fees in the churchyard were £1 17s 2d for adults and £1 10s 2d for children. In accordance with the English principle that the parish took responsibility for burying its own dead, there was a higher fee for non-parishioners, £2 15s 10d for adults.

Enon's 15s fee for burial, only 200 yards away and within St Clement Dane's parish, proved especially attractive. Howse's work was still profitable: some central-London incumbents were receiving less than two-fifths of this sum as their funeral fee (Jupp, 1993 pp. 195–9). Howse was not denomination-ally strict:

> Are all the persons of the Baptist persuasion in that neighbourhood buried there? – No; but it was so cheap, that the poorer classes in the neighbourhood, not, perhaps, religious persons, were buried there.
>
>   You account for the vast number of persons buried there from the cheapness of the fee? – Yes. (*PP*, 1842, QQ. 191–2)

Nor was Enon unusual, as a non-Anglican Church, in seeking income from burial fees. The Congregationalists in Fetter Lane buried their dead in their own vaults, whilst those in Whitefields Tabernacle, Tottenham Court Road, had their own burial grounds beside the chapel. In some instances, burial fees were used to prime chapel building funds. The Presbyterian Church in Regent Square was built in the 1820s:

> the vaults under the church (were) ... excavated and built as a preliminary to the superstructure, they were sold as Burial Vaults, the proceeds going to swell the Building Fund, of course they were not freehold, but the lease was for 999 years and they cost £40 each. (Adamson n.d., p. 1)

In the period of chapel-building which followed the Napoleonic Wars, the attraction of burial-vaults was stimulated by fears of body-snatching. Until the Anatomy Act 1832 (Richardson, 1987), churches and chapels with vaults could literally make capital out of human deposits. The connection was explicitly made by Walker:

> (this) chapel is a specimen of one of the evils which sprang up during the operation of certain laws that were hostile to the cultivation of anatomical science, which have happily now been repealed. The professed security of the dead was made the pretext; individual advantage was the real object for depositories of this description. (Walker, 1839, pp. 156–7)

This use of burial-vaults to finance chapel building did not last long. Rugg describes below (chapter seven) the Nonconformist pressure behind the private cemetery movement of 1820–50. The repeal of the Test and Corporation Acts in 1828 gave a stimulus for wealthier Nonconformists to celebrate their funerals in the new Nonconformist chapels which were being built, alongside Anglican, in the new commercial cemeteries. This all made little difference to the unchurched poor. If they wished to avoid pauper burial in common graves in churchyards, inexpensive alternatives could be found in the commercial Green Grounds and the Dissenting Enon Chapels. Walker commented that the only private burial places, so called, were, strictly, 'vaults underneath, or grounds connected with, Dissenting meeting-houses' (Walker, 1839, press reviews p. 2).

Baptist Dissenters, rich or poor, suffered one specific handicap: the children of convinced Baptists were not baptised. Baptism was reserved for believers. When Baptist babies and children died before undergoing believers' baptism, and if the Baptist congregation had no burying ground of its own, then they were usually buried (by Anglican clergy) in that part of the parochial Churchyard reserved for the unbaptised, suicides and infidels.

This social slight could function as Christian testimony. If citizenship in Heaven was facilitated by, for instance, Baptist loyalty on earth, then the social slight was bearable, especially for as long as Baptists were few in number and economically powerless. This confidence was made more plausible by a Calvinist tradition which held that only the elect were redeemed for Heaven: for Baptists this meant that the baptism of children imparted no special Heavenly or post-mortem benefits. The Evangelical Revival of the eighteenth century began to weaken this tradition, suggesting that access to Heaven was open to all who believed in Christ. This shift in belief was accompanied by the rise, first, of a new understanding of Heaven as a location for the reunion of family members, and, second, of a sentiment towards children as members of families whose loss was to be mourned more seriously than heretofore. This connection, with its secularising theme, is complex and has yet to be delineated for Britain, as Stannard has explored for the United States (Stannard, 1977).

In previous centuries, Dissenters' identity as denominations and as social groups was underlined by the provision of their own burial places. This provision was a necessity for many Baptist churches, especially in areas where Anglican tradition militated against them. It was similarly a necessity for some other non-Anglican minority groups (Holmes, 1896). When Dissenters began to share in the wider spread of wealth brought by industrialisation, they sought more denominational control over burials (Rugg, chapter 7 below); for instance the conduct in parish churchyards of Dissenting funerals by Dissenting ministers. The ground rules for burial were changed in 1850 and 1852, when the Burial Acts established secular cemeteries. In 1880, Nonconformists were permitted to conduct burials according to their own rites in parish churchyards (Fletcher, 1974).

The story of Enon Chapel can now be set within its Dissenting context.

Enon Chapel's lower storey was reached either from the street or from the chapel interior, by a flight of five or six wooden steps beneath a trapdoor. There was no baptistry. A boarded floor separated the cellar from the chapel, that is, there was no lath-and-plaster to guard against smells, rodents or insects from below. Undertakers christened the cellar 'the dust-hole'. The space measured 59 feet by 29, large enough, by Walker's calculations, for only 1361 coffined bodies (Walker, 1846, p. 25).[6] He calculated this figure by allowing for equal numbers of adults and children and with coffins stacked in piles of six (Walker, 1847, pp. 15–16).

Howse was clearly successful in attracting the funeral trade. His income between 1822 and 1828 was calculated at £951 5s (Walker, 1846, p. 29). Any fear of body-snatching as the major criterion at Enon must have been replaced by the cheapness of burial fees. From the first interment (1822) until the last, it was claimed that between ten and twelve thousand people had been buried at Enon (Walker, 1839, p. 157; *PP*, 1842, Q. 135).

The cheap funeral facilities attracted poor people. They also attracted disease. Walker held the miasmatist hypothesis whereby disease was airborne. The proximity of so concentrated a deposit of decaying matter, and in so confined a space, to human beings sitting and breathing a few feet above it at regular Sunday worship, was clearly insanitary. It affected the health even of the undertakers who compounded the danger. An undertaker named Tombleson (of 4, Warwick Street, Golden Square) told Walker he had attended the funeral of an Oddfellow one Sunday at Enon Chapel. He had 'smelled a disgusting stench; he was seized within forty hours, with a violent pain in the back of his left hand, continuing about an hour'; the patient kept his bed nine weeks, with a malignant typhus. This was 1831/2. In July 1838 Walker was called to a house in Grays Inn Square where the housekeeper, a widow called Mrs Adams, was afflicted with pain around the liver. This was typhus 'accompanied with symptoms of extreme putrescency'. She died on 22 July. She had been a regular attender at Enon (Walker, 1839, p. 137).

A third witness places in context the introductory quotation from Chadwick. Samuel Pitts, a cabinet-maker, of 14, Catherine Street, Strand, attended Enon regularly from 1828 to 1834–5. He testified to the Select Committee:

At the time I attended it.... there were interments, and the place was in a very filthy state; the smell was most abominable and very injurious; I have frequently gone home myself with a severe headache, which I suppose to have been occasioned by the smell, more particularly in the summer time; also, there were insects, something similar to a bug in shape and appearance, only with wings, about the size of a small bug; I have seen in the summertime hundreds of them flying about the chapel; I have taken them home in my hat, and my wife has taken them home in her clothes; we always considered that they proceeded from the dead bodies underneath. (*PP*, 1842, Q. 128)

Pitts had had a son buried at Enon himself (*PP*, 1842, Q. 193). Yet like nearly everyone else, he had tolerated Enon's conditions. Why? Firstly, they were poor and Enon burials were cheap. Secondly, they probably knew that, by the Anatomy Act 1832, the unclaimed bodies of those dying in workhouses (the Portugal Street Workhouse was only 100 yards away) could be taken away for anatomical dissection. Secure burial evaded the student's knife. Thirdly, they all knew that all the vaulted churches nearby operated and tolerated almost similar conditions. In the era of the Poor Law Report (1834), burial at Enon was a bargain.

The exposure of the scandals at Enon is so intimately connected with Dr Walker, that his early career as a burial reformer must at this point be briefly rehearsed. Walker set up his practice in 1837 as a surgeon at 101, Drury Lane.

The ground level at St Martin's Drury Lane burial ground was five feet above the level of the neighbouring tenements. Walker saw, at first hand, the conditions of the poor: with open sewers and poor water supplies. Following the miasmic hypothesis, he believed that the gases emanating from human putrefaction could be fatal. His campaign for burial reform was based on his first-hand knowledge of health, sanitation and mortality. Seven burial grounds lay between his home and St Clements Dane's. Everybody knew of the peculiar smell of the metropolitan graveyards. Walker was concerned to prove that the smell not only sapped the health and physique of those who ate and slept nearby, but could prove fatal.

In *Gatherings from Graveyards* (1839) Walker expounded his connection between disease and burial. It drew attention to the appalling state of urban graveyards, whether owned by church, chapel or private entrepreneurs. The book was widely reviewed in the provincial press. The reasons for the astonishing reception accorded Walker are complex. They include the fact that in growing towns all over the country, aldermen, journalists and reformers had been made conscious of the danger of disease by the cholera epidemic of 1831–2. They sought to copy in their own localities the success of those cities which had opened private cemeteries. Many will have chafed for the end of the Church of England's near-monopoly of existing burial grounds. Walker fuelled their aspirations. His remedy, that intramural interment should be prohibited and new cemeteries be provided outside the towns, was attractive. His proposal, that only government legislation could upset the vested interests that obstructed reform, was controversial.

The story of Walker's campaign awaits full narration. Short accounts are provided in Brooks (1989) and Jupp (1993). *Gatherings from Graveyards* (1839) was the first in a series of publications which included *The Graveyards of London* (1841), a series of letters to the *Morning Herald* between November 1842 and February 1843, published as *Interment and Disinterment* (1843), *Burial Ground Incendiarism* (1846), *A Series of Lectures on the actual conditions of the Metropolitan Graveyards* (1847).

In January 1842 he addressed a petition to the Home Secretary, Sir James Graham. He itemised his concerns: the insanitary condition of urban burial grounds; the inability of exhausted soil to effect proper decomposition; the failure to supply more land for burials; the resort by graveyard staff to nefarious mutilation, burning or removal of dead bodies; the blind eye turned to these practices by clergy, ministers and vestry authorities. Compared, for example, with the arrangements on the continent and especially at Père Lachaise, such practices shed a poor light upon the reputation of civilised English society.

With the help of W.A. MacKinnon (MP for Lymington) Walker secured a Commons Select Committee of investigation. This concluded that 'the nuisance of interments in towns and the injury arising to the health of the community therefrom had been proved'. Another force behind the Committee on *Health of Towns* (*PP*, 1842) and its supplementary report *Interment in Towns* (Chadwick, 1843) was the Benthamite reformer Edwin Chadwick. Relations between Chadwick and Walker were not good, and it may be supposed that this lies behind Walker's apparent reliance upon a more individual campaign, pursued through lectures, writings and the establishment of a Society for the Abolition of Burial in Towns in 1845 (Walker, 1847, p. 29).

Walker faced considerable opposition from Anglican clergy.

> I am sorry to find the apathy of my reverend brethren, from the Bishop to the curate, so universally prevalent. It must arise from apathy or from interest... They are upholders of the practice [of intra-mural interment]: the sight of gold acts as an open sesame to the marble floors of our cathedrals and churches... (Walker, 1847, p. 21)

The clergy of the Established church were caught in a double trap. On the one hand, burial fees in London provided between a third and a half of clergy incomes. On the other, clergy played a key role in the very power structures that could have promoted reform, at vestry level. There were 68 vestries in North London alone: the very complexity of local government at that time militated against joint action to secure burial reform.

Nonconformist clergy could prove as defensive. The minister of Whitefields Tabernacle, John Campbell, was one who depended considerably upon burial fees. In *The Patriot*, he attacked Walker and MacKinnon for their attack upon chapel incomes, interpreting this also as a wider attack upon Nonconformist interests:

> no means whatever were taken by MacKinnon MP to ascertain the true condition of the Nonconformist burial grounds and the effect which this bill would have on Dissenting property... We can prove he was fully apprised of the ruinous results of this Bill to many of the most important congregations of the Nonconformist community. This Bill is very largely a question of property. (*Patriot*, 6 October 1842 p. 669)

The secular array of entrenched interests was as wide. Some religious authorities, fearful for their burial monopoly and fees, thought Walker represented the private cemetery interest. Certain private cemetery entrepreneurs, like those at Spa Fields, sought to reject his attack upon their livelihoods (Walker, 1846). He posed a threat to non-miasmatist doctors, in that government investment in Walker's schemes would have shown up the failure of their own analysis. As Pinfold showed in chapter 5, Walker drew the fire even of reformist doctors like Todd of Kings College Hospital. Todd claimed that Walker could not distinguish between the stenches of corpses and cooking-fat (*The Times*, 9 January 1849).

Walker paid special attention to Enon Chapel, situated so near to his home and practice. While the circumstances are unclear, sometime before 1839 the parish authorities of St Clement Dane's intervened in Enon Chapel: they forbad interments for one year (Walker, 1839, p. 154). Almost immediately, burials recommenced. By 1842, it was claimed, Enon had buried 12 000 corpses in 20 years. By what means could such a number have been accommodated? 'The expanding pavilion of the Fairy Tales was nothing compared to this', commented Saunders in 1843. How could such miracles of disposal be performed? He concluded that similar miracles of disposal were being worked at Enon as at St Anne's, Soho, where he commented of the sexton, 'that man that is dead has done most wonderful things in the vault' (Knight, 1843, p. 164).

Enon Chapel provided Walker and MacKinnon with critical evidence in their campaign for the prohibition of intramural burial. Enon featured in the Select Committee evidence of the undertaker Whittaker, the cabinet-maker Pitts and the master carman Burn. Pitts had worshipped at Enon between 1828 and 1835 and claimed to have learned of the abuses only afterwards. Bodies had been removed to make room for others; the minister's copper, used for washing, and his kitchen fire were regularly heated with coffin wood; the convenient sewer enabled the clandestine removal of further waste (*PP*, 1842, Q. 128 and *passim*).

Not only is the chronology difficult to unravel from contemporary records but it affects the estimate of Howse's work and his reputation. Clearly, the claim that he had disposed of 12 000 bodies was a major plank in Walker's case for reform. Yet, the figure was questioned at the time. The first known estimate is 10 – 12 000 (Walker, 1839, p. 154). Pitts, asked for an estimate of 'dead bodies...in this place', replied, 'I should suppose 10 – 12 000' (*PP*, 1842, Q. 135). Thereafter, the Select Committee adopted the higher figure (*ibid.*, QQ. 149, 190, 201).

Campbell was incorrect to claim that Walker's whole case depended upon 'three or four insignificant and notorious cases' of which Enon and the Green Ground were two (*Patriot*, 3 October 1842): the burial ground problem was London-wide (Walker, 1839, 1841). Campbell may have been on stronger grounds when he claimed that 12 000 was an exaggeration. He claimed to have been shown Howse's burial register by Mrs Howse who, further, denied the charges against her husband (*Patriot, ibid.*). Campbell's own estimate, for the seven years 1828–35 (the years Pitts had worshipped at Enon) was

3 503 burials. If this annual rate was representative of the whole period 1822–42, an estimate of 10 – 12 000 was not unfair. Did Pitts and Walker rely on such an estimate? One critical factor is the absence of the minister himself. It is clear that, sometime before 1842, Howse had died.

Critical questions await their answers, before the true significance of Enon can be assessed. When did Howse die? How many had he buried at Enon? Does his burial register exist, as Campbell claimed it once did? Did burials cease with his death? (*PP*, 1842, QQ. 132, 171, suggest not). The chapel was closed by 1842 (*ibid.*, 132, 169–70) but had chapel worship continued after Howse's death and had other ministers, with his widow, continued the burial practices? How genuine were the witnesses? Did MacKinnon and Walker deliberately exaggerate their case?

A further set of problems relates to alterations to the sewer and the action of external authorities. Walker claims the Parish temporarily closed Enon for burials. He also claims that the Commissioner had a new sewer laid under the chapel prior to 1839 (Walker, 1839, pp. 154–7). According to *The Patriot* it was concern for the removal of bodies via the sewer that caused the Commissioner to be 'strict in bridging it over' (*Patriot*, 3 October 1842). Pitts may mean that Howse himself supervised alterations to the sewer, saying '(the drain) was open when I first attended, and the Commissioners compelled Mr. Howse to build this arch over' (*PP*, 1842, Q. 155). Yet while Pitts claimed the 'arching over' was prior to his leaving the chapel in 1835, Burn testified that it was 'at the time the sewer was being built' that he was employed to remove 60 loads of rubbish. Burn was the master carman who supervised the operation on behalf of the Commissioner of Sewers when the sewer was enlarged, by being arched over. He had then shot this rubbish, consisting of putrefying human bodies, at the north side of Waterloo Bridge (*PP*, 1842, QQ. 260ff.) Burn's testimony elides too many facts.

There is, in W.H. Prescott's phrase, a 'snarl in chronology'. The whole evidence omits precise dating. Later commentators could not disentangle the dating problem. Knight wrote that the Commissioner compelled Howse to cover the open drain sometime before 1842, after which Howse resorted to burning more corpses (Knight, 1843, p. 164). According to Diprose, the Commissioner only acted in 1844 by closing the Chapel after becoming aware of the extent of the scandal (Diprose, 1868, p. 83).[7]

Enon undoubtedly had an enormous trade in funerals and drew its dead from many parishes. The establishment of more exact figures and the assessment of the use of the Enon story in Walker's campaign must await further attention which, like the other questions awaiting solution, lies beyond the limits of this chapter.

Clearly, the means of disposal by quicklime, fire and water must have been very effective if the carman was only able to take away 60 loads of 'rubbish' for Waterloo Bridge. The conjuring trick, it was afterward revealed, involved a secret door.

By August 1844 Mrs Howse and her son had moved. A new tenant, Fitzpatrick, occupied the house formerly occupied by the minister. Finding the kitchen ceiling too low, he employed one John Mars to work for him on Sundays, excavating the floor of the kitchen to provide more headroom. Mars took up all the flagstones, from the front of the house to the back. He found an enormous quantity of bones. He also found a door made in the brick wall dividing the kitchen from the burial vault. At this moment, neither Mars nor, presumably, his employer Fitzpatrick displayed an altruistic streak of character. Mars first filled the chapel cellar with bones, then the doorway. He dug down two feet in all directions. 'Finding after his utmost efforts, his labour must be interminable without actual removal of the enormous masses of bones' (Walker, 1847, p. 18), Mars failed to fulfil his engagement.

With the chapel closed, the bones remained for at least four more years, left 'to lie there and rot' (Diprose, 1868, p. 83). The chapel was then let to a teetotal group who held dances. This *danse macabre,* with couples crowding the ballroom floor, beneath which coffins and bodies festered, was featured as an illustration in the *Sanatory Progress* of 1850 (Morley, 1971, illustration 61).

Yet *Sanatory Progress* was outmoded. By 1850, the bodies had gone. Sometime in 1846–7, Walker bought or leased the Chapel with the intention of removing the remains. 6 000 people came to witness the removal of 'this Golgotha' whose detritus constituted 'four upheaved van loads'. Walker certainly contacted Abney Park, an unconsecrated, private cemetery, established in 1840 specially for Dissenters. Abney Park would only accept the remains of the Enon Dissenters on payment of £30. Walker then successfully approached the directors of Norwood Cemetery, established by the South Metropolitan Cemetery Company in 1837. Walker had the Enon congregation buried there at his own expense. The coffin wood was burned in Sydenham (Diprose, 1868, pp. 83–4).

Thereafter Enon Chapel went through 14 years of mixed fortunes. It was used as a concert room, a casino, a prize-fighting ring, a penny theatre and a bath-house. About 1861, it was fitted out by St Clement Dane's as a schoolroom-cum-chapel and renamed Clare Market Chapel. Supported by the Additional Curates Society and the Bishop of London's Fund, the Chapel also enjoyed the patronage of the Twinings and W.H. Smith families (Diprose, 1868, pp. 19–20).

The upward-mobility of Enon from Baptist Golgotha to Anglican Chapel paralleled the change in the Strand's fortunes. The Green Ground was closed in 1850, no longer providing a dismal outlook for patients at King's College Hospital. The Hospital itself was redeveloped in 1862, its nursing reorganised along Florence Nightingale lines, and ultimately transferred to Denmark Hill in 1909. In 1876 the entire north-east side of St Clement's Lane was demolished for the new Law Courts. Nineteen years later, the Webbs founded their London School of Economics in Houghton Street. Within ten more years the streets to the west and south – the location of Shaw's *Widowers' Houses* – were cut through to form the Aldwych and Holborn Kingsway and to facilitate increased traffic. With the decline of a resident population, the prospect of ill-health and premature death receded from the local streets.

The social context which produced burial practices like Enon's depended upon a complex of specific social conditions. These included:

1 A densely-packed urban population, prey to disease and premature death, in an era symbolised by inadequacy in the provision of fresh water and waste disposal.
2 An area of great poverty where the inhabitants, not unreasonably, bargained for the most economic fee that competing churches, chapels and funeral directors, supplemented by generosity, could manage.
3 The traditional form of disposal of the dead by burial, which was symbolically consistent with Christian doctrine but which also supported a Church monopoly interest in presidency at funerals.
4 A situation where the restricted availability of burial space, provided locally by the Established Church, could be partially and economically solved by the competition of Dissenting Chapels, albeit (in Enon's case) by its immoral if not criminal resort to the recycling of coffin space.
5 A prevailing Christian culture which was undergirded by a virtual Church monopoly where death was given a religious interpretation: funerals were all conducted by clergy, burial was the sole mode of disposal, and burial land was overwhelmingly supplied by the church.
6 An era where the law supported the system whereby the place of residence and the place of burial were linked, and were reinforced by systems of differential fees.
7 An era and an area where both the public and public institutions were insufficiently organised either to promote or to accommodate change.

The return of cholera in 1848 magnified the growing cries of the reformers into an irresistible imperative. Morris (1976) has charted how cholera in 1831–32 galvanised the public health movement, by positing a link between health and environment.

Cholera in 1848 reactivated the call for reforms in just those conditions that had promoted Enon: reorganisation of water supplies, sanitation and sewers; the abolition of intramural burial and the provision of new and extensive burial grounds outside the city boundaries, the funding, ownership and maintenance of which was to be by public authorities; the severing of the link between place of residence and place of disposal, which lifted responsibility for burial from parish-based government and transferred it to elected, secular authorities representing a wider constituency. These broad-based authorities could fund much larger pieces of land outside London if the poor would consent to travel there by train. The dead of central London need no longer be shot to ground near Waterloo Bridge, but could be sped from Waterloo to Woking, or from King's Cross to New Southgate.

The combined pressures of locality upon funerals – local undertakers, local clergy, local disposal, the conservative and perhaps superstitious instincts of neighbours, all in an area of acute poverty – were dispersed. There was a general readjustment of interest groups in death. In a long Victorian perspective, the bereaved family steadily lost the help of relatives, neighbours and clergy and accepted the proffered and additional service of other entre-preneurial groups, including funeral directors, drapers, memorial masons, cemetery staff and later, medical professionals (Howarth, chapter 8).

As Rugg (chapter 7) will suggest, the public cemetery movement blurred the public face of death: it displaced funerals from local burial grounds to distant cemeteries beyond the city. The walking funeral was set to be replaced by the train- and carriage-wheel. Death was also subject to the twin and rational forms of efficiency: the mid century reform of funeral directing and the development of Industrial Assurance pioneered by the Royal Liver and the Prudential (whose early headquarters were in Portugal Street, adjacent to the Green Ground). These developments were paralleled by statistical development: the life tables promoted by the Registration Act of 1837 helped to secularise the Providential view of mortality in which the Lord both gave and took away (Prior, chapter 12).

Until 1850 God's controlling interest in death in England was undergirded by an established Church. Thereafter successive burial laws transferred measures of control to secular authorities. Correspondingly, the Dissenting churches gained greater control over funerals of their own people. Throughout the 1850s and 1860s, the Dissenters pressed for an increased measure of their civil liberties which included burial rights (Manning, 1952; Mackintosh, 1972).

Their campaign came to a head in 1878. An Anglican clergyman refused burial rites to a Baptist child aged two. The public outcry proved the catalyst for the passing of the Burial Laws Amendment Act 1880 by which people of all denominations or none could be buried in rural Anglican churchyards

(Fletcher, 1974). In 1884, at the William Price trial at Cardiff, cremation was declared not illegal. This revitalised the Cremation Society, founded (1874) by a former Baptist, Sir Henry Thompson. The days of burial as the traditional mode of disposal in Christian England were numbered (Jupp, 1993). The era of the Churches' controlling interest in burial had already passed.

Enon was briefly unearthed. Around 1897 a building afterwards used as a Government laboratory was built on its site. Eighty years later, the London School of Economics bought the site for its new St Clement's Building. On 1 September 1967, an excavator uncovered 'a large quantity of human bones, among them four or five complete skulls'. The site architect suggested that the site was a plague pit.[8] This cannot be the plague of 1665, as the neighbourhood was then respectably inhabited. The site as photographed in the Magazine is precisely that of Enon Chapel.

NOTES

1   I thank Dr Clyde Binfield (Sheffield University) and Mr John Creasey (Dr Williams' Librarian) for their comments on earlier drafts, and the Reverend Dr Roger Scopes and Ms Helen Jobber for providing archive material from Regent Square Church and the LSE respectively.
2   Its course under the Chapel area may be traced from maps e.g. Greater London Record Office, WCS Plan 50 (originally no. 54) of 1808 and WCS Plan 69 (originally no. 200) of 1812. The neighbouring Great Queen Street Chapel was also built over the Essex Street Sewer. (GLRO WCS vol. 176, p. 58 re. 7 August 1818).
3   Alternative dates are given for the minister's arrival, 1821 (Whitley) and 1823 (Diprose).
4   Committee of Works, Fair Minutes 1820 –. GLRO WCS 177 vol. 21, p. 165 (6 July 1821).
5   GLRO WCS 177 vol. 21, p. 232 (4 January 1822). A rolled plan of 1820–25 shows the Essex Street Sewer crossing under the 'Sawyer's Yard' from Clare Market to Clement's Lane. GLRO WCS PR/62.
6   The Chapel's external dimensions were 71 feet 6 inches x 28 feet, according to Robert Sibley, *Plans of Property not hitherto rated to the Sewer,* July 1840, GLRO WCS 914.
7   The Commissioner frequently records delayed sewer repair work and insufficient funds.
8   *Beaver,* the LSE Union newspaper, 12 October 1967. *LSE Magazine,* December 1967, p. 28.

REFERENCES

Adamson, n.d., p. 1 in Regent Square United Reformed Church archives.
C. Brooks, *Mortal Remains*, (Exeter: Wheaton, 1989).

E. Chadwick, 'A Supplementary Report on the Results of an Enquiry into the Practice of Interment in Towns' [*PP*] (1843)

O. Chadwick, *The Victorian Church*, Part 1 (London: A & C Black, 1966).

J. Diprose, *Some account of the Parish of Saint Clement Danes, past and present*, (London: Diprose & Bateman, 1868 (vol. 1), 1876 (vol. 2)).

R. Fletcher, *The Akenham Burial Case*, (London: Wildwood House, 1974).

F.J.C. Hearnshaw, *The Centenary History of King's College, London, 1828–1928*, (London: Harrap, 1929).

Mrs B. Holmes, *The London Burial Grounds*, (London: T. Fisher Unwin, 1896).

P. C. Jupp, *The Development of Cremation in England, 1820–1990: a sociological account*, (University of London, unpublished PhD thesis, 1993).

C. Knight (ed.), *London*, (London: C. Knight & Co., vol. 3, 1843).

J. Litten, *The English Way of Death: The Common Funeral Since 1450*, (London: Robert Hale, 1991).

W. H. Mackintosh, *Disestablishment and Liberation*, (London: Epworth Press, 1972).

B. L. Manning, *The Protestant Dissenting Deputies*, (Cambridge: The University Press, 1952).

J. Morley, *Death, Heaven and the Victorians*, (London: Studio Vista, 1971).

R. J. Morris, *Cholera, 1832*, (London: Croom Helm, 1976).

The Patriot, issues of 1 September 1842–6 October 1842.

'Report from the Select Committee on Improvement of the Health of Towns. Effect of Interment of Bodies in Towns', [*PP*], X (1842).

R. Richardson, *Death, Dissection and the Destitute*, (London: Routledge and Kegan Paul, 1987).

D. E. Stannard, *The Puritan Way of Death*, (New York: Oxford University Press, 1977).

G. A. Walker, *Gatherings from Graveyards, particularly those of London*, (London: Longman and Co., 1839).

G. A. Walker, *Interment and Disinterment*, (London: Longman and Co., 1843).

G. A. Walker, *Burial-Ground Incendiarism*, (London: Longman and Co., 1846).

G. A. Walker, *A Series of Lectures on the actual conditions of the Metropolitan Graveyards*, I–IV (London: Longman and Co., 1847).

W. T. Whitley, *The Baptists of London 1612–1928*, (London: The Kingsgate Press, 1928).

7 The Origins and Progress of Cemetery Establishment in Britain

Julie Rugg

The second quarter of the nineteenth century saw radical alteration to the provision of land for burial. Since the eighth century, the majority of interments had taken place in the acre or so of land surrounding parish churches. From the 1820s, however, a significant challenge to this practice arose with the introduction of cemeteries. These were large, often attractively landscaped tracts of land usually located on the outskirts of towns (extramural), and commonly free from Anglican control. In towns and cities all over Britain, the laying out of cemeteries broke the centuries-old pattern of burial provision, sometimes in a matter of less than a decade. It took just seven years for the General Cemetery in Northampton, for example, to establish its position as the main location for burials in the town (Bill of Mortality, 1856). By the 1850s, the virtual monopoly of the churchyard in accommodating the last remains of the deceased had been irrevocably broken.

Despite the radical nature of this development, there has been only limited analysis of the transition and the principal agency of the change: cemetery companies. These companies, which financed the laying out of cemeteries with money raised through the sale of shares, proliferated between 1820 and 1853. At least 113 companies were founded, operating in towns and cities from Truro to Perth. In many places companies were the means by which the first large-scale provision was made of new space for burial (Rugg, 1992). Analysis of the nature and chronology of cemetery company establishment leads to fresh conclusions on the origins and progress of cemetery foundation in Britain in the first half of the century. A specific challenge is posed to long-standing orthodoxies relating to both the vital influence of the French cemetery, Père Lachaise, in inspiring an effective cemetery movement in Britain; and the centrality of Edwin Chadwick to burial reform in the 1840s is called into question.

The importance of cemetery companies has long been obscured, since they have generally been characterised by historians as either a further example of eccentric 'necropolitan' enterprise, to be set in the context of the burgeoning funerary trade in black-edged visiting cards, mourning hatbands and jet jewellery (Morley, 1971); or evidence of a rather morbid continuation of class divides, since it is popularly believed that the companies sought profit by catering only for the monied minority (Brooks, 1989). Other historians take a more prosaic view, and interpret cemetery companies as little more than attempts to exploit the need for new burial grounds made imperative by the population explosion of the early nineteenth century: thus these companies were 'vested interests' which sanitary reformers had to circumvent (Finer, 1952).

Perhaps the main cause of confusion in interpreting the nature of cemetery companies was their use of the joint-stock format. When cemeteries are founded through the sale of shares and shareholders paid a dividend, it looks very much like profiteering from death. Certainly, there can be no doubt that some cemetery companies were established with that very intention. Perhaps the most famous example of a such an enterprise was the London Cemetery Company, which laid out a cemetery at Highgate, and flourished by selling a luxury burial service. What became evident from extended study of company foundation, however, was that these types of company were very much a minority. Only eleven companies operating strictly for profit were successfully founded in the first half of the nineteenth century, and the majority of these were restricted to London and Edinburgh. There were many more attempts to float such companies, but their shares remained unsold; exploiting the need for such a service was not considered acceptable, and the public withheld support.

The lack of success of these sorts of cemetery company did not mean that joint-stock financing for cemeteries was considered inappropriate. A feature of urban life in the first half of the nineteenth century which is often overlooked is the widespread reliance on the use of the joint-stock format for all kinds of enterprises (Grady, 1987). Much of the town improvement which took place in the period 1820–40 was financed through the sale of shares, bought by local people eager to see better local amenities and loath to pay for these through increased rates. Shareholders were assured of the improving intent of such companies by their directorates, which were dominated by local worthies – many of whom served on the town council. Such was the close connection between some joint-stock companies and town councils, it can be seen that councils chose to act through these companies rather than operate though sometimes unwieldy municipal agencies. It is perhaps often overlooked that *laissez-faire* attitudes within local government did not mean inaction, but rather the willingness to find solutions in alternative approaches which did not impose increases on the ratepayer.

For communities to found cemeteries using the joint-stock format, then, is hardly remarkable, and does not automatically convey the simple desire to make financial gains. For this reason, study of the nature and chronology of company establishment reveals much about the pattern of multi-faceted responses to the inadequacies of existing burial practice. Close analysis of company literature and prosopographical research on company directorates reveals that there were at least two types of company aside from the small number of speculative concerns. Companies established by religious denominations predominated in the early period from 1820–34, and intended to lay out land which would be independent from the control of the Church of England. There were 20 such companies successfully operating in the period 1820–53. A second, and larger, group of companies involved those laying out burial grounds because of a concern for public health. The majority of these companies were founded in the 1840s, and by 1853 26 were in operation. It is by distinguishing company types and examining the pattern of their development that wider conclusions can be drawn on the origins and progress of cemetery establishment.

Research which has been completed on the introduction of cemeteries in Britain has largely agreed a standard interpretation of events (Curl, 1993; Brooks 1989). This interpretation places great emphasis on the importance of the cemetery of Père Lachaise in Paris. Commissioned by Napoleon, and laid out in 1804 – in the currently fashionable neoclassical mode – the French cemetery was quickly acknowledged as the epitome of cemetery design. Curl, for example, claims that 'most burial reformers took Père Lachaise as their model', and attributes the introduction of cemeteries in England to the efforts of one man: George Carden – evidently a vociferous admirer of the cemetery. Indeed, it is claimed, 'it is not until [Carden] began his campaign for cemeteries that the idea had any following in England' (Curl, 1993). The view of Carden's importance seems to have been derived from an article written in the *Penny Magazine* in 1834, which simply noted that the barrister 'was the first to draw attention to the necessity for extra-mural cemeteries' (*Penny Magazine*, 1834, p. 299). Certainly, Carden was active in the capital. By 1830 he had aroused the interest of some of the most prestigious Londoners – bankers, politicians and the nobility – in a scheme to found the General Cemetery Company, which eventually established the All Saints Cemetery at Kensal Green. H.E. Kendall's early designs for the cemetery obviously echoed the rural delights of Père Lachaise (*Gentleman's Magazine*, 1832, p. 245). According to Curl, 'the success of Kensal Green encouraged the formation of other cemeteries that followed in rapid succession from 1836' (Curl, 1993, p. 223).

This interpretation of the origins of cemetery establishment in Britain contains, however, a number of debatable assumptions. The supposed widespread and immediate popularity of Père Lachaise, for example, is open to question. Much is made of Carden's success in convening a meeting to establish the General Cemetery Company in 1830, which is often given as evidence of the energy of an articulated, Père Lachaise-inspired 'cemetery movement'. Little attention, however, is given to the fact that Carden's first proposal, the '(British Père Lachaise) General Burial Ground Association' of 1825 failed to attract any support at all, largely because the style of Père Lachaise was not immediately uniformly popular. An article in the *Quarterly Review* on cemeteries and catacombs in Paris, written in 1819, barely mentioned Père Lachaise, aside from a remark denigrating the cemetery, laid out, as it was 'for a promenade':

> it would hardly happen in the neighbourhood of London that we should have a guide to the burial grounds ... that parties should be made to visit them. (*Quarterly Review,* 1819)

The essayist William Hazlitt thought the French cemetery, like the French, 'frivolous and trifling' (*Kaleidoscope,* 1827), and in reviewing the Père Lachaise-influenced designs for a national cemetery in Britain, the *Morning Chronicle* testily commented:

> Nor do we think that the sentimentality of the French, in visiting Père Lachaise, is communicable by means of tombs or temples or gardens to the English, who prefer to indulge their sorrows in domestic privacy. (*Morning Chronicle*, 12 April 1830)

Even as late as 1834, the *Penny Magazine* described the cemetery as 'studiously picturesque and...obtrusively fashionable' (*Penny Magazine,* 1834, p. 270). Enthusiasm for the French cemetery became general only after the mid 1830s, by which time the establishment of cemeteries was well under way.

The lack of a consensus on the appeal of the cemetery before this period does not deny the fact that Père Lachaise was welcomed by an artistic élite with almost delirious excitement, and provoked an enthusiasm for all manner of cemetery designs. Much of this excitement and debate centred on schemes for 'national' cemeteries which were notable for their grandiose impracticality. The late 1820s saw heated battles between proposers of rival plans. Carden put forward proposals for a national cemetery, perhaps to be located on London's Primrose Hill, and preliminary designs of which included the erection of temples and '*fac similes* of some of the most celebrated remains of Greek and Roman architecture' (*Gentleman's Magazine*, 1830, p. 351). The architect Thomas Wilson, on the other hand, planned to build a vast pyramid standing on an 18-acre site and capable of containing five million bodies in catacomb-style chambers. Allegedly, Carden had written to Wilson to ask him to withdraw his scheme, since it distracted attention from plans for his Père Lachaise-inspired model. Wilson was less than accommodating, and criticised the scheme as 'a servile imitation of what requires no ingenuity to be carried into effect' (Wilson, 1830, p. 236). In London during this time, much of the comment on cemetery matters was largely characterised by discussion of the virtues of 'the pyramid' versus the 'Père Lachaise'. Neither of these grand schemes were followed through, a fact which must point to the conclusion that an effective 'cemetery movement' or 'an articulated campaign for the provision of cemeteries' was limited to an inconclusive debate conducted largely between cemetery architects. Indeed, as Brooks tellingly admits: 'the Cemetery movement got off to a stuttering start...it may hardly be regarded as a movement at all' (Brooks, 1989).

In conclusion, Père Lachaise cannot be afforded a central place in inspiring the introduction of cemeteries in Britain, since there was no initial consensus on the attraction of the cemetery; and the designs it inspired initially were hardly practicable. There can be no doubt that the history of cemetery design owes much to the French cemetery, but the history of cemetery establishment in Britain relies on trends much more complex than a simple dissatisfaction with British burial grounds induced by a visit to Père Lachaise. Brooks intimates as much through his reference to two cemeteries opened by Dissenters in the early 1820s: the Rosary Burial Ground at Norwich, and the Rusholme Road Cemetery in Manchester. Brooks draws no conclusions from these two examples, aside from comment that the Manchester cemetery was essentially middle class and commercial (Brooks, 1989, p. 9). However, it is the dominance of Dissenters – specifically as religious denominations – in cemetery company establishment which most convincingly explains the origin of cemeteries in Britain. Of the 13 companies successfully founding cemeteries before 1835 (see Table 7.1), ten were closely affiliated to Nonconformist congregations. Furthermore, none of the Nonconformist companies floated during this period failed to attract sufficient capital to lay out a cemetery. It becomes clear that cemetery establishment in Britain had its origins in the burgeoning power of provincial Nonconformity, its growing congregations increasing the need for burial provision which was – most importantly – free from the control of the Church of England.

The first cemetery company in Britain – the Rusholme Road Proprietary Cemetery – was founded in Manchester in 1820. It seems that one man should be credited with the idea of providing burial ground using this method: George Hadfield, the doyen of Dissenting agitators. Hadfield was evidently acting in response to burial grievances, since he says of the new cemetery, 'it was a particular advantage, to get our own ministers enabled to preside at our funerals' (Personal Narrative, 1882, p. 81). Hadfield chose to act at a propitious time, since Dissent in Manchester in 1820 was particularly strong. The city had seen the growth of Dissenting congregations – indeed, Hadfield himself was involved in the building of two new chapels. Existing burial grounds were insufficient for the needs of the rising congregations, as the cemetery company's Articles of Agreement intimated: it was considered that 'a public place of burial for the use of all persons dissenting from the Established Church in or near Manchester is highly necessary' (Articles, 1820).

Table 7.1: Early successful cemetery companies, 1820–34

Date	Town	Company
1820	Manchester	Rusholme Road Proprietary Cem. Co.*
1823	Liverpool	Proprietors of the Low Hill Gen. Cem.*
1824	Norwich	Rosary Burial Ground Trust*
1825	Liverpool	St James Cem. Co.
1825	Newcastle	Westgate Hill Cem. Co.*
1828	Great Yarmouth	Gen. Cem. Co.*
1830	London	Gen. Cem. Co.
1830	Portsmouth	Portsea Island Cem. Co.*
1832	Birmingham	Gen. Cem. Co.*
1833	Leeds	Proprietors of the Leeds Gen. Cem. Co.*
1834	Sheffield	Gen. Cem. Co.*
1834	York	Cem. Co.
1834	Newcastle	Gen. Cem. Co.*

*Denotes a Nonconformist cemetery company
(Rugg, 1992).

Rusholme Road Cemetery set a crucial precedent. Hadfield noted that 'Many towns followed our example' with regard to the cemetery (Personal Narrative, 1882, p. 811) and there is extensive evidence to show that he was right. Undoubtedly Hadfield's influence in the Dissenting world, and the centrality of Manchester to the general progress of Dissenting affairs, meant that news of the foundation of Rusholme Road Cemetery travelled to many Nonconformist congregations. Reference to Rusholme Road is common among the documents of other early cemetery companies: the Westgate Hill Cemetery in Newcastle (Fenwick, 1825), the Portsea Island Cemetery Company (Minute Book, 1830), and the Leeds General Cemetery (Leeds, not dated) all had material relating to the Manchester cemetery, or referred to the company at the time of their establishment. Indeed, Miss Martha Hope, who was first to be buried at Liverpool's Necropolis, was related to the lady first interred in the Manchester Cemetery (*Liverpool Daily Post*, 8 November 1905).

The example of Manchester illustrates the duality of the impulse which led to the dominance of Dissenting communities in the establishment of cemeteries in Britain. At the heart of Dissenting action to found new cemeteries was the need to provide additional burial space. Although the majority of Dissenters was interred in parish graveyards, there was a strong tradition of provision – albeit limited – outwith the Church. Bunhill Fields – an unconsecrated burial ground which Dissenters had been using since the seventeenth century – is perhaps the most famous example of this sort of burial ground, exceptional as it was in terms of its size and eminence. In most towns, Dissenting burial grounds were only small, comprising the grounds attached to chapels or meeting houses. Limited resources were taxed by rapidly increasing Dissenting populations, which doubled in the years between 1800 and 1820, and doubled again in the next two decades (Currie *et al.*, 1977). Most of the places which had cemetery companies founded by Dissenters were towns in which such congregations comprised the majority of worshippers (Rugg, 1992), and in these towns company literature makes clear that existing independent burial provision was limited. For example, Birmingham's General Cemetery Company of 1832 was advertised 'in consequence of the general want of burial grounds' amongst the Dissenting congregations (*Aris's Birmingham Gazette*, 1832). In Liverpool and Portsmouth, Nonconformist cemetery companies were set up following periods in which Dissenting congregations saw rapid and even spectacular growth. The Liverpool Necropolis was closely associated with the town's Congregational Newington Chapel, which had seen a massive increase in attendance during the 1810s. Thomas Raffles, the Chapel's charismatic minister, regularly preached to congregations of 2000 (Sellers, 1969). In Portsmouth, similar growth had also taken place, and the Baptist Meeting House chapel emerged as the leading congregation. This chapel closed its burial ground in 1830, and it is significant that members of the Meeting House dominated the directorate of the new Dissenting cemetery company (Phillips, 1979).

Although in all these cases the desire to increase burial space was evidently a priority, it was critical that such cemeteries should be free from the control of the Established Church. Conflict had arisen over the Church's near-monopoly of land for burial, and controversy had attached to three issues. In the first place, it was possible for clergymen to refuse burial to certain types of Dissenter. Church of England ministers were, by church law, forbidden to bury suicides and those dying unbaptised, or who were not baptised with phrases invoking the blessing of the Holy Trinity. Some clergymen therefore refused burial to the children of Baptists and to Unitarians. A second point of contention was the consecration of the churchyard. Most Dissenters concurred with John Wesley's view that consecration was 'wrong in itself' (Collison, 1840, p. 192), especially since some clergy believed that burial in non-consecrated soil could threaten the salvation of the soul (*op.*

cit., p. 182). If the churchyard was deemed to belong to the community, then it should serve both Dissenters and Church of England congregations and should have a portion that was not consecrated – a view which provoked passionate disagreement. A final controversy related to the burial service. Nonconformists buried in churchyards were compelled to be buried according to the service of the Church of England, from whose tenets they had consciously dissented. Dissenting ministers were by law unable to take such services in churchyards, although there had been some attempts to sidestep this regulation by having the minister take the service from a point just outside the churchyard boundary. The troublesome nature of the disputes arising from these issues was such that the Protestant Dissenting Deputies addressed the question of burial more frequently than any other, and had even at one point applied to the Home Secretary for clarification on the ownership of the churchyard (Protestant Dissenting Deputies, 1827–36, p. 310).

The new Dissenting cemeteries stressed their resolution of these grievances, by proclaiming that burial in their grounds would be open to all, with no restriction in the type of service used or on the minister taking the service, and that the ground would remain unconsecrated. Birmingham's General Cemetery Company, for example, was open to 'all shades of religious opinion' (Manning, 1905, p. 7). The liberality of Newcastle's Westgate Hill Cemetery Company was similarly emphasised: each of its annual reports was printed with the rubric, redolent of mild Dickensian satire, 'Westgate Hill Cemetery: open alike to the Whole Human Family without difference or distinction' (Annual Reports, various dates). A handbill produced by Nottingham's General Cemetery stressed that the company offered 'free burial form' (Nottingham General Cemetery Company, 1841), and the Portsea Island General Cemetery's prospectus announced:

> Those who bring their own minister with them, will be at liberty to use what form they please; while others, who prefer it, may inter their dead without any service whatever. (*Prospectus*, 1830)

None of these companies consecrated their cemeteries, with the exception of the Nottingham General, where it was agreed in principle that if the ground were to be truly open to all, then part of the cemetery should be consecrated and so be available to members of the Church of England.

Thus the origin of cemetery establishment in Britain should be traced to Manchester rather than Paris. In the period up to the mid 1830s, the dominance of Dissenters in the establishment of new cemeteries was widely acknowledged. Even up to the 1840s, when reformers were pressing for new burial grounds for sanitary reasons, commentators were stressing that it was not always necessary for cemeteries to be Nonconformist. Years before Kensal Green was supposedly setting the example that was to galvanise cemetery establishment in Britain, Dissenting communities had demonstrated that cemeteries were a workable alternative to graveyards. Even Carden himself admitted as much in a petition to the Commons for a new cemetery for London, where he attempted to raise interest through reference to the successful establishment of cemeteries in 'several parts of the kingdom' (*Prospectus*, 1825).

As has been seen, earlier interpretations of the origin of cemeteries in Britain have been dominated by the supposed influence of Père Lachaise. In a similar fashion, histories of the progress of burial reform have been overshadowed by discussion of the attempts by sanitary reformer Edwin Chadwick to pass legislation regulating all aspects of burial practice. Again, an orthodox version of events is usually presented. Chadwick is cast in the 'hero as bureaucrat' mode, with his *Interment Report* of 1843 praised for ruthlessly exposing exploitative and insanitary burial practice; and his range of recommendations seen as an admirable response to all the revealed abuses. Although the substance of the report was acceptable to the general public, its recommendations, including the introduction of state provision of funeral and burial services, provoked a hostile response. Chadwick is depicted almost as a lone voice, battling against the intransigence of vested interests – the Church, the undertaking business and private cemetery companies – which were threatened by his recommendations (Finer, 1952; Lewis, 1952; Jones, 1991). Again it must be emphasised that a study of cemetery companies undermines the orthodox interpretation of events, by revealing new primary material and by encouraging the use of localised productions such as newspapers – sources which facilitate sidestepping the long-standing reliance on documents produced by Chadwick himself. The company documents and provincial newspapers offer a contrasting interpretation of the progress of burial reform, calling into question the generally positive view normally held of Chadwick's involvement in the interment debate; and proposing that cemetery companies offered a blueprint on which future burial provision could be based.

There can be no doubt that the 1840s saw a general consensus on the need for new burial grounds, to combat the supposed evils – both moral and medical – arising from chronic overcrowding in inner-city graveyards. It is often the case that credit for turning public opinion is given to Edwin Chadwick. Analysis of company literature, however, reveals significant debate on the insanitary nature of inner-city (intramural) interment taking place long before Chadwick's *Interment Report* was published. During the 1820s, Dr John Armstrong had discovered what he considered to be a connection between the prevalence of fever in a particular location, and its proximity to an overcrowded graveyard. Armstrong was a popular and well-respected authority in the area of fevers, and his conclusions were accepted without criticism (Pelling, 1978). From the late 1820s, the view that graveyards posed a threat to health was never seriously questioned. As a result, the 1830s saw an increasing number of cemetery companies established with the intention of improving provision for public health reasons.

The trend had been slow to gather pace, perhaps because the death of Dr Armstrong in 1829 had lost the cause of extramural interment an authoritative voice. It was clear, however, that by the 1840s, some transformation had taken place in the way in which the whole issue of burials was discussed, and that the question acquired an almost hysterical urgency. During the 1830s, company prospectuses often simply mentioned that there was only limited space in the existing sites, and that these sites were already overcrowded. Prospectuses in the 1840s, however, were much more elaborate, and were likely to dwell on the consequences of intramural interment, add a degree of grisly descriptive detail of the overcrowding, and give some sort of scientific evidence to support the claim that burial in the city was harmful to the health of the community. There can have been no significant deterioration in the evidently appalling burial conditions between the two decades – something radical broke the habit of finding chronic overcrowding acceptable. Credit for this change should not go to Chadwick, but to a previously little-known doctor, George Alfred Walker. Walker's *Gatherings from Graveyards* was published in 1839, and treated its readership to an exposé of burial conditions of such force that it transformed the language then used to describe graveyards, and allowed an almost Gothic relish of the worst conditions which accelerated demand for change (Walker, 1839). Indeed, by 1850 *The Times* could declare that the first legislation on burials was 'mostly owing to his exertions' (*The Times*, 1850).

Gatherings from Graveyards follows a simple structure, constituting a history of burial; examples of the public health consequences of overcrowded graveyards; and descriptions of a selection of the burial grounds in London. What was radical about Walker's approach was the language used. All his medical case studies were drawn out with sickening detail, and his descriptions of conditions in graveyards dwelt unremittingly on stench and gore. A single typical example gives a flavour of the work: in describing a graveyard in Southwark, Walker noted that

> a body partly decomposed was dug up and placed on the surface, at the side slightly covered with earth; a mourner stepped upon it, and the loosened skin peeled off, he slipped forward and had nearly fallen into the grave. (Walker, 1839, pp. 201–2)

Despite the melodramatic nature of his writing, Walker's authority on the question was widely accepted. The medical community accepted his assertions of the fatal nature of graveyard emanations, and corroborating case studies were reported at length in the *Lancet*. Walker was called as a witness to the Select Committee on the Health of Towns in 1840, and to the more specialised Committee, which dealt with interments only, two years later. Details of his research and extracts from his book spread throughout the country, through extensive reviews in the quality periodicals. Provincial newspapers also produced extracts from his work, and cemetery company prospectuses made reference to him. It was clear that Walker had been successful in 'awakening an unusual degree of attention to the subject' (*Lancet*, 1839). By the time Chadwick's *Interment Report* had been produced, a receptive audience had already been created.

Thus Chadwick was acting in a context where the need for new burial ground – for public health reasons – had already been established. In 1840–53, cemetery companies with a primary concern for public health were successful in opening 19 cemeteries. However, Chadwick pointedly stressed that such action was ineffective. Writing in the *Interment Report*, he dismissed such enterprises with brief, condemnatory comment, claiming that the directors of such grounds had made no study on the evils of intramural interment, and that the cemeteries were deficient on a number of points (Chadwick, 1843, p. 27). In a further report, produced in 1850, and relating to burial in the provinces, Chadwick continued the attack, commenting that 'instances are rare in which even essential conditions are fulfilled which are required to render them proper places of sepulture' (Report, 1851, p. 31). Chadwick clearly did not consider that the establishment of a company cemetery could be considered a public health measure.

Company literature, however, reveals that Chadwick's opposition to cemetery companies was perhaps based less on reasoned assessment than on bias. It was evident, for example, that directors of public health cemetery companies were well informed on the issues surrounding intramural interments. For example, in Paisley in 1845, the local newspaper had included extensive discussion of burials, and of Walker's work. The Paisley Cemetery Company prospectus referred to such debate and concluded that: 'the social evils of interment, in the midst of towns are now universally acknowledged' (*Renfrewshire Advertiser*, 1 February 1845). Indeed, the strength of feeling on burials in Paisley was such that two companies were formed; these were united harmoniously and had opened a new cemetery within a year of the issue being mentioned in the local newspapers.

Perhaps a more telling indicator of the cemetery company directors' understanding of the burial issue was the fact that in many of the new cemeteries, concern was expressed to make burial affordable. Chadwick himself had stressed that the key to the interment problem was the inability of the poorer classes to afford quick and sanitary interment, away from the heart of the city. Thus many of the public health cemetery companies offered to the poorer classes burial at cost (Circular, 1845; *Deed of Settlement*, 1838), and 'at the least possible expense' (Norwich, 1845). The Sighthill Cemetery Company in Glasgow stressed that its burial costs for the poor would always be the lowest in the city (Minute Book, 1840). Furthermore, it was widely expressed that the poor should have good quality interment. Suggestions for a common or pauper cemetery in Wolverhampton were met with this response from a company director:

> A *common* cemetery! Perhaps a disused *coal pit?*...A hard lot indeed is that of the *poor*. Unremitting toil and 'coarser' food during life, and after death, an anatomy act and a *common* cemetery. (*Wolverhampton Chronicle*, 31 March 1847)

Many companies were concerned to offer burial of good quality to the poor. Despite being cheaper, interments would still be of 'equal security with the rich that their graves would not be disturbed' (Norwich, 1845).

There is extensive evidence of the intention of public health companies to uphold sanitary practice and, furthermore, evidence that Chadwick knew this was the case. His own inspectors sent to Chadwick details of companies operating efficiently and according to sanitary principles. James Smith, General Board of Health Inspector, visited Hull in 1850, and made extensive study of the town's General Cemetery Company site at Spring Bank. Smith could find no objection to the site, and could only conclude that the cemetery offered 'ample accommodation, with every necessary precaution as to public health, and at moderate charges' (Smith, 1850). Similarly, William Lee – another General Board of Health Inspector – praised the company cemetery at Reading. The cemetery had done 'good service to the town', and was succeeding in drawing burials away from the overcrowded town churchyards (Lee, 1852).

Chadwick chose to ignore these reports, however, and continued to press for state provision of cemeteries. In the long run, however, it was the example of cemetery companies which had most influence with the passage of legislation on burials in the 1850s – legislation which some commentators have viewed as evidence of the 'failure' of the cemetery company (Brooks, 1989). Chadwick's Metropolitan Interment Act of 1850, passed in haste by a Commons panicked by cholera scares, was repealed almost as soon as the cholera epidemic faded away (Finer, 1952). It was the succeeding legislation which underlined the importance of cemetery companies in setting a precedent for effective provision. The Burial Acts of 1852 and 1853 allowed the setting up of burial boards which were empowered to provide cemeteries financed with money raised on the poor rate. There were close similarities between the burial boards and cemetery companies – indeed, burial boards evolved from cemetery companies without conflict of interests. Private company cemeteries were hardly less concerned about the provision of sanitary burial than the boards, and cemetery companies were not a vested interest which the boards had to circumvent. Indeed, in at least two cases, companies willingly sold their cemeteries to boards, making no profit from the transaction. Most importantly, the success of the boards lies with the fact that they honoured the tradition of local initiative which had been crucial to the establishment of private cemeteries. In organisational terms all power under the new legislation was vested in the parish, and so the provision of cemeteries still remained a community response to a local problem, with the added advantage that the new boards were permitted to close intramural graveyards – action which cemetery companies could never take. Cemetery companies did not therefore 'fail' because they were superseded by burial boards. Rather, burial boards succeeded because they were founded on the same principle as cemetery companies – local initiative.

This chapter has shown that detailed study of the cemetery company introduces fresh material relating to the origins and progress of cemetery establishment. These sources undermine current orthodoxies, and encourage the development of new interpretations which point towards a revision of the previously dismissive view of company cemeteries. In conclusion, perhaps it should be contended that only an independent local agency could have wrested control of burial provision from the Established Church, since national legislation failed so dismally to make any impact at all on this near-monopoly. The passage of the Burial Acts in the 1850s, in handing control to burial boards, signalled acknowledgement of the pioneering work of cemetery companies in providing cemeteries both free from the domination of the Church of England, and operating on sanitary principles.

REFERENCES

The place of publication or printing is London, unless otherwise indicated.

Annual Reports of the Westgate Hill Cemetery Company, (Newcastle Central Library, Local History Library).

Aris's Birmingham Gazette, 22 Oct. 1832.

Articles of Agreement of the Rushholme Road Cemetery Company, (Manchester Archive Office, MS document, 1820).

Bill of Mortality (1856), (Northampton Central Library, Local Studies Collection).

C. Brooks, *Mortal Remains*, (Exeter: Wheaton, 1989).

E. Chadwick, *A Supplementary Report on the Results of an Enquiry into the Practice of Interment in Towns*, (1843).

Circular reproduced in the MS Minutes of the Edinburgh Cemetery Company, (Scottish Record Office, Edinburgh, 29 Apr. 1845).

G. Collison, *Cemetery Interment*, (1840).

J. S. Curl, *A Celebration of death*, (Batsford, 1993).

R. Currie, A. Gilbert, and L. Horsley, *Churches and Churchgoers*, (Oxford: Clarendon Press, 1977).

Deed of Settlement of the York Public Cemetery Company, (York Archive Office, MS document, 1838).

Fenwick, *Substance of the Speech given at the General Meeting of the Various Denominations of Protestant Dissenters, of Newcastle upon Tyne, to take into Consideration the Propriety of Obtaining an New Place of Sepultre*, (Newcastle Central Library: Local History Library, 1825).

S. E. Finer, *The Life and Times of Sir Edwin Chadwick*, (Methuen, 1952).

Gentleman's Magazine, C (1830) i.

Gentleman's Magazine, CII (1832) ii.

K. Grady, *The Georgian Public Buildings of Leeds and the West Riding*, (Leeds: Thoresby Society, 1987).

G. Hadfield, *Personal Narrative of George Hadfield*, (Manchester Archive Office: MS memoir, 1882).

K. Jones, *The Making of Social Policy in Britain 1830–1900*, (Athlone, 1991).

Kaleidoscope, 19 Dec. 1827.

Lancet, I (1839).

W. Lee, *Report to the General Board of Health on an Enquiry Respecting the Conditions of the Burial Grounds in the District and Borough of Reading*, (1852).

Leeds General Cemetery Company: miscellaneous correspondence, (University of Leeds, Brotherton Library).

R. A. Lewis, *Edwin Chadwick and the Public Health Movement*, (Longmans, 1952).

Liverpool Daily Post, 8 Nov. 1905.

E. Manning, *Guide to Birmingham General Cemetery*, (Birmingham: 1905).

Minute Book of the Portsea Island General Cemetery Company, 24 Nov. 1830. MS document, Portsmouth Record Office.

Minute Book of the City Burial Grounds Institute and Père Lachaise of Sighthill, 25 Feb. 1840. MS document, Glasgow Archive Office.

J. Morley, *Death, Heaven and the Victorians*, (Studio Vista, 1971).

Morning Chronicle, 12 Apr. 1830.

Norwich Church of England Burial Ground Company (1845). In the scrapbook of John Greene Crosse, Norfolk Record Office, Norwich.

Nottingham General Cemetery Company: Handbill (1841). Local History Library, Nottingham Central Library.

M. Pelling, *Cholera, Fever and British Medicine*, (Oxford: Oxford University Press, 1978).

Penny Magazine, III (1834).

R. Phillips, *Burial administration in Portsmouth and Portsea 1820–1900*, (Portsmouth Polytechnic, unpublished diploma for English Local History dissertation, 1979).

Prospectus of the General Burial Ground Association (1825), appended to *Prospectus of the General Cemetery Company* (1830). British Library, London.

Prospectus of the Portsea Island Cemetery Company (1830). Sanderson Collection, Local History Library, Portsmouth Central Library.

Protestant Dissenting Deputies Minute Books 1827–36, (Dr William's Library, London, MS document).

Quarterly Review, XXI (1819).

Renfrewshire Advertiser, 1 Feb. 1845.

Report on a General Scheme of Extra-mural Sepulture for County Towns (1851). *Parliamentary Papers*, [1348] XXIII.

J. Rugg, *The rise of cemetery companies in Britain 1820–53*, (University of Stirling, unpublished PhD thesis, 1992).

I. Sellers, *Liverpool Nonconformity*, (University of Keele, unpublished PhD thesis, 1969).

J. Smith, *Report to the General Board of Health on a Preliminary Inquiry into the Sewerage, Drainage and Supply of Water, and the Sanitary Condition of the Inhabitants of the Town and Borough of Kingston Upon Hull*, (1850).

The Times, 23 August 1850.

G. A. Walker, *Gatherings from Graveyards*, (Longman & Co., 1839).

T. Wilson, 'On the Pyramid and Père Lachaise', *Lancet* (1830) i.

Wolverhampton Chronicle, 31 Mar. 1847.

8 Professionalising the Funeral Industry in England 1700–1960

Glennys Howarth

In 1689, coffin maker William Russell undertook to provide clients with all the requirements for a funeral.[1] Gaining the blessing of the College of Arms whose heralds he proposed to employ, Russell seized the initiative for the embryonic undertaking profession. The trade has since flourished; presently enjoying a virtual monopoly of funeral services. This chapter will explore the undertaking industry as part of a process which commercialised death. The economic exploitation of death rites is discussed in relation to Victorian funerals and the nineteenth-century reform movement, with its central concern for public health and sanitation. The consequences for the funeral industry and the mechanisms it employed to ensure its survival are examined in a consideration of twentieth-century innovation.

THE EMERGENCE OF THE UNDERTAKER

Prior to the emergence of the undertaking trade, executors were responsible for employing a range of artisans to provide the upper-class funeral. The development of the trade, however, precipitated the demise of executors' authority as undertakers took control of procuring and centralised the labour of other agencies. A commensurate proportion of decision-making power was consigned to these experts who soon came to exert their own preferences over funeral rituals (Gittings, 1984).

This shift, from executor-power to undertaker-control, requires explanation. The growing perception of death as a social problem provides a wider perspective, offering clues to this innovation. Society was witnessing the earliest effects of a revolution in industry; the growth of towns and ensuing social disruption promoted an awareness of the need for stability and order. Institutions were established dedicated to solving the problems of social order, among them the forerunners of the modern prison and hospital. As people began to appreciate the primacy of the individual over the collective, death, or rather the disorder threatened by death, was added to the list of social problems demanding attention (Stone, 1979).

The creation and success of a separate undertaking business resulted from a combination of factors. First, Protestant rejection of the doctrine of Purgatory led people to question the value of death rites for the salvation of the deceased. As character and achievements during life took on greater significance for spiritual salvation the efficacy of chantries, doles and prayers were viewed with scepticism. Funerals now focused less on the future of the deceased and more on sentiment for the bereaved. Efforts previously expended praying for the souls of the dead were transferred to the care and protection of the corpse (Houlbrooke, 1989).

Second, the effects of the Reformation were keenly felt in the Church's funeral rituals – reducing the role of the clergy in the dying and death process (Chaunu, 1978). The death-bed rituals of the Middle Ages where the priest played an influential role – absolving sin and assisting in the structuring of final speeches and will-making[2] – lost their authority. Will-making now took place prior to the onset of dying and this obviated the need for the customary gathering of people to witness the final speech – rich with piety and practical instructions (Beier, 1989). The dying process, before the Reformation the realm of the clergy, became the responsibility of the doctor (Porter, 1989). As the sickroom became the domain of the doctor, so the undertaker assumed control of the corpse.

Third, the increasing importance of individualism heightened awareness of the significance and distinction between life and death (Gittings, 1984) and an expanding consciousness of the self led to the desire to mark and mourn loss. Change was further compounded by the decline of a collective conscience heralding a gradual move away from a public expression to a privatisation of death, affirmed through an intensified nuclear family (McManners, 1981). Rapid urbanisation and industrialisation meant less time and fewer individuals to organise sometimes highly complex funeral rituals. Handing over the organisational aspects of the obsequies to an expert would recoup time and unburden the family.

Finally, in an age of entrepreneurialism and industrialisation where the bereaved required ostentation but lacked the leisure to organise it, demand for a specialist agency spiralled. In this context the expansion of undertaking as a trade of convenience formed a key strand in the commercialisation of death. There were four primary mechanisms contributing to undertakers' profit: the promotion of funereal goods and services; the purchase of corpses for dissection; the provision of private and municipal cemeteries; and the burial club movement. A glance at each will aid an appreciation of the role of undertakers in this commercial trend.

THE COMMERCIALISATION OF DEATH

Funereal Goods and Services

The demise of the heraldic funeral was in part a consequence of an aristocratic rebellion against the dictates of the College of Heralds and the high cost of funerals (Gittings, 1984). This fomented an ideal environment for the emerging undertaker-entrepreneurs to spawn a new profession. They began by handling the funerals of the middle class, imitating procedures established by the Heralds whose business they eventually usurped. The display of opulence emulated in funerals of non-aristocracy was manifestation of commercialisation. Trades such as drapery, carpentry, blackstuffs, wreath-making and metal working specialised in the production of trappings, and furnished an ever multiplying array of commodities presented as essential components of the 'respectable funeral'. Undertakers handled the provision of all that was considered necessary for a funeral; the measure of which was informally set out in a 'code of status' and varied according to rank and wealth. It was the funeral expert who applied the code.

A Trade in Corpses

Richardson (1987) points to the selling of corpses to surgeons and anatomists as evidence of economic exploitation. She notes the coincidental rise of undertaking during this eighteenth-century commercialisation of the body, and comments that undertakers and bodysnatchers 'developed in tandem'. Undertakers, she contends, benefited from the public fear of bodysnatching and dissection as people were prepared to pay to ensure they did not end up on the dissecting table.

Apart from protecting the corpse from theft before burial, undertakers supplied a number of mechanisms to protect the body once in the ground. Fortified or double coffins with rows of nails were used to deter the resurrectionists. Iron straps around the coffin and the erection of railings sunk deep into the ground were further measures for those who could afford them. More sophisticated protection escalated the cost and these accessories became associated with rank and status. The poor were largely unprotected.

Private and Municipal Cemeteries

Whilst the undertaker was pursuing proliferation of goods and services, urban churchyards were becoming obscene. Immigration to the industrialising towns and cities (with their great mortality rate), resulted in overcrowded urban burial grounds in the metropolis which rapidly degenerated into public health hazards. The Church of England generally failed to provide additional burial ground in towns and cities, thus intensifying pressure on existing space (Jupp, 1993). Corpses were buried in shallow graves and often disinterred after a brief period, usually in a state of semi-decay, to make room for others.

Fears of overcrowding and bodysnatching were significant factors in prompting the provision of private cemeteries.[3] Burial in these cemeteries, however, was invariably expensive and the Romantic Movement encouraged the fashionable purchase of an impressive monument to mark the status of the family and proclaim the loss. Those who could afford it attempted to avoid the social mix of the increasingly overcrowded parish churchyards by selecting a private burial ground and employing an undertaker to organise and perform the funeral.[4]

Private burial grounds were followed by large municipal extramural cemeteries. Reports such as Edwin Chadwick's *Supplementary Report* on interment in towns (1843), stressed the health risks posed by overcrowded churchyards. The Metropolitan Interments Act 1850 contained the solution to the dangers posed to the living of pollution by the dead: separation. Amongst its provisions the Act empowered the Board of Health to establish extramural cemeteries to compensate for the closure of overcrowded burial grounds and to ensure that no corpse was interred within 200 yards of any house. No longer were urban churchyards to be used for the disposal of human remains.

Of paramount significance for the funeral industry was that the increased distance between the home and the grave necessitated improved transport for the body and entourage. For undertakers this meant greater reliance on carriage-masters who now stood to make a profitable business from the bereaved poor as well as their wealthier counterparts. The extended distances demanded of the funeral parade were an opportunity to advertise an ever-growing collection of funeral apparel which varied according to rank and purse.

The Burial Club Movement

For poor people the new cemeteries were a further barrier to acquiring a 'decent' burial. Their predicament provided an additional line of business for the entrepreneur-undertaker who invested heavily in the burial club movement. In return for weekly payments the club guaranteed a funeral according to prevailing custom. Many clubs were administered by undertakers and it was not unknown for them to resort to unscrupulous methods to secure the business. One common ploy was to use some pretext for withholding payment whilst offering to furnish the funeral 'on credit' until the family received their benefit. Although there were instances of dishonesty on the part of both management and membership of the clubs, their value for the poor is clearly gauged by the fact that they thrived well into the twentieth century.

REFORMING THE FUNERAL INDUSTRY

During the late Hanoverian period profits from death reached new heights. As early as the 1830s however, a powerful and vociferous reform lobby emerged. In addition to concern with improving health, the reformers called for measures to limit expenditure and extravagance.

The Victorian Period

From the middle of the century, other institutions entered the field of burial expenses. The Royal Liver and the Liverpool Victoria were two collecting societies concentrating on burial insurance. The Prudential was an industrial assurance company whose policies were commonly used for funeral expenses. Industrial assurance did not decline until after 1945.

Chadwick's 1843 Report recommending extramural cemeteries, concluded that £4–5 million was 'annually thrown into the grave'. Paradoxically, a substantial proportion of this sum came from the funerals of the poor. Their expenditure was condemned by wealthier sectors of society who readily adopted the stereotype of a working class who would rather see their children starve than undergo a pauper's burial. Reports also appeared of people hoarding dead bodies until they were able to meet the costs of the funeral.[5] This not only horrified the middle class sense of decency but also heightened their fear of contamination by the diseased poor. If the latter could not be persuaded to limit their unreasonable expenditure then the cost of interment and its associated display had to be reduced.

Ardent campaigners for reform laid the blame for extravagant funerals on undertakers whom they depicted as greedy, heartless men enforcing an expensive hierarchy of funeral goods on the victimised poor.

Impetus for reform came from many sections of society including the Church of England, whose nineteenth-century reforms began in the 1830s. The new Anglo-Catholic movement was particularly interested in funeral reform, criticising funeral practice for employing pagan imagery and symbolism.

The Ecclesiological Society was an Anglo-Catholic Society which sought to rescue the Church from the power of the State and to retrieve some of its medieval authority. The Society devoted considerable energy to denouncing excessive expenditure on funeral paraphernalia and proposed its own, ethically Christian, burial rituals. One preoccupation was the burial of the poor. The Church, they believed, had neglected its duty to bury everyone, regardless of wealth or privilege, according to Christian custom. With local parish priests as the flag-bearers of funeral reform they demanded remedial action.

Although the majority of urban clergy was unperturbed by the rise of undertaking, this campaign by the Ecclesiological Society can be interpreted as an attempt to retrieve some of the power and influence over death services rapidly being usurped by undertakers and cemetery managers. There was also alarm at the loss of burial fees suffered by the clergy following the creation of private graveyards. Some even urged the Church to speculate in cemeteries as a means of compensation. The 1850 Act addressed some clergy concerns by providing remuneration for loss of funeral work. Overall, the Act effectively institutionalised the separation of the Church from the organisation and supervision of funeral rites and freed them from the responsibility to provide burial land.

The Early Twentieth Century

By the end of the nineteenth century funerals and mourning procedures were subject to marked revision. Undertakers were putting their houses in order and succumbing to calls to temper flamboyant practice. Early this century, the *Undertakers' Journal* noted that the 'parade of private grief' was becoming unfashionable for,

> ... there are many nowadays who, when the private bereavement comes, refuse to make themselves conspicuously sorry. (*Undertakers' Journal* (UJ), July 1910, p. 169)

Along with the new reluctance to parade grief, many of the middle classes tried to avoid the patterns of conspicuous consumption associated with the purchase of mourning apparel. Indeed, toward the end of the First World War undertakers, weary of constant criticism, were eagerly disassociating themselves from drapers whom they depicted as the real offenders:

> Whenever and wherever the undertaker is found guilty, or even suspected, of encouraging extravagance in funerals, county court judges and others make it their delight to mount the pulpit of righteousness and lecture him and his class ad nauseam; while the draper may beat the drum to hurry silly women up to buy their foolish and expensive mourning without a

word said in reproof or discouragement ... Undertakers would perhaps do well to associate themselves as little as possible with the drapery side of the funeral business. (*UJ*, May 1918, p.128)

Furthermore, it came to be seen as poor taste for undertakers to display their wares. As a 'halfpenny sheet' in 1910 informed,

> Of course, coffin makers can show samples of their wares with as much reason as butchers show their beef, but a number of people who do not like to be reminded that they will have to die have taken objection to the practice. (Quoted in *UJ*, February 1910, p. 25)

While extravagant funerals declined among the middle classes, many of these practices survived in the funerals of the poor until well into this century. The discrepancy between death mores of the wealthy and those of the poor may be partly explained by the variance in demographic changes. With greater emphasis placed on nutrition, sanitation and health the 1870s witnessed a declining mortality rate. This was more significant for higher status groups than for the poor for whom the decline in fertility, which particularly accompanied and underlined these improvements, was negligible until the interwar period (Mitchison, 1977). Large families continued to be viewed as the solution to poverty – many babies were born, few survived infancy, fewer still achieved adulthood. Whilst the reform movement emanated from the wealthy classes, funerals continued to play a familiar and relevant role in working-class life. It could thus be argued that death held less fear for the wealthy and, therefore, no longer warranted such public displays of significance.

The Effect of Two World Wars on Attitudes to Death

Social attitudes to death undoubtedly stimulate change in funeral practice. The possible effect of the world wars on approaches to death therefore requires some attention (Wilkinson, chapter 10). Although the First World War is held by Cannadine (1981) to have had momentous consequences for attitudes to death, there does not appear to have been any meaningful shift in outlook within the funeral industry. True, there were modifications during the first half of the century but these were essentially self-imposed and issued from the nineteenth-century reform movement. It was not until after the Second World War that the industry underwent accelerated revision.

The critical factor, a fundamental distinction between the First and Second Wars, was the degree to which civilian life was threatened. The years 1914–19 saw colossal loss of life, and some 722785 British citizens died

(Winter, 1976). For the British, however, the killing was overseas and largely confined to men on active service. Although it is likely that most English families lost at least one male, they were nevertheless distanced from the physical horrors of the bloodshed and many found comfort in the conviction that their loved ones had died an 'honourable death'. During the Second World War the conflict reached the home front. Night bombing raids destroyed buildings and services and led to enormous civilian loss of life. With war on the doorstep, the regular exposure to the daily and nightly terrors of air raids gave life a fragile, impermanent quality as people were forced once again, to accept death as a fact of living. The exigencies of a society at war forced the survivors to abbreviate their normal mourning rituals; life had to go on, there was a war to be won.

Once the fighting was over, this refusal to dwell on death and dying persisted. This helps to explain why, rather than erecting new monuments to dead warriors, names were simply added to those already dedicated to the Great War (Cannadine, 1981). The relative lack of ceremony necessitated by wartime conditions was carried over into postwar society and became one component in a kaleidoscope of attitudes toward mortality. A relatively low-key approach to funeral ritual was established and continues to influence contemporary ceremonies.

Let us now consider the radical changes in the death industry during the twentieth century.

INNOVATION IN FUNERAL PRACTICE

Several factors have been responsible for re-styling undertaking practice. Roughly in chronological order,[6] the first of these was the creation of protective associations, and this was closely followed and in many ways entwined with the desire to gain professional status. The introduction and popularisation of cremation revolutionised disposal customs but had only indirect influence on the undertaking trade. Of greater significance were the provision of the chapel of rest and the adoption of the motor vehicle. Each of these changes is addressed in turn.

Protective Associations

The turn of the century was a particularly appropriate time to establish alliances as the industry was in a state of flux responding to the reform movement. In addition to attacks from reform groups, other industries were keen to carve themselves sections of this profitable business. If the industry was to survive it needed to organise. The British Undertaker's Association (BUA) was created in 1905 and the industry's first code of ethics formulated in 1908. The editor of a trade journal commented,

> We may be wrong, but we think if the association movement is to thrive it must take in all branches of the undertaking trade – must not exclude even the draper-undertaker if he can be got to come in. And this because the coffin manufacturer has come, and he has come to stay ... The whole trade is undergoing a profound change, and no one knows how that change will look in 20 years time. (*UJ*, August 1910, p. 195)

As in other industries, trade associations were created to protect members' interests. For the funeral business this was primarily resort to defence against related trades such as the carriage-masters. Prior to the introduction of the new cemeteries undertakers supplied bearers to carry the coffin to the churchyard. The increased distances to the cemeteries required better transport and placed non-vehicle-owning undertakers in the hands of the carriage-masters. The lucrative nature of the burial business prompted some carriage-masters to invest heavily in funeral conveyances, supplying services in competition with undertakers. Realising the essential nature of the carriage-master's services, undertakers began to buy rather than hire horses and carriages and so to reap economies of scale. In other cases undertakers complained of being unfairly treated by the carriage-proprietor. The latter was accused of forcing them to sell their own horses and to hire at inflated prices. This situation prompted the formation of protective associations to ensure the industry's monopoly over the provision of after-death services.

Although associations were created to fight a rear-guard action, undertakers soon recognised the need to expand and 'professionalise' their services. In pursuit of expansion they manufactured a range of funereal goods enabling them to sever reliance on other sectors of the industry. Thus the entreaty to all branches of undertaking was really a call for amalgamation to provide the totality of services required for human disposal.

Aspiring Professionals

Treated with scorn by some sectors of Victorian society and the target of reform groups, undertakers toiled to achieve respectability. One tactic in the attempt to gain higher status for their beleaguered occupation was the gradual replacement of the designation 'undertaker' by that of 'funeral director'. By 1940 this nomenclature had been adopted in most branches of the trade. In 1935 The British Undertakers Association became the National Association of Funeral Directors (NAFD). The industry's journal, once 'The B.U.A.

Monthly', simultaneously became 'The National Funeral Director' – simplified to 'The Funeral Director' in 1953. The title appealed to those undertakers who aspired to professional status.[7] As a trade journal commented of the possession of 'professional skills', there is, 'something very alluring in the prospect of rubbing shoulders on a basis of equality of status with doctors and parsons' (*UJ*, April 1910, p. 195).

Professionalisation for British undertakers, like their North American counterparts, with the emphasis on education (Habenstein, 1962), was related to expansion. It also attempted to exclude imposters. Millerson (1964) describes six characteristics which distinguish an occupation as professional. These are: skill based on theoretical knowledge; training and education; demonstration of competence by passing a test; maintenance of integrity by adherence to a code of conduct; a professional organisation; and the provision of a service for the public good. Throughout the twentieth century undertakers have cultivated all these attributes. The BUA/NAFD was the professional organisation regulating members through a code of conduct. Funeral directors promoted a view of their deathwork as a public service protecting the bereaved. The level of skill in funeral work and the knowledge involved in such techniques as embalming require education, training and qualifications.

Although undertakers' pursuit of professionalism has been modelled on both religious and medical vocations, the initial inclination was towards religious association. They adopted Christian symbolism to replace items such as coffins in their window displays and, later, to embellish the chapel of rest. As the twentieth century progressed the accent on institutionalised Christianity declined and the demand for ethnic and religious minority funerals increased. Undertakers' trust in religion was eclipsed by resort to science as they turned their eyes to the medical profession. One of the central planks of this approach to professionalisation was the 'science' of embalming.

As early as 1910, when the British undertaker was busy fashioning a pseudo-religious vocation, Professor George B. Dodge, President of the Massachusetts College of Embalming, who maintained a regular feature in a British trade journal, advocated embalming as the key to professional respectability.

> Why every undertaker in this country does not prepare himself to use these methods ... is something that is very hard to understand. The reputation he would gain for keeping bodies in good condition would rapidly spread and give him a vast advantage over his competitors who do absolutely nothing to prevent those most disagreeable conditions. (*UJ*, January 1910, p. 6)

The revival of embalming was couched in terms of 'hygienic treatment' and intended to arrest decomposition. Its other characteristic was to give undertakers an advantage over non-embalming competitors. It was only a short time before the advantages of preservation were bound up with the art of presentation (Parsons, 1995). This encouraged 'viewing' when the chapel of rest was developed.

Cremation

Funeral directors largely opposed cremation before 1939 (Jupp, 1993). Previously cremation had not posed a great threat to their industry but required an increase in time and administration. It also demanded a reappraisal of coffin types. Although some undertakers continued to produce coffins on demand until the 1960s, large scale manufacturers were emerging. They constructed boxes specifically for cremation using cheaper wood selected for its narrower gauge and flammable quality. In the previous century the purchaser had checked the thickness and quality of the wood as a barrier against natural recycling and the dangers of bodysnatching. The popularisation of cremation and consequent use of poorer quality materials may have led to criticisms that undertakers were instrumental in offering cheap, substandard coffins and using plastic rather than metal furnishings.

Providing Shelter for the Corpse

During the 1920s use of public mortuaries was encouraged as sanctuary for the dead. This was justified in terms of health and sanitisation. These places had long been viewed with disgust and their use was largely spurned. Puckle, a contemporary social observer, found them abhorrent:

> The thought that the bodies of friends and relations should be taken to a mortuary suggests to the average mind an indignity, a social degradation ... we associate it mentally with the prison and the workhouse ... for ... outcasts picked up from the gutter ... the river, or ... where the suicide ... is impounded till a jury can be called. (Puckle, 1926, p. 28)

It was suggested that undertakers should provide mortuary accommodation for the masses instead of simply for the rich – as they had been doing for some time. One implication was that bereaved people no longer wished to care for the corpse and preferred to rely on experts to provide for its shelter and protection. A decade elapsed before this advice was adopted by the trade; the first funeral home incorporating a chapel of rest was reported in the *Undertakers' Journal* in 1935.

This innovation must be set in the context of concern with health and an increasing propensity towards the distancing of death. Improved diet and sanitation had an astounding effect on mortality and fertility rates – in the interwar period this was evident in all social groups. Relocation of the cemetery to the outskirts of the city, together with the introduction of cremation meant that people were more able to escape constant reminders of mortality. The work of laying-out the corpse had traditionally been undertaken by women: female kin, midwives or neighbourhood layers-out (Adams, 1993). The increase in the number of women working outside the home; legislation which effectively barred midwives from laying-out; and the exclusion by professionalising funeral directors of women from body-handling work culminated in transference of these tasks to the male expert. The desire of undertakers to utilise their newly acquired 'scientific' techniques, combined with the realisation that the body was fast becoming the key to funeral rituals, meant that they were keen to take custody of the corpse.

After 1945 and with the development of the National Health Service the provision of shelter for the corpse became elevated to the status of necessity. In addition to the reasons already outlined, a further explanation is that death more frequently occurred in the hospital than in the home: by 1959 over 50 per cent of people died in institutions (Autton, 1966). In a hospital setting a body is removed to the mortuary and from there undertakers simply transfer it to their mortuary or chapel. Relatives seldom request return of the body to the home. Modern housing design, bereft of a parlour where the body would once have lain, and the popularity of the through-lounge were further factors contributing to the requirement for the chapel of rest.

Introducing the Motor Vehicle

The invention of the motor vehicle had notable repercussions for the funeral industry. The motor-drawn hearse began its career in America. First used in this country in 1905 it was rather clumsily known as the 'automorguemo-bilc'. The name was soon replaced. In its early days it was used not for the funeral but for the collection and long-distance transportation of bodies. As the combustion engine was more widely adopted it began to succeed the horse-drawn hearse and carriage at the funeral. At first a mark of wealth and status, this change accelerated during the First World War when horses were scarce, due to confiscation by the War Office. The final demise of the horse-drawn vehicle came in the Second World War when the Belgian Black horse, specially bred for the funeral industry in now Occupied Holland, was no longer obtainable.

Although the motor hearse was usually decked in flowers and its windows decorated with ornate engravings it bore little resemblance to the spectacle of the horse-drawn hearse with decorated horses and elaborately carved hearse. As such, the motor hearse fuelled the fashion for simplification of the funeral. The advantages of the motor vehicle were that it was cheaper and easier to care for than the horse. More poignant, it was substantially faster. The pace of the funeral procession was quickened and the time required for each ceremony reduced. This was marketed as a benefit to mourners who had other growing demands on their time. Clearly, there were also significant economies for undertakers for whom was opened up the possibility of performing more than one funeral in a day.

CONCLUSION

The origins of the funeral director lie in the role of the Heralds in the funerals of the aristocracy. Created and evolving during a dynamic period of commercialisation of death, undertaker-entrepreneurs seized power from the College of Arms and came to supply burial rituals for all social classes. The early Victorian preoccupation with health and sanitation resulted in the creation of extramural cemeteries and the greater travelling distances entailed in using these cemeteries had repercussions for funeral practice. Reaching its profit-making zenith in the mid nineteenth century, the industry was subject to criticism and censure from an influential reform movement. Since 1900 undertaking has undergone radical transformation in an attempt to survive the novel and limiting propensities of the consumer élite.

Prompted by changes in dying and disposal mores, death, burial and the funeral have been allocated as the concerns of a small number of experts. Cremation for example saves time and money. Furthermore, it obviates the need to assign a geographical place for the dead and so encourages their separation from the living. Locating the hospital, rather than the home, as the centre for dying has exaggerated that division. One consequence of this development has been the requirement for experts to handle the practical necessities associated with preparing the corpse and organising the rituals which accompany its disposal. Funeral directors now house the body and one aspect of their work is the presentation of the corpse – using technology such as embalming.

The orchestration of the funeral ritual has been greatly modified since the Victorian celebration. In responding to the nineteenth–century reform movement undertakers adopted the rhetoric of public health and protection, and (like the medical profession) they have exposed death to science. Rather than tame it, they have sanitised it.

As we approach a new century, however, this sanitised way of death is increasingly under attack. Individuals and reform groups are beginning to demand more meaningful rituals surrounding mortality, and greater control over them. And so, the industry is again fighting a defensive action against a strengthening reform movement. The aims of this movement, however, are quite at odds with the sanitary goals of their predecessors. The survival of the funeral industry will depend on its capacity to change. As I suggest elsewhere (Howarth, 1996) the evolution of new forms will entail dismantling the image of professionalism and nurturing the quality of care.

NOTES

1 See Litten's chapter in this volume for a detailed discussion of early undertakers.
2 The medieval church held a key place in people's lives and the clergy were involved in all rites of passage. Sickness and death took on special prominence vis-à-vis belief in Purgatory (see Duffy, 1992).
3 See Rugg's chapter in this volume for a discussion of changes in cemetery provision.
4 Many of the smaller nineteenth-century private grounds were owned by undertakers profiting both from the sale of the funeral and use of the burial plot.
5 Some of these reports confused the delay attributable to lack of funds with that imposed by the necessity for Sunday funerals. People laboured six days a week leaving only the Sunday free for funerals. If death occurred early or, alternatively, too late in the week to arrange a burial, the corpse would remain in the house a number of days.
6 The time period during which particular reforms took place varied according to the geographical area.
7 The term 'undertaker', however, is still used by the trade in private.

REFERENCES

S. Adams, 'A Gendered History of the Social Management of Death and Dying in Foleshill, Coventry, during the Inter-War Years', in D. Clark (ed.) *The Sociology of Death*, (Oxford: Blackwell, 1993).
N. Autton, *The Pastoral Care of the Dying*, (London: S.P.C.K., 1966).
L. McCray Beier, 'The Good Death in Seventeenth Century England', in R. Houlbrooke (ed.), *op. cit.*
D. Cannadine, 'War and Death, Grief and Mourning in Modern Britain', in J. Whaley (ed.) *Mirrors of Mortality: Studies in the Social History of Death*, (London: Europa Publications, 1981).
E. Chadwick, 'A Supplementary Report on the Results of an Enquiry into the Practice of Interment in Towns', (*PP*, 1843).
P. Chaunu, *La Mort à Paris: 16è, 17è, 18è Siècles*, (Paris: Librairie Arthème Fayard, 1978).
E. Duffy, *The Stripping of the Altars: Traditional Religion in England, 1400–1580*, paperback edn. (New Haven and London: Yale University Press, 1992).

C. Gittings, *Death, Burial and the Individual in Early Modern England*, (London: Croom Helm, 1984).

R. Habenstein, 'Sociology of Occupations: The Case of the American Funeral Director', in A.M. Rose (ed.) *Human Behaviour and Social Processes*, (London: Routledge & Kegan Paul, 1962).

R. Houlbrooke (ed.), *Death, Ritual and Bereavement*, (London: Routledge, 1989).

G. Howarth, *Last Rites: The Work of the Modern Funeral Director*, (Amityville, New York: Baywood, 1996).

P. C. Jupp, *The Development of Cremation in England 1820–1990: a sociological account*, (University of London, unpublished PhD thesis, 1993).

J. McManners, *Death and the Enlightenment: Changing Attitudes to Death among Christians and Unbelievers in Eighteenth-Century France*, (Oxford: Clarendon Press, 1981).

G. Millerson, *The Qualifying Professions*, (London: Routledge & Kegan Paul, 1964).

R. Mitchison, *British Population Change since 1860*, (London: Macmillan, 1977).

B. Parsons, 'The Pioneers of Presentation', *The Embalmer*, vol. 38, no.1 (1995) pp. 16–24.

R. Porter, 'Death and Doctors in Georgian England', in R. Houlbrooke (ed.), *op. cit.*

B. Puckle, *Funeral Customs: Their Origin and Development*, (London: Werner Laurie, 1926).

R. Richardson, *Death, Dissection and the Destitute*, (London: Routledge & Kegan Paul, 1987).

L. Stone, *The Family, Sex and Marriage in England 1500–1800*, abridged edition (Harmondsworth: Penguin, 1979).

J. M. Winter, 'Some Aspects of the Demographic Consequences of the First World War in Britain', *Population Studies*, XXX (1976) pp. 539–52.

9 Hindu Cremations in Britain
Stephen White[1]

INTRODUCTION

It is generally thought that to burn human remains otherwise than in accordance with the provisions of the Cremation Acts and Regulations is unlawful; that these require all cremations to be carried out 'in a crematorium', that is to say 'a building fitted with appliances for the purpose of burning human remains';[2] and that, consequently, they do not permit a cremation on a pyre in the open air. Although it may be that these notions are misconceived,[3] the Home Office could be expected to defend them resolutely. It is, therefore, particularly interesting to inquire how, on at least two occasions since the passing of the Cremation Act in 1902, it came about that a series of cremations was conducted alfresco yet with official approval and how as a result of the second series a permanent facility for the performance of such cremations came close to being established.

CREMATIONS OF HINDUS AND SIKHS IN THE FIRST WORLD WAR[4]

At the end of 1914 several hospitals were hurriedly established in Sussex and Hampshire to receive Indian soldiers who had been wounded fighting in France. There were three at Brighton; the others were at Brockenhurst, Netley, New Milton, Barton-on-Sea, and Bournemouth. Britain had involved its Dominions in the war without consulting them and bringing Indians to fight in Europe had been controversial. The War and India Offices were especially concerned that nothing done in the treatment of the soldiers should fuel political agitation against British rule in India and to this end, some thought,[5] were prepared to treat the Indians better than their British counterparts. Accordingly elaborate culinary, sanitary and other arrangements were made to allow the various groups among the wounded in the hospitals to follow their own social and religious practices.

One result of this policy was the provision of special burial grounds. Another was the provision of crematoria. Exactly how many crematoria there were, how many cremations took place and what their nature was is uncertain. But certainly there were cremations on the Downs at Patcham behind Brighton, at Netley and at the Lady Hardinge Hospital at Brockenhurst. There

135

were also cremations in France: at Hardelot and Marseilles and, possibly, at Bolougne. Thirty are said to have taken place at Brighton and 83 at Marseilles.

Fullest details are available about the arrangements at Brighton. On a high, isolated spot some five miles behind the town three concrete slabs were laid on which pyres were built. An observer of one cremation there[6] described a 'very ugly little screen and shelter of corrugated iron' enclosing the ghats, access to which was given by a gate. He also described the body being laid on the pyre and then covered and surrounded with blocks of wood and straw. The ashes and remains of cremations at Brighton were cast into the sea.

At Brighton at least, then, the arrangements did not obviously comply with the usual understanding of the Cremation Act. How were they reconciled with its requirements? The answer is that they were not. When first approached the Home Office recognised immediately that the cremations would be unlawful. It was far from obvious that they would be taking place 'in a crematorium'. Other requirements of the Act to be dispensed with were the application for a cremation from the executors or relatives of the deceased, the two death certificates and the authorisation from the medical referee of a cremation authority. True it was that these precautions against the concealment of evidence of crime were hardly necessary in the cases of those dying in the military hospitals. Nevertheless the Home Office official dealing with the matter minuted 'The proposed action is of course quite illegal': and then changed his draft to 'extra-legal' – a nice but not, in Home Office circles, novel jurisprudential distinction. He suggested that any difficulty that might arise could be met by emergency legislation.[7] The Officers at the hospitals were told that the Home Secretary regarded the anticipated cremations as 'quite outside the restrictions of the Cremation Act and the regulations under it' and asked simply to keep a register recording the cremations and the causes of death.

NEPALESE CREMATIONS IN THE 1930s

The second series of cremations consisted of just three. They took place in the grounds of the London Cremation Company's crematorium at Woking in 1934, 1935 and 1937. This time, however, much regard was had to the requirements of the Cremation Act and Regulations; and the negotiations between the Company, the Foreign, India and Home Offices, and the Government of Nepal shed an interesting light on their interpretation. It is curious, however, that in none of the discussions about the legality of this set of cremations was any reference made to the earlier ones. But just as political considerations had influenced the sanctioning of the cremations in 1915 so did they in 1934.

British and Nepalese Diplomatic Relations[8]

At the time of these cremations diplomatic relations between Britain and Nepal had just been upgraded. Article 8 of the Treaty of Segowlie, which had been made in 1815, had provided that:

> In order to secure and improve the relations of amity and peace hereby established between the 2 States, accredited Ministers from each shall reside at the Court of the other.

For this article the Nepalese had no practical use: the treaty had been imposed on the Nepalese by the British and article 8 inserted so that the British could establish a permanent representative at Kathmandu.[9] But implicit in the article was a recognition of Nepal's sovereign independence, since only sovereign states exchange ambassadors. As the rulers of Nepal began to pursue a policy of friendship towards Britain and the lands ceded to Britain under the treaty were restored to Nepal, the treaty came to be regarded as the corner-stone of an increasingly close relationship between the two countries, whose high-points from the British point of view were the assistance given by Nepal firstly in suppressing the Indian Mutiny in 1859 and then in defeating Germany in the First World War.

Nevertheless Nepal and Britain had not exchanged Ministers. Until 1920 Britain was represented in Kathmandu by a Resident only, and thereafter by an Envoy. For their part the Nepalese had no permanent diplomatic representatives in London or indeed anywhere else. Nepal was a very isolated and enclosed country, just beginning to look outwards. Only a few select foreigners were welcomed as visitors, and caste rules and the tenets of Hinduism, which prevented all but the very few from crossing the sea, made it very difficult for her to have diplomatic representation in other lands.

The continuing British failure to accredit a proper ambassador to Kathmandu affronted the Nepalese on two counts. The first was that in the diplomatic world at large Residents stood at the foot of a hierarchy topped by Ambassadors or Ministers. The second, and perhaps more galling, aspect of the arrangement was that in India British Residents were unlike Residents in the diplomatic world at large. There the Residency was the symbol of British suzerainty over the Princely States and the Residents were the means by which the Government of India exercised political control over them. This led foreign, if not British, diplomats and writers to mistake the true state of diplomatic relations between Nepal, India and Britain. When in 1920 the British Resident became an Envoy, the Nepalese suspected that Britain saw this as a change in name only, and Britain's continuing to appoint the Envoy from the ranks of the Indian Political Service rather than from the diplomatic staff of the Foreign Office merely confirmed their suspicion. In the 1930s several other countries began to woo Nepal, and the anomaly of Nepal granting precedence to the British Envoy over fully-fledged ambassadors caused embarrassments. In 1933 the new Nepalese Prime Minister revived a proposal to exchange ambassadors.

The Foreign Office was concerned that agreeing to the proposal might encourage other nations, such as Russia and China, to establish diplomatic relations with Nepal and it toyed with the idea of seeking an undertaking from Nepal that she would not enter into diplomatic relations elsewhere. The India Office's view was that refusing the request would offend the Nepalese, especially if other nations did seek diplomatic relations with them, and that to seek such an undertaking would do so all the more. India Office officials felt that the Nepalese were extremely sensitive about their sovereign independence and were anxious to avoid any risk of offending Nepalese susceptibilities. Their view prevailed and on 28 May 1934 the Nepalese Legation arrived in London. It was led by General Bahadur Shumshere Jung Bahadur Rana, the eldest son of the Prime Minister and effective ruler of Nepal, which had a titular monarchy and a dynastic prime ministership.

The First Cremation[10]

The General was accompanied by his wife. She was seriously ill even before her departure from Nepal. On 18 July, while he was in Italy on diplomatic business, she died.

The Rani's impending demise caused consternation among the members of the Legation and of the ruling family in Nepal. The General's father wrote to his London agent who passed the letter to George V's Private Secretary. The letter explained that Nepalese Hinduism required that a dying person take their last breath beside a sacred piece of water, preferably the sea; that within 24 hours of death the body be cremated on a pyre of sandalwood, camphor and oils in the open air; that no non-Hindus touch or carry the body; and that the corpse be carried uncoffined on a stretcher and on foot from the place of death to the site of the cremation.[11] Failure to secure that the cremation was carried out in this fashion would have disastrous consequences for the General's standing in Nepal.

The Legation had asked the London Cremation Company how far these conditions could be met at its crematorium at Golders Green. The Company told him that the most it could do was to use sandalwood as fuel in one of its ordinary furnaces, an open air cremation being out of the question at Golders Green. There were three provisions of the Cremation Act and Regulations which particularly concerned Home Office officials. Firstly, section 5 of the Act prohibited the building of a crematorium within 200 yards of a dwelling house without the owner's, lessee's and occupier's consents or within 50 yards of a public highway. Secondly, regulation 3 prohibited any 'cremation of human remains ... except in a crematorium of the opening of which notice has been given to the Secretary of State'. Thirdly, section 2 of the Act defined 'crematorium' as 'a building fitted with appliances for the purpose of burning human remains'. On 11 July, after a discussion with the Private Secretary to the General, the officials decided that if a cremation authority could be found which could conduct the cremation in the open without causing a nuisance and if the notice required by regulation 3 were given, the pyre itself might be regarded as a 'crematorium' for the purpose of the Act and Regulations. In the meantime Dr Thomas Herring, the Managing Director of the Company, had come up with the idea of conducting the cremation in a field in Woking, some 300 yards from its crematorium building there.[12] There were two houses possibly within 200 yards of the field but one was his own and he was confident of obtaining the necessary permission from the cottager in the other. Nor would the site be within 50 yards of a road. As for the need for water, the Basingstoke canal, which bounded the Company's land, might supply it. Furthermore on the south side of the Crematorium was a large estate named after the house on it, The Hermitage, and the house was standing uninhabited awaiting demolition. It could probably be bought cheaply by the Legation and the Rani could be moved immediately to it to prepare for her death.

In fact by 13 July the use of another house, The Chalet, St John's Lye, had been acquired and the Rani moved to that. It was set back from the main Woking to Aldershot road on the north-east corner of the Lye and on the east bank of the Canal in the village of St John's. On the 16th Herring wrote to the Home Office formally requesting permission for the cremation and giving further details of how it was to be conducted. A circle of some 50 yards was to be enclosed by a six feet high screen and the cremation would take place within. The Home Office treated this letter as the notice required by regulation 3 of the Regulations. Permission was given and the Superintendent of Police alerted to ensure that the ceremony did not turn into a public spectacle.

The funeral ceremony began at 6 o'clock in the evening of 18 July. The bier, shrouded in red or pink and gold silk, was borne from the house by four high-caste Hindus, one in sports coat and flannels, the others in lounge suits, and all wearing rubber-soled canvas plimsolls. The bier was placed on a tumbril and the cortège, with more than 200 villagers in its wake, processed towards the main road, crossed the Kiln Bridge over the Canal,[13] and entered the grounds of the crematorium at the rear via Temple Bar and the banks of the Canal, a distance in all of about half a mile. Copper and silver coins were scattered along the route by the cortège. When the procession reached the site of the cremation three policemen held back the onlookers while it was surrounded with the canvas screen. The pyre, some five feet high, was built of 400 lb of sandalwood and a quantity of other woods, 20 lb of camphor, incense, two tins of butter and other oils, gums and spices. The bier was placed on the pyre and a Brahmin pundit walked round it seven times chanting mantras. He then set fire to it with a sandalwood torch dipped in butter. The cremation itself lasted about two hours. Estimates of its cost varied from £400 to over £500 but the bill submitted by the Cremation Company to the Legation was for 100 guineas. The Rani's ashes were collected and sent to be scattered on the Ganges.[14]

The Aftermath

No sooner had this cremation been completed than the London Cremation Company and the Nepalese Legation began to ponder whether a permanent facility could be provided for cremations of members of the Legation to be conducted in accordance with the dictates of their religion.

If it had been a matter simply of ensuring that the field at Woking was kept available for open-air cremations there would have been no insurmountable problems. The Home Office had already stretched a point in being prepared to accept that the funeral pyre itself could be regarded as a crematorium, that is to say 'a building fitted with appliances for the purpose of burning human remains', and, presumably, that a body burned on a pyre was cremated 'in' such a building. It does not appear that anyone suggested that, if a cremation took place in the open air in the grounds of an already opened crematorium, it was unnecessary to regard the pyre as the building (or give notice of its opening) since the term 'crematorium' included not only the building but 'everything incidental and ancillary thereto'. But, on the assumption that the pyre had to be regarded as the building, the further question arose: once the pyre had been totally consumed by fire was there still a crematorium where it had stood?

The answer to this intriguing conundrum was of practical importance. For if there was still a crematorium, cremations could continue to be carried out without the Home Office being informed every time even if houses should subsequently be built within 200 yards or roads within 50 yards of it; but if there was not, then every time a pyre was built a new notice of opening would have to be given to the Home Office and, once a house or road had been built within the prohibited distance, cremations there would no longer be possible. And development in the vicinity of the field was anticipated. Herring was told that for the site to be permanently recognised as a crematorium 'something in the nature of a building' would have to be constructed on it. He replied that the Company would be prepared to build 'what might be called an altar and plant a circle of trees round the ground'. However, the matter was taken no further than this by the Company when it emerged that it and the Home Office had each been overestimating the other's enthusiasm for the scheme. Herring was told that, should the need arise in the future for an isolated cremation, the notice already given might be regarded as sufficient.

It is clear from an internal minute that the Home Office officials thought that this would enable it to retain control over Hindu cremations and prevent them becoming scandalous. The minute records that the notice might be regarded as sufficient 'in the unlikely event of it being desired on grounds of policy to facilitate the cremation of an Hindu potentate'. But if the notice was sufficient for one cremation it must have been sufficient for all since if notice of the opening of the crematorium had been properly given the Home Secretary had no power to prevent a cremation that was otherwise in accordance with the Act and Regulations. When on the morning of 23 December the following year Herring telephoned the Home Office to inform it of the cremation in the afternoon of Dadi Lal, a 23-year-old male cook at the Legation, he was told that his telephone message would be treated as 'the official notification'. Whatever the strict legal position the cremation went off quietly. The Home Office minute of the telephone conversation with Herring records 'Steps will be taken to prevent any show – but happily today's fog will prevent any crowd assembling'. And so it proved. Not even the local newspapers reported the cremation.

Securing a field at Woking for cremations, however, was not the only problem. Shortly after the Rani's cremation the General went to the Foreign Office with several complaints: certain of the formalities attendant on the Rani's death had been objectionable to his religion: the Foreign Office had given no assistance when asked but had simply passed responsibility to the Home Office: and he been disappointed that no ceremony, not even 'some soldiers and a band', had been laid on for the funeral, an omission in striking contrast to the solicitude displayed by the Nepalese to even the most insignificant British soldier in Nepal. The patience of some Foreign Office officials was wearing thin. One minuted:

The Minister has produced abundant arguments to show that London is no place for a Nepalese mission. It is difficult to see how we can either meet the Minister or refuse him in such as way as to avoid injuring Nepalese susceptibilities. Surely the I.O. or Government of India should have foreseen these complications when the questions of establishing the Mission was brought forward.......What a nuisance this man is.

The General was told that his request was receiving 'sympathetic consideration' but that it presented 'great difficulty'. Eventually it was considered at a meeting at the Foreign Office with representatives of the Home Office, India Office, Ministry of Health and Registrar-General's Department.

The British Reply

Although the use of the field in Woking could have been guaranteed, accommodating the wishes of the Nepalese in other respects proved more difficult. The Minister wanted a site to be made available by a river. He wanted the dead body to be borne uncoffined and on foot by high-caste Hindus from the place of death to the site. He wanted no non-Hindu to touch the body after death. And, since the cremation had to take place within 24 hours of death, he wanted a death certificate from the Nepalese Minister or Chargé d'Affaires to serve the purpose of the two medical certificates and certificate of the medical referee required by the Cremation Act. Everyone was relieved to learn that the Nepalese were not expecting to be made the gift of a site like the cemetery the British had accepted in Nepal. So the first requirement could be met by the Legation buying a suitable site and building a sanatorium on it to which the moribund could be transferred. The second desideratum the Legation relaxed. The Foreign Office had initially led the Minister to believe that there would be no obstacle to uncoffined corpses being carried through the streets but the Home Office certainly did not want any such public processions and, where death occurred away from the sanatorium, the Legation was prepared to use a hearse driven by high-caste Hindus.

The third and fourth requirements proved more difficult. Even where the circumstances surrounding a death were not such as to give a coroner jurisdiction there might need to be a post-mortem. When the deceased had been attended during their last illness by a doctor who had seen the body after death, both that doctor and another who had also seen the body after death had to provide certificates to the effect that there were no circumstances surrounding the death of which the coroner should be told. In some cases it would be possible for both certificates to be lawfully supplied without either doctor touching the body after death and, if the death was anticipated, arrangements could be made so that the authorisation from the medical referee of the cremation authority was forthcoming in time for the cremation to take place within 24 hours of death. But either doctor would be entitled to refuse to supply a certificate unless allowed to touch the body; and where the deceased had not been attended by a doctor during their last illness a post-mortem was inevitable. To cater for such cases the Legation was advised to retain a duly qualified doctor who was also a high-caste Hindu. The Legation was further told that in some cases where a coroner would have to be involved an inquest or post-mortem under the coroner's direction and perhaps both would be required. In fact the Home Office habitually discouraged coroners from conducting inquests into the deaths of members of embassies and legations, whether the death occurred on official or private premises. But the only case where the regulations allowed the Home Office to dispense with the necessary medical certificates was where a body was brought from abroad for cremation. All that the officials could suggest here was that the members of the Legation undergo regular medical check-ups to reduce their chances of succumbing to sudden, unexpected deaths.

There was much relief all round at the appreciative response of the Nepalese to the eventual reply to their request, though the Foreign Office doubted whether this did not conceal some dissatisfaction at the British authorities' inability to accommodate Nepalese wishes further. 'They are people', noted Sir Denys Bray, 'who need the most delicate handling.' The letter finally sent to the General suggested that he seek the assistance of the London Cremation Company, which the Home Office was especially keen to have act as the cremation authority in respect of any cremations that might be carried out.

The Negotiations between the Nepalese and the London Cremation Company[15]

The Legation lost no time in approaching the Company and it was soon agreed that it was more sensible for the Company to grant the Legation an exclusive licence over the land on which the recent cremation had taken place than for the Legation to buy the land. After prolonged and intermittent negotiations the terms for this were agreed and Herring wrote to the Home Office to ascertain that the Home Office approved them. In particular the Legation wanted an assurance that as the site presently complied with section 5 of the Act, there being no dwellings within 200 yards and no road within 50 yards of it, subsequent developments within those distances would not prevent the use of the site for cremations.

A Home Office official noted that the Home Office was in no position to approve and sanction the arrangement, adding 'As the site will be used only for cremations of Nepalese diplomats we cannot object to them'. But there continued to be uncertainty about whether the notice required by regulation 3 had already been given. The same official minuted:

> To regularise the position the Company should either notify us formally when the negotiations are completed that this open air crematorium has been opened – Reg. 3 – or inform us before each cremation. The latter seems preferable as Reg. 3 hardly contemplates an open air crematorium.

But if regulation 3 did not contemplate an open air crematorium (and surely it did not) then either the cremation would be unlawful and no giving of notice could legalise it or it was lawful and no giving of notice was necessary. A subsequent minute by another official noted 'The notice required by s. 3 of the Cremation Regulations made by S of S has already been given'.

Both the Legation and Company were officially told that the Home Office had no objection to the proposal so long as the site was surrounded with a fence which would ensure the privacy of any cremations on it; that the London Cremation Company continued to act as the cremation authority in respect of it; and that the Company formally notify the Home Office of any impending cremation. The Company's solicitors saw the matter more clearly – though arguably not more correctly – than the Home Office officials. They commented:

> The Home Office letter ..... protects you, though the position will not be in accordance with the Cremation Act and Regulations, unless the Nepalese Minister's site is considered as being part of your Crematorium.

The Licence was granted in November 1936 for 21 years. Subsequently the Legation bought some land from the Hermitage Estate and on it they built a large house with splendid gardens. By 1954, however, the house had become derelict. In 1957 the Licence expired and was not renewed. In 1962 the Nepalese sold their land but the site over which they had their licence continues to be marked off by a circle of pine trees.

CONCLUSION

Shortly after the licence had been granted one more cremation took place. On 26 February 1937 Hasta Bahadur, a 24-year-old valet at the Legation, died at The Chalet and Noble telephoned the Home Office to report that on the following day Bahadur was to be cremated on the site. To this day the question of whether this site is permanently licensed for open-air cremations appears to be a matter of some confusion. In 1985 the present Superintendent of the Crematorium at Woking wrote:

Woking is the only crematorium licensed to carry out open air cremations to this day, again presumably with the express permission of the Home Office.[16]

But, to repeat, if it is licensed because of the notice served in 1934 the Home Office has no right to insist on a notification of every impending cremation; and if it is not licensed because of the notice in 1934, and a notice must be served before each cremation, then it is incorrect to say that it is licensed. Moreover, there is now a considerable body of statutory law relating to the prevention of atmospheric pollution and while it seems that it might be possible to carry out an open-air cremation without falling foul of it, the cremation would have to be extremely carefully planned.

The Nepalese cremations took place some 20 years before mass Hindu immigration.[17] Legal and bureaucratic requirements[18] still impede the observance of the rites of social or religious groups whose traditional method of disposing of corpses is by funeral pyre[19] but attempts have been made to facilitate their observance in other ways. In 1971 the possibility of allowing Hindus and Sikhs to cast ashes into the River Thames between Richmond and Teddington was investigated. The Severn-Trent and Anglian Water Authorities have refused permission to scatter ashes in watercourses under their control but they can be scattered in certain tidal and estuary waters with a licence from the Ministry of Agriculture, Fisheries and Food.[20] Edinburgh is set to become the first authority to provide – at Cramond on the Almond – a facility for scattering ashes on a river from its bank.[21]

Christian symbols in crematoria can be replaced by others when non-Christian cremations take place and the corpse can be surrounded with sandalwood inside the coffin. In several crematoria too it is possible to watch the coffin enter the cremator and to touch it and in some to observe it being reduced to ash. For the benefit of mourners who are comforted by the sight of smoke from a cremation oily rags have on occasions been placed in the cremators. In 1983 a funeral director in an inner-city area in Leicester promoted a private bill in Parliament to have section 5 waived. If passed the Bill would have allowed him to conduct cremations on his premises and thus offer a comprehensive 24-hour funeral service which would meet the needs of the Asian community within which his premises were situated. After lengthy Committee proceedings, which provided the unusual spectacle of a local authority petitioning against the establishment of a crematorium for which it had given planning permission, the bill was defeated.[22] There was of course no question here of there being open-air cremations in the middle of a city. In India itself attempts are now being made, for environmental reasons, to convert people to the use of incinerators, and, as far as I am aware, since

1937 there have been no further attempts in this country to carry out cremations in traditional Hindu fashion.

NOTES

1 I am indebted to Roger Arber, Secretary of the Cremation Society, Bryan Fenner, Superintendent of St John's Crematorium, Woking, Kathleen Garland, Evelyn Gibbons, Doris Harwood, Ken Halls, Martin Humphrey, Gladys Newlyn and W.H.C. Woolvett, all of Woking, A.T. Lloyd of New Milton, Dr Argarwall and Pandit Krishnatraye of the Hindu Centre and Raj Malhotra of Raj Funeral Services, Ilford, for help given me in the preparation of this article. Crown-copyright material in the Public Record Office is reproduced by kind permission of the Controller of Her Majesty's Stationery Office. This chapter is adapted from a fuller article, a copy of which I will send to anyone who asks.

2 Cremation Act 1902 s. 2.

3 Stephen White, 'An End to D-I-Y Cremation?', *Medicine, Science and the Law*, 33 (1992) 151. On the compatibility of non-Christian funeral practice with English law see Sebastian Poulter, *English Law and Ethnic Minority Customs*, (London: Butterworth, 1986), pp. 234–41 and Sebastian Poulter, *Asian Traditions and English Law: A Handbook*, (Stoke-on-Trent: Runnymede Trust, 1990) pp. 120–6.

4 I was alerted to these cremations by Rozina Visram's *Ayahs, Lascars and Princes: Indians in Britain, 1700–1947*, (London: Pluto Press, 1986), and would like to acknowledge her advice about sources on them. I have relied mainly on the following sources in my account: Public Record Office (hereafter PRO): HO 45/27022, f. 5; Papers of Walter Roper Lawrence, the Commissioner for the Indian Sick and Wounded in England and France, in the India Office Library, MS EUR F. 163; the Kitchener Papers, PRO: WO 159/17; Sir Charles Burtchaell's *Collection of Reports etc. re Medical Services (1903–1920)*, and the War Diaries of Lieutenant Colonel Beveridge, Contemporary Medical Archives Centre, Wellcome Institute for the History of Medicine, RAMC 446, f. 7 and RAMC 543, vol. 5, respectively; Brighton Corporation, *A Short History in English, Gurmukhi and Urdu of the Royal Pavilion, Brighton and a Description of it as a Hospital for Indian Soldiers*, (Brighton, 1915); and Scrapbook about the Royal Visit to The Chattri, 1 February 1921, Brighton Reference Library.

5 Letter from Colonel Arthur Lee MP to Lord Kitchener, 13 December 1914, in Sir Charles Burtchaell's Collection of Reports, *op. cit.*

6 'An Indian Funeral: Strange Rites on Sussex Downs: The Burning Ghat', *The Times*, 16 October 1915, 11d.

7 The Cremation Regulations had been amended in September 1914 to allow the cremation of combatants where coroners, following Home Office advice, had foregone holding inquests, PRO: HO 45/152635, f. 37.

8 For this section I have relied mainly on R.L. Kennion, 'England and Nepal', *Nineteenth Century*, 91 (1922), 45; Perceval Landon, *Nepal*, (London: Constable, 1928); *Confidential Memorandum on Nepal: History and Constitution*, by Col. Keyes; *Leading Personages* by Lt-Col Daukes and Daukes' *Political Memoir of Events from 1929–34*, IO L/P & S/12/3011 and PRO: FO 371/18164, f. 234; and material in the following Foreign Office and India Office [hereafter IO]

papers: PRO: FO 371/1862, 1863, 1864 and 372/2973, 2996 and 2997 and IO L/P & S/12/3028, 3039, 3040 and 3444.

9   John Pemble, *The Invasion of Nepal: John Company at War*, (Oxford: Clarendon Press, 1971) p. 83.

10   For the following account of the Nepalese cremations I have relied mainly on PRO: FO 372/3026, IO L/P & S/12/3043, and PRO: HO 45/17075/676866.

11   C.A. Bayly, 'From Ritual to Ceremony: Death Ritual and Society in Hindu North India since 1600' in Joachim Whaley (ed.), *Mirrors of Mortality: Studies in the Social History of Death*, (London: Europa Publications, 1981) p. 154.

12   The Company had been formed in 1900 by members of the Cremation Society to establish the crematorium at Golders Green. In 1933 the Society sold its crematorium at Woking to the Company in return for shares in the Company. So the connection between the Company and the Society was very close. In 1934 Herring was also Honorary Secretary to the Council of the Society and George A. Noble was Secretary to both the Society and the Company.

13   The Rani's corpse may have been rowed across the Canal.

14   This paragraph is based on the not wholly consistent accounts of the funeral in *Daily Telegraph*, 19 July 1934; *The Times*, 19 July 1934, 16b; *Surrey Advertiser and County Times*, 21 July 1934; *Woking News and Mail*, 20 July 1934, 5c; *Daily Mirror*, 19 July 1934, 4d; *News Chronicle*, 19 July 1934, 1d; *Daily Express*, 19 July 1934, 1c; and *Daily Mail*, 19 July 1934, (which also has a photograph of the cremation); also on R.B. Pole, 'Memories of St. John's' in Programme for the St John's Fete, 25 August 1973.

15   I am indebted to Bryan Fenner for allowing me to see the correspondence in his possession between the Company and the Legation.

16   Bryan G. Fenner, 'The History of Woking Crematorium', *Pharos International*, 51 (1985) pp. 85 to 91.

17   Richard Burghart, 'Introduction: The Diffusion of Hinduism to Great Britain', in Richard Burghart (ed.), *Hinduism in Great Britain: The Perpetuation of Religion in an Alien Culture*, (1986) p. 6.

18   Shirley Firth, 'The Good Death: Attitudes of British Hindus', in Glennys Howarth and Peter C. Jupp (eds), *Contemporary Issues in the Sociology of Death, Dying and Disposal*, (London: Macmillan, 1996) p. 125.

19   On the funeral customs of Hindus see Mary Levin, 'Mummification and Cremation in India', *Man*, 30 (1930) 29, 44, 64; the articles by Jonathan Parry, 'Ghosts, Greed and Sin: the Occupational Identity of the Benares Funeral Priests', *Man*, 15 (1980), 'Death and Cosmogony in Kashi', *Contributions to Indian Sociology*, 15 (1981) 337, 'Sacrificial Death and the Necrophagous Ascetic', in Maurice Bloch and Jonathan Parry (eds), *Death and the Regeneration of Life*, (Cambridge: Cambridge University Press, 1982) p. 74, 'Death and Digestion: The Symbolism of Food and Eating in North Indian Mortuary Rites', *Man*, 20 (1985) 612, and his book *Death in Banaras*, (Cambridge: Cambridge University Press, 1994); and the work of Shirley Firth, 'The Good Death: Approaches to Death, Dying and Bereavement among British Hindus', in Arthur Berger *et al.* (eds), *Perspectives on Death and Dying: Cross Cultural and Multi-Disciplinary Views*, (Philadelphia: Charles Press, 1989) p. 66, 'Changing Patterns in Hindu Death Rituals in Britain', in Dermot Killingley *et al.* (eds), *Hindu Ritual and Society*, (Newcastle-upon-Tyne: S.Y. Killingley, 1991), 'Approaches to Death in Hindu and Sikh Communities in Britain' and

'Cross-cultural Perspectives on Bereavement', in Donna Dickenson and Malcolm Johnson (eds), *Death, Dying and Bereavement*, (London: Sage Publications, 1993) p. 26 and p. 254. Firth points out that ritual which in India would be performed by the pyre has been translated in Britain to the home.

20   Sebastian Poulter, 'The Scattering of Cremated Ashes, River Pollution and the Law', *Land Management and Environmental Law Report*, 3 (1989) 83.

21   James McGhee, 'River Funerals Plan', *Evening News* (Edinburgh), 11 August 1994.

22   Ginns and Gutteridge, Leicester (Crematorium) Bill, 1983; H.C. Debs., ser. 6, v. 37, col. 69 (14 February 1983); H.C. Debs., ser. 6, v. 57, col 1166 (5 April 1984); Minutes of Evidence of the House of Commons Committee on the Ginns and Gutteridge (Crematorium) Bill, Sessions 1982–83 and 1983–84; Report by the Local Ombudsman on an Investigation into Complaint 476/J/84 against Leicester City Council, 1986.

10 Changing English Attitudes to Death in the Two World Wars

Alan Wilkinson

THE FIRST WORLD WAR

So many dead

> What do your clear bells ring to me
> In this glad hour of jubilee?
> Not joy, not joy. I hear instead:
> So many dead! so many dead!

In these words Austin Dobson expressed what many British felt as they approached Christmas 1914. Britain had not fought a major war for a century. It had forgotten what war was really like. In 1915 a group of patriotic soldiers arrived on a beach in the Dardanelles and rushed up to a marquee. It reminded them of village fetes. They unlaced it. 'It was full of corpses. Dead Englishmen, lines and lines of them, and with their eyes wide open. We all stopped talking...Nobody had mentioned this' (Blythe, 1969, p. 39). Those who hurried to enlist loved their country and were angry about Belgium. For some it was a way out of a dull job or unemployment; for others it was a religious vocation. A young man on his way to the front wrote: 'entering into this war seems to me like entering some vast Cathedral, full of God's Presence and of prayer and praise'.

In the First World War some 745 000 British soldiers died – ten per cent of the army (compared with five per cent in the Anglo–Boer war). Some of the losses were horrifyingly concentrated. Of the 60 000 men who went over the top in the first waves of the Somme offensive on 1 July 1916, half became casualties within 30 minutes. Inscriptions on the headstones of the Accrington Pals Valhalla attempted to vindicate their deaths: 'The French are a great nation worth fighting for'; 'The Lord giveth and the Lord taketh away'; 'I heard the voice of Jesus say, Come unto me and rest'.

When all allowances have been made, the Great War remains arguably different from any other war. For the first time young men from all areas and social classes died over a long period, with speed of notification in the national press making the widespread nature of the sacrifice clear to everyone. The loss became national, and above all, the dead were civilians.

149

However wrongly, the death of a professional soldier was put in a different
category, an occupational risk... (Winter, 1978, p. 204)

What was it that persuaded a democracy to accept bereavement on such a
scale? Firstly, the invasion of 'little Belgium' caused moral outrage; it
threatened British ideals as well as British interests. Secondly, the Bryce Report
(1915) on German atrocities confirmed for many that Germans were sub-
human and that therefore any means could be used against them. Thirdly, it
became more and more impossible to turn back as the war developed its own
irresistible momentum. On 4 August 1918, Portsmouth citizens gathered and
resolved to do all in their power 'to achieve the ideals on behalf of which
so great sacrifice has already been made'. For combatants, the initial motive
of patriotism was quickly overtaken by the determination not to let themselves
and their comrades down. Hatred for Germans spurted up intermittently at
the front, but some felt that they had more in common with the enemy than
with those at home who romanticised war (Wilkinson, 1978, pp. 208–29).

To what resources did the nation turn as it struggled to cope with the
numbing casualty lists? People were too desperate to look only in a single
direction, so they often drew upon a combination of some or all of the
following theodicies.

The crucified soldier

Many facing death or bereavement were inspired by the stories of the
compassionate Jesus, his sufferings, death and resurrection. The most popular
text for war memorials described Jesus' own preparation for death: 'Greater
love hath no man than this that a man lay down his life for his friends' (John
15:13). A young officer told his mother before he went into battle in 1916
that he had received Communion and faced testing in Gethsemane and was
now able to say with Jesus 'not what I will but what Thou willest' (Housman,
1930, p. 277). The most popular picture of the war 'The Great Sacrifice'
portrayed a dead soldier on the battlefield clutching the feet of a spectral,
crucified Christ. The most popular wartime hymn, 'O valiant hearts', versified
that theme. The image of the incognito Christ encountered in the trenches
was expressed not only in ephemeral pictures and verse, but also explored
in the poems of Owen and Sassoon (Wilkinson, 1978, pp. 169–96; 1985,
pp. 14–9). Many Conscientious Objectors also looked to the crucified Christ.
In Richmond Castle, Yorkshire, as they faced the possibility of execution
they wrote texts on the whitewashed walls such as 'If any man will come
after me, let him deny himself, and take up his cross, and follow me'
(Matthew 16:24).

The belief that redemption could only be achieved by the shedding of blood had pre-Christian as well as Christian roots. Some argue that Abel was slain ceremonially by Cain to fertilise the land with blood. For the liberal-minded hero of H.G. Wells' novel *Mr Britling Sees It Through* (1916) rational explanations of the war no longer sufficed; he pondered instead the text of so many contemporary sermons: 'without shedding of blood is no remission' (Hebrews 9:22). John Oxenham, a best-selling writer, described Vimy Ridge as 'truly an altar bathed in the rich red blood of thousands of high and gallant hearts' (Oxenham, 1918, p. 27).

The cross now became a public symbol. Though it was common to see crosses or crucifixes on Anglican or Roman Catholic altars, it had been rare to find either in a public place in England. But when British servicemen went to France they grew to prize the wayside crucifixes, and remarked how often they stood unscathed amid the devastation. A favourite picture 'Eyes Right' showed soldiers looking with fellow-feeling upon Jesus on his cross. The Anglican *Church Times* argued that this was the moment to rebuild the old Catholic wayside calvaries (13 August 1915). Thus public crosses and crucifixes began to appear as war shrines, particularly if the parish priest was of the Catholic tradition, as at St Matthew's Southsea where an outdoor crucifix was erected in 1916 to commemorate the dead of Jutland. When that year the people of Dalderby, Lincolnshire, achieved the highest proportion of enlistments in the county, the Lincoln Chamber of Commerce decided that a village cross was the most fitting reward.

Wartime calls for self-sacrifice fell on prepared ground. The churches taught Christianity as struggle and warfare. Baptism was a sharing in Christ's death and resurrection. Stories of recent heroes like Scott and his Antarctic companions were often used to illustrate the text 'Greater love...' Many popular hymns like 'Onward Christian Soldiers'; the Psalms, *Pilgrim's Progress* and the baptism rite all used images of warfare. Psalm 23, which most soldiers knew by heart, gave an assurance of God's presence through 'the valley of the shadow of death'. The Anglican Holy Communion focused upon Christ's sacrificial death and the communicants' sacrificial response: 'And here we offer and present unto thee, O Lord, ourselves, our souls and bodies, to be a reasonable, holy, and lively sacrifice unto thee...' Imagine the impact of those solemn words upon soldiers on the eve of battle.

The Christian knight

People also interpreted their war experiences through the images and stories of Christian chivalry. Revived by the nineteenth-century Romantics, they were central to the public school ethos, but also widely diffused through the Volunteer Movement, Boy Scouts, Church Lads' and Boys' Brigades. For Christian Socialists too, helping the poor and the weak was a form of Christian chivalry. Thus rescuing Belgium from 'rape' was described in chivalric imagery; recruiting posters showed St George in armour slaying the dragon; war memorials depicted soldiers as knights. The chapter headings of John Masefield's account of Gallipoli were taken from the medieval epic *The Song of Roland* (Girouard, 1981; Morris, 1983; Parker, 1987; Wilkinson, 1978; Wilkinson, 1986b).

Yet the best of war poetry was fired by anger against the chivalric tradition for having deceived the people about war. Vera Brittain sent Rupert Brooke's wartime sonnets to her fiancé, also a poet, at the front. He responded with a bitter account of the actualities of trench life using sardonically a phrase from Sonnet II (here italicised):

> The dug-outs have been nearly all blown in, the wire entanglements are a wreck, and in among this chaos of twisted iron and splintered timber and shapeless earth are the fleshless, blackened bones of simple men who *poured out their red, sweet wine of youth*, unknowing, for nothing more tangible than Honour or their Country's Glory or another's Lust of Power. (Brittain, 1982, pp. 287, 344)

Despite such scepticism, the hymn which millions wanted to sing each Armistice-tide, 'O valiant hearts', continued to offer the traditional images of Christian chivalry:

> Tranquil you lie, your knightly virtues proved,
> Your memory hallowed in the land you loved.

The classical warrior

The officer class was largely recruited from schools and universities dominated by the Classics. Northern industrial towns selected Latin mottoes for their new coats of arms and aspiring schools displayed gold-lettered boards headed 'Victor Ludorum'. 'He whom the gods favour dies young' (Plautus) was a favourite tag. Educated soldiers regularly used the Classics as sources for battle tactics and models for heroism in war (Housman 1930, pp. 111, 136, 198). However Herbert Read in 'The Happy Warrior' contended that the Classical virtues expounded in Wordsworth's poem of that name could not be exercised in modern warfare:

Bloody saliva
Dribbles down his shapeless jacket.
I saw him stab
And stab again
A well-killed Boche.
This is the happy warrior.
This is he...

In July 1914 the chaplain at Sandhurst had preached on *Dulce et Decorum est pro patria mori* – recently inscribed in gold above the chancel arch in memory of the dead of the Anglo–Boer war. Owen's poem employed that text to savage the whole Classical tradition of war.

The uneasy relationship between the Classical and Christian traditions of the warrior became evident when the Imperial War Graves Commission chose a Renaissance humanist architectural tradition for its cemeteries, in which the only unambiguously Christian symbol was the Cross of Sacrifice. Explicitly Christian texts from 1 Corinthians 15 (used in the Prayer Book burial rite) were rejected in favour of texts from Ecclesiasticus which are neither specifically Jewish nor Christian. Religiously neutral headstones (on which relatives could have their own religious emblems) replaced temporary wooden crosses, despite protests from the churches. Thus in 1919, the wife of the Bishop of Exeter, who had lost three sons, lamented:

It is only through the hope of the cross that most of us were able to carry on the life from which all the sunshine seems to have gone, and to deny us the emblem of that strength and hope adds heavily to the burden of our sorrow. (Longworth, 1967, pp. 47–9)

Some national decisions about war memorials seemed to imply that Britain was now a post-Christian society. A shared death had become more important than a shared religion. The Whitehall Cenotaph, cool and agnostic, was designed without Christian texts or symbols so that it could be reverenced by those of any religion or none. However, many public memorials in smaller (and therefore often less secular) English towns included Christian iconography and language. These were civilian memorials paid for by local people as tributes to those buried far away in official (and then still stark) cemeteries. Local memorials could include those elements of local religious and folk culture which the War Graves Commission architects were committed to exclude. Such memorials gathered and named the local dead in an identifiable public place as a focus for pride, sadness and tributes. The erection of memorials and the completion of the cemeteries marked the end of the war and brought some order after years of chaotic emotions (Boorman, 1988; Longworth, 1967; Moriarty, 1992; Wilkinson, 1978, pp. 294–305).

Other sources of meaning

Those who believed that the war had a moral purpose – to end war or uphold international law, for example – could cling to the belief that their sacrifices contributed to the wider good. So a newly-bereaved father wrote to his son's commanding officer:

> These losses are very terrible, but I can assure you make us here all the more determined that they shall not be in vain. I would sooner see all my Boys go and myself too than that the German Military Power should not be crushed. (Liddle, 1979, p. 41)

Christian leaders frequently quoted J. B. Mozley's sermon preached in 1871 during the Franco–Prussian war in which he argued that in God's providence people have to suffer for one another: 'it is this serious and sacred function which consecrates war'. Others contended that war was a concentrated form of the ordinary trials of life. The description of Jesus in Hebrews 2:10 – 'Made perfect through sufferings' – was inscribed on some war memorials. Preachers made much use of the monitory value of war; it reminded people of the fragility of life and the proximity of death. Some argued with Tennyson and Ruskin that war roused citizens from sloth and united the nation, or with the neo-Darwinians that war was in accordance with the evolutionary process (Wilkinson, 1978, pp. 10–20).

People tried to control the randomness of death and injury through superstition, fatalism, humour or religious faith. A surprising escape might be regarded as the result of prayer, absolution, a charm or luck. Vera Brittain, though rational and religious, stopped accompanying friends to the station because she came to believe that if she did so, she would never see them again. Humour, like fatalism, steadied the nerves. It domesticated the horrific: a trench became 'Park Lane', Ypres became 'Wipers'. But there was much experience which was intractable. Studdert Kennedy, the memorable chaplain, came across a mutilated soldier to whom he had given Communion three days before, praying that the body of Christ would preserve his body and soul unto everlasting life. He wondered what those words had meant to that soldier. Studdert Kennedy could no longer believe in an almighty, transcendent God; only the suffering God of the cross made any sense (Wilkinson, 1985, pp. 14–16)

Responses to death

In the context of such a war, what the churches taught about life after death had a political as well as a pastoral significance. Belief in heaven can nerve soldiers to face death and induce families more readily to accept the sacrifice of their loved ones. In the nineteenth century the churches' eschatology had been criticised on moral grounds. This led some Christians to take a more inclusive view, but others continued to teach that those without explicit faith would go to hell. Roman Catholics and Anglo-Catholics taught an intermediate state which provided opportunities for further growth. Most soldiers thought that the churches offered only heaven or hell; that heaven was primarily a reunion of friends and relations; that hell could usually be discounted. It seemed only fair to them that God should give them a second chance and only natural to pray for their dead comrades. It was widely believed (and taught by some Christians) that a patriotic soldier was saved by his own self-sacrifice (Cairns, 1919). In Gallipoli, a badly wounded soldier asked his officer 'Shall I go to heaven or hell, sir?' The officer replied with confidence 'To heaven'. Not even the most conservative pastor would tell a dying soldier or his bereaved relations that he was destined for hell.

Thus the war completed, except in conservative circles, the removal of hell from English Christianity. Cardinal Bourne said of the war: 'God has peopled Heaven with saints who, without it, would hardly have reached Heaven's door-sill' (Oldmeadow, 1944, p. 108). Wilfred Owen's mother inscribed on her son's grave his words, 'Shall life renew these bodies? Of a truth all death will he annul.' But by omitting Wilfred's question mark at the end, she tried to turn her agnostic son back into a believer.

Prayers for the dead had been rare in the Church of England, except among Anglo-Catholics, and abhorrent to the Free Church tradition. The war made them a widespread practice. Controversy was swept aside by the tide of grief. Roman Catholicism gained a reputation for knowing what to do about death, because of its clear rituals of confession, anointing and communion, a pattern more and more adopted by many Anglican priests. In the Roman, and increasingly in the Anglican tradition, the eucharist was presented as the place where heaven and earth met. 'The Place of Meeting' a deeply valued picture of an Anglo-Catholic requiem, portrayed figures of departed servicemen mingling with the saints in a cloud of incense. Memorial services were greatly appreciated as the bereaved had had no opportunity to say farewell at a funeral. The Russian 'Contakion for the Dead', included in the *English Hymnal* became almost a part of the Anglican liturgy, sung for Edith Cavell (1915) and Lord Kitchener (1916) at St Paul's and for the Unknown Warrior at Westminster Abbey (1920). In Toc H the 'Elder Brethren' were remembered at every meeting when 'They shall grow not old...' was recited.

However to some of the bereaved what the churches offered was inadequate. They wanted tangible communication with and reassurance directly from the dead. During the war the number of Spiritualist societies doubled. Sir Oliver Lodges's *Raymond* (1916) about his son killed the year before, gave spiritualism the prestige of his scientific reputation. But some found Raymond's messages banal. Church leaders distrusted spiritualism. They feared charlatanism. They believed that it cheapened heaven by making it autonomous, not God-centred; but they conceded that it had grown because of inadequacies in church teaching and practice (Cannadine, 1981; Wilkinson, 1978, pp. 173–86; Winter, 1992).

Public rituals expressed the nation's grief and pride and reduced the isolation of the bereaved. To be widely acceptable, ceremonies had to evoke a diffused religious sense through ritual rather than through doctrine. Many rituals had simply evolved – war memorials from street shrines; two minutes silence from silent prayer at noon; the Reveille added onto the Last Post to express future hope. The Unknown Warrior had been buried according to Anglican rite, but the public was assured that he might have been anyone, of any country, of any faith. A war fought in the name of democracy required that all the dead should be traced and named, either on headstones or on monuments, like Thiepval, erected to record the missing. 'What passing-bells for these who die as cattle?' asked Wilfred Owen. In fact, chaplains and others went to great lengths to bury all the dead as far as this was feasible. Neville Talbot, a chaplain, who had crawled out under fire to pray over and bring back his brother's body for burial, wrote: 'How strong is the sense of outrage at non-burial!' In another area, many dead lay beyond reach in No Man's Land. The chaplain said prayers for them; then he, an officer and an NCO sang this hymn together:

> On the Resurrection morning,
> Soul and body meet again;
> No more sorrow, no more weeping,
> > No more pain!

When they got up next morning, snow had fallen and covered all the bodies. But bodies sometimes reappeared after a bombardment. Macabre rituals developed – those coming on duty were sometimes expected to shake the corpse's hand. It was easy to grow callous (Cannadine, 1981; Moriarty, 1992; Wilkinson, 1978, 1981).

At home the bereaved were torn between grief and patriotism. Was it unpatriotic to grieve? Relatives also desperately wanted to piece together the last hours of the deceased. Official letters were vague: 'He died bravely without pain.' Vera Brittain sought help from her fiancé's fellow officers, chaplain and servant. She discovered he had been killed reconnoitring in the moonlight and cried with anguish 'Why *did* you?' Then his personal effects arrived, including his blood-stained tunic, smelling of decay (Brittain, 1978, pp. 251–2; 1982, pp. 9–10, 376f.). Relatives of those executed for cowardice or desertion were usually told that they had died of wounds. But sometimes the truth leaked out, leaving a bitter legacy. At the trial a chaplain often acted as Prisoner's Friend; he spent the last night with him in his cell, then accompanied him to the execution (Andrews, 1975; Bickersteth, 1991).

'Inter-war Britain was probably more obsessed with death than any other period in modern history' (Cannadine, 1981, p. 189). Doris Lessing describes how in Rhodesia in the 1920s almost every family, like hers, was blighted by the war. The houses were full of photographs of dead men (Lessing, 1994). Those who survived sometimes felt guilty because they had not been killed and that their war experiences had cut them off from their families. Or had they, as Toc H urged, been preserved by God to serve others?

In 1921 Vera Brittain decided to visit her brother's grave in Italy and her fiancé's in France. She had recently been moved at the arrival of the wooden cross, wrapped in canvas, which had stood for three years over her brother's body. It had now been replaced by a headstone. She planted a fern hoping it would long survive. At her fiancé's grave she felt that her 'impetuous warrior slept calmly'. She left thinking that she was getting over her loss but went to bed in tears (Brittain, 1978, pp. 521–34). In May 1922 the King and Queen went as pilgrims to the cemeteries. At Étaples he placed forget-me-nots given by a mother on her son's grave. When the visits were completed, he said: 'In the course of my pilgrimage I have many times asked myself whether there can be more potent advocates of peace... than this massed multitude of silent witnesses to the desolation of war' (Longworth, 1967, p. 80).

By 1931, 140000 bereaved were visiting the cemeteries every year. Those who came to visit a grave, discover a name or take a photograph for some widow's shrine often experienced an unexpected emotional release. One survivor felt guilty for years because he had been unable to save a wounded friend. But when he saw his friend's name on a memorial to the missing he felt his friend was safe and his guilt dropped away. Many still return home believing that the beautifully tended and patterned graves have brought order to their chaotic emotions. People say: 'I felt complete having seen his gravestone'; 'I felt I wanted to kiss my son's name when I saw it. I feel so happy to have seen that name' (Kipling, 1926; Walter, 1993).

However, remembrance was sometimes bitter. On Armistice Day 1921 thousands of unemployed marched on the Cenotaph with pawn tickets instead of medals. Scathing poems and memoirs from ex-servicemen deepened doubts about official concepts like 'honour', 'glory', 'sacrifice'. The bereaved and ex-servicemen were outraged. E.C. Hoskyns, Dean of Corpus Christi College, Cambridge, and a former army chaplain reacted sharply:

> It appears as though we have permitted sorrow for the dead to absorb our observance. But rejoicing ought to be our chief note of the [Armistice] day, gratitude for a victory by which our country was freed... Are we to say that it was all a ghastly mistake? Are we to say that there was no issue and that human life was merely thrown away? (Hoskyns, 1938, pp. 47, 168)

THE SECOND WORLD WAR

A very different kind of war

The evidence about English attitudes to death in the Second World War is both less varied and more prosaic. This indicates both the different character of the Second War and how much society had changed since 1918. In the First War, we are in touch with Wagner and Tennyson. In the Second War, we can envisage Pinter and Beckett.

The Second War, unlike the First, was long expected. The number of British servicemen who died (300000) was much less than half the dead of the First War. Politicians and military leaders knew that the public would not accept losses on the scale of 1914–18. They could no longer rely on that strong belief in life after death or in the virtue of war to undergird heavy losses. Conscription had begun in May 1939, so there was no need for hyperbolic recruiting propaganda. In any case, few by September 1939 needed convincing that Nazism was evil. Nor was there that gulf between people at home and in the services which made communication about the real nature of the war so impossible. By the end of 1940 more people had been killed in air raids than in the forces. The First War began with excitement but ended in disillusionment. The Second War began without high emotion but each year support for it grew while the proportion of Conscientious Objectors declined. The ideological basis for the war has remained remarkably durable. No-one ever celebrated the jubilee of the battle of the Somme, but the fiftieth anniversary of D-Day was commemorated with genuine pride and enthusiasm. The trapped men of the trenches seem victims. The dead of the Second War do not, because it was in many ways 'The People's War' (Wilkinson, 1986a, pp. 232–51).

A British film of 1943, *Millions Like Us* (a characteristic title of the period) followed the lives of a group of young women called up to work in a factory. Leaving their families they are sustained by their new community. One marries an airman, but he is very soon killed over Germany. Not long after, at a lunch-time concert in the works canteen she feels sad and isolated by her bereavement. At first she cannot bring herself to share in the community singing, but gradually casting aside her private grief, she begins to join in. The film illustrates the Second War theme that the community's needs take precedence over those of individuals.

Settling for half-loaves

The poetry of the Second War was written in a laconic, anti-heroic style as though a nerve had been severed by the First War. So in 'O Dreams, O Destinations' C. Day Lewis meditates on the loss of the 'appetite for wholeness'; now we are content with 'Half-loaves, half-truths – enough for the half-hearted'. In 'Where are the War Poets?' he depicts the war as a defence of 'the bad against the worse'. Herbert Read who in the First War had described his men as 'my modern Christs' now wrote 'To a Conscript of 1940':

> We think we gave in vain. The world was not renewed...
> But you, my brother and my ghost, if you can go
> Knowing that there is no reward, no certain use
> In all your sacrifice, then honour is reprieved.

The identification of the deaths of soldiers with the sacrifice of Christ, so common in the First War, was almost unknown in the Second. The title of the most famous of Second War books *The Last Enemy* by Richard Hillary, a study of inverted heroism, was derived from I Corinthians 15 in the burial service. Hillary believed that the war gave his generation a cause in which they could lose themselves, for it 'demanded no heroics, but gave us the opportunity to demonstrate in action our dislike of organised emotion and patriotism' (Hillary, 1961, p. 35). Whilst on active service, Dennis McHarrie wrote:

> 'He died who loved to live,' they'll say,
> 'Unselfishly so we might have today!'
> Like Hell! He fought because we had to fight;
> He died that's all. It was his unlucky night.

Another serviceman's poem ended 'No poppy, thank you.' (Selwyn, 1985, pp. xxx, 58).

Most Anglican and Free Church leaders rejected any simple identification of Christ with the national cause. Lessons had been learned since 1918. Indeed, quasi-pacifism was now so widespread that Archbishop Temple, who deeply valued the pacifist vocation, thought it necessary to say in November 1939: 'this notion that physiological life is absolutely sacred is Hindu or Buddhist, not Christian' (Temple, 1940, p. 29). The English Roman Catholic Church, however, supported both wars more uncritically than either the Church of England or the Free Churches. Cardinal Hinsley (a Christian nationalist whom Churchill preferred to the internationalist Temple) addressed the forces in curiously dated romantic language: 'I like to think of the soldier as a knight of olden chivalry who laid his armour on the altar of God and spent his midnight vigil there beside it, striving to fit himself for his life's grand work' (Hinsley, 1941, p. 104). Whereas Hillary when he thought he was dying was relieved that he did not give way to prayer, in 1940 another airman wrote a last letter to his mother, reminiscent of 1914: 'My death would not mean that your struggle had been in vain. Far from it. It means that your sacrifice is as great as mine.' Within a month of its appearance in *The Times*, half a million copies had been sold. This incident, together with the widespread admiration for Churchill's rhetoric suggests that more patriotic emotion bubbled beneath the laconic English surface than people admitted (Wilkinson, 1986a).

Fetch out no shroud

Christian eschatology which had been common property in the First War was now more confined to believers. There was little or no public anxiety about hell, judgement or the fate of the dead. These once central Christian themes had been eroded by liberal theology and secular thought. By a parallel process, interest in spiritualism also reduced. Those who fought or were bereaved faced similar feelings as before and the churches again ministered to the dying and the mourners. But the context had changed. For example, *Pilgrim's Progress*, much quoted by soldiers in the First War, and which for centuries had taught the English to set their lives within a cosmic drama with its goal in heaven, was now discarded (Cannadine, 1981, p. 232; Fussell, 1975, 1989). Yet it is said that 'society experiences a crisis of meaning when the threat of death pervades the atmosphere, yet cannot be incorporated into a religious or philosophical context' (Blauner, 1966, p. 392).

The successful yet subtle film *The Way to the Stars* (1945), as its title suggests, explores death and immortality in the lives of aircrew and their families. The airmen are laconic about death ('The CO bought it this afternoon...Yes, it's a bad show') and ambivalent about the supernatural. One of the pilots is killed after leaving his mascot behind. But another pilot reassures the widow that this was not the cause of his death. (The sceptical spirit eroded superstition as well as religion.) Two terse poems by John Pudney,

'Missing' and 'Johnny', provide a quasi-liturgical framework. 'Missing' quoted by a pilot to his fiancée to prepare her for his possible death includes such lines as 'Less said the better' and 'Last words don't matter'. The widow tells another pilot not to hesitate to marry even though he might also be killed. 'Fetch out no shroud' says the poem 'Johnny':

> Better by far
> For Johnny-the-bright-star,
> To keep your head,
> And see his children fed.
> (Gardner, 1977, pp. 77–8)

The film ends with a pilot sacrificing his life by staying in his doomed plane to avoid destroying the village and particularly its children. The vicar makes a brief appearance, not as a priest who knows about death, but as the organiser of the children's party. Do we only live on after death through our children?

When the war ended fewer special memorials were built. The new names – far fewer this time – could simply be added to the old. Some new memorials depicted soldiers in battle dress not armour, but some reverted to First War iconography and texts, particularly in the North. Individual memorials in churches were discouraged as contrary to the war's communal spirit. The official national memorial was the National Land Fund, a world away from the Cenotaph or the Menin Gate. The old remembrance rituals returned. Now confined to a Sunday, they no longer involved the whole community, so the churches exercised more control over them. 'O valiant hearts' was increasingly replaced by internationalist hymns – often, as with two out of three hymns at the 1994 Southsea Common D-Day service, unknown to the general public. The gradual spread of cremation loosened the Christian character of and clerical control over funerals. Cremation made it easier to take a pantheistic view of death, especially when (despite clerical disapproval) ashes were scattered in some favourite spot of the deceased, not buried in the churchyard. Thus a significant part of the rite passed into lay control and took place outside the sacred arena.

The increasingly diffuse attitudes of English people to death and an afterlife did not affect the national determination to locate and name the war dead. There were 370 000 graves to be marked, 250 000 missing to be commemorated and damaged First War cemeteries to be repaired. Those who died in a disorderly and chaotic manner were once again to be arranged in symmetrical patterns. Since the Falklands War and the fortieth anniversary of D-Day, interest in remembrance rituals and the war cemeteries, which had declined, has notably grown. More and more commemorations are also acts of international reconciliation as at Dresden in 1995 (Walter, 1993; Wilkinson, 1986a, pp. 310–12).

The English have remained ambivalent about death in war. The nation entered the Second War protesting against Hitler's bombing of civilian targets. Later, despite the protests of Bishop Bell and others, they accepted obliteration bombing of Germany as the way to avoid the huge Allied casualties of the First War. The liberation of the death camps in Spring 1945 intensified the nation's horror of Nazism; yet in August the people supported the destruction of thousands of Japanese civilians by atomic bombs to avoid huge Allied losses.

If the interwar years were blighted by the casualties of the First War, the years since 1945 have been haunted by the Jewish Holocaust and by the spectre of nuclear war. Death on such a scale confronts all human beings with their shadow side, and believers with the shadow side of God. It also threatens the secular concept of immortality as the participation in an unbroken chain from the past which reaches infinitely into the future (Hick, 1979, p. 89).

REFERENCES

M. Andrews, *Canon's Folly*, (London: Michael Joseph, 1975).

J. Bickersteth, 'The Bickersteth War Diaries', *Spectator*, (28 September 1991).

R. Blauner, 'Death and Social Structure', *Psychiatry*, XXIX (1966), pp. 378–94.

R. Blythe, *Akenfield*, (London: Allen Lane, 1969).

D. Boorman, *At the Going Down of the Sun, British First World War Memorials*, (York: Boorman, 1988).

V. Brittain, *Testament of Youth*, (London: Virago, 1978).

V. Brittain, *Chronicle of Youth*, (London: Fontana, 1982).

D. Cairns (ed.), *The Army and Religion*, (London: Macmillan, 1919).

D. Cannadine, 'War and Death, Grief and Mourning in Modern Britain', in J. Whaley (ed.), *Mirrors of Mortality* (London: Europa, 1981).

P. Fussell, *The Great War and Modern Memory*, (London: Oxford University Press, 1975).

P. Fussell, *Wartime*, (London: Oxford University Press, 1989).

B. Gardner (ed.), *The Terrible Rain, The War Poets 1939–1945*, (London: Magnum, 1977).

M. Girouard, *The Return to Camelot*, (London: Yale, 1981).

J. Hick, *Death and Eternal Life*, (London: Fount, 1979).

R. Hillary, *The Last Enemy*, (London: Macmillan, 1961).

A. Hinsley, *The Bond of Peace*, (London: Burns Oates, 1941).

E. Hoskyns, *Cambridge Sermons*, (London: S.P.C.K., 1938).

L. Housman, *War-Letters of Fallen Englishmen*, (London: Gollancz, 1930).

R. Kipling, 'The Gardener', in *Debits and Credits*, (London: Macmillan, 1926).

D. Lessing, *Under my skin*, (London: Harper Collins, 1994).

P. Liddle, *Testimony of War 1914–1918*, (Salisbury: Michael Russell, 1979).

P. Longworth, *The Unending Vigil, A History of the Commonwealth War Graves Commission 1917–1967*, (London: Constable, 1967).

C. Moriarty, 'Christian Iconography and First World War Memorials', *Imperial War Museum Review*, No. 6 (1992) 63–75.

P. Morris, *Leeds and the Amateur Military Tradition*, (Leeds University unpublished PhD thesis, 1983).

E. Oldmeadow, *Francis, Cardinal Bourne*, (London: Burns Oates, 1944).

J. Oxenham, *High Altars: The Battlefields of France and Flanders as I saw them*, (London: Methuen, 1918).

P. Parker, *The Old Lie, The Great War and the Public School Ethos*, (London: Constable, 1987).

V. Selwyn (ed.), *Poems of the Second World War, The Oasis Selection*, (London: Dent, 1985).

W. Temple, *Thoughts in War-Time*, (London: Macmillan, 1940).

T. Walter, 'War Grave Pilgrimage', in I. Reader and T. Walter (eds), *Pilgrimage in Popular Culture*, (London: Macmillan, 1993).

A. Wilkinson, *The Church of England and the First World War*, (London: S.P.C.K., 1978).

A. Wilkinson, 'The Paradox of the Military Chaplain', *Theology*, LXXXIV (1981) 249–57.

A. Wilkinson, 'Searching for Meaning in time of War: Theological themes in First World War Literature', *Modern Churchman*, NSXXVII No. 2 (1985) 13–21.

A. Wilkinson (1986a), *Dissent or Conform? War, Peace and the English Churches, 1900-1945*, (London: SCM, 1986).

A. Wilkinson (1986b), 'The Poetry of War', *Theology*, LXXXIX (1986) 459–70.

D. Winter, *Death's Men*, (London: Allen Lane, 1978).

J. Winter, 'Spiritualism and the First World War', in R. W. Davis and R. J. Helmstadter (eds), *Religion and Irreligion in Victorian Society*, (London: Routledge, 1992).

11 The Death of a King: Elvis Presley (1935–1977)

Christine King

'ELVIS DIES AND THE AGE OF ROCK IS OVER'

Beneath this headline the *Manchester Guardian* of 17 August 1977 continued,

> The King is dead and there will be no replacement. Elvis Presley, the founder, the greatest exponent, and the most passionate figure in rock and roll, died last night in the emergency ward of Memphis Baptist Hospital of 'acute respiratory distress'. A hospital spokesman said Presley was found unconscious at his home by his road manager, Joe Esposito, who called the fire department ambulance. Ambulance personnel tried to resuscitate the singer as he was being rushed to hospital, but Presley's personal physician, Dr George Nichopoules, pronounced him dead.

Nearly 20 years after his death, Elvis Presley regularly attracts more attention than any other comparable cultural icon, including James Dean and Marilyn Monroe. The continuing interest in Presley shown by biographers, music critics and students of American society, is matched by the sustained enthusiasm of the media for stories of Elvis and his contemporary fans. The popular press runs regular stories about whether Elvis is 'really dead', with reports of sightings that take ever more fantastic forms. Not only in his home town, but throughout the United States, car bumper stickers may be seen asserting 'Elvis Lives!'

Elvis earns more for his estate today than he ever did in his lifetime. His graveside at Graceland receives regular pilgrims and is the scene of a spectacular annual international Festival which culminates in a candle-lit vigil. Elvis impersonators all over the world offer tribute to Presley either for money or for love and often for both. This chapter examines elements of the fascination with Elvis Presley, a musician who has gained a special significance, both in and by his death.

Fans all over the world responded to the unexpected news of his death with a sense of shock and of personal loss (King, 1993). Presley had symbolised the fulfilment of American dreams; he also transcended national boundaries, transmitting American popular culture across the world. Fans as far apart as Russia and Japan mourned his death. Their expressions of grief were matched by formal media tributes, which admitted his significance for contemporary social history. This was particularly true of the United Kingdom, where his music, in the late 1950s, offered teenagers a new way of life and where Presley had a large following. Elvis, had, in his way, been more of a missionary for the American way of life then had been the visiting GIs during the Second World War. These fans have stayed loyal and in the UK, as elsewhere, younger generations have taken up the flag. Thus the mourners who gathered in August 1977 as the news of his death was received, included old as well as young, with a predominance of those who had been teenagers with Elvis. Tabloid and broadsheet newspapers shared the grief.

For the next few months, the world's media was flooded with obituaries and tributes to Presley. Most extensive coverage was to be found, not surprisingly, in America. There radio and TV stations often abandoned scheduled programmes to play his music and show his films. Elvis was predominantly the hero of America, the country he loved so patriotically, and which he symbolised as much as Coca-Cola or the Cadillac. America gave him the attention customarily given to its heroes at their death. Huge crowds gathered at the gates of Graceland, his home in Memphis. Television cameras revealed many fans being carried away, overcome by emotion and heat. Photographs of mourning fans appeared on TV and on the front pages of newspapers all over the world.

In Britain as elsewhere some local churches organised memorial services. On the day of the funeral, a church in Cockfosters was packed with mourners, many in extreme distress. Hundreds of people, unable to get into the church, waited outside in silence. The decision was taken to hold the memorial service twice. Mourners were told 'We're going to close the service by playing "Peace in the Valley" – if you can stand it.' Few could: people had been steadily breaking down as the sound of Elvis' voice echoed through the church. As people left the church and gathered in the churchyard, they leant on each other for support, bodies heaving. After the service, a fan called 'Mouse' told the *Manchester Guardian* 'Elvis is dead bodily, but spiritually he lives on. He was wild, untamed. He *made* people like me, who are still rebels and boys at heart' (The *Manchester Guardian*, 19 August 1977).

Fans, worldwide, had shared in the American way of life through Presley's music and films; now they were sharing something of the American way of death. Mouse's conviction that Elvis Presley was to have abiding meaning for his fans proved correct; that Elvis was 'dead bodily' was a premise imminently to be challenged. Just as Elvis had brought to British youth in the 1950s an undefined optimism, so, worldwide, his fans shared a new hope, that he would 'live on'. Elvis, who had escaped death, just like his childhood hero Captain Marvel Junior, was about to enter the mythology, offering hope to a postwar generation that death was not the end. For some this was to be a spiritual truth; for others it would take a more tangible form.

Elvis' new lease of life took a specifically tangible form for those with the responsibility for promoting his music. For the rest of the year his voice was regularly heard on 'Top Forty' radio. Clayson comments:

> A death in pop sells records. Before they had a chance to dry their tears, music industry moguls would be obliged to meet the demand kindled by tragedy and rush-release the product while the corpse was still warm. On 16th August 1977, record-store windows bloomed with the King's splendour... It was a boom time for Presley's manager, Colonel Tom Parker, who regarded his client's absence as no more a hindrance than back in 1958 when Elvis had been drafted into the US army for two years. (Clayson, 1992, pp. 88–9).

The death of Elvis produced a scale of mourning which at least matched that which followed the deaths of Marilyn Monroe and John F. Kennedy. His death was not simply the public face of fans' private grief. His death was a challenge to American popular culture and to its self-confidence. The press coverage reflected an international recognition that Elvis' death represented some kind of landmark. He had long been identified as the herald of a new phase in Western social life and popular culture. Even amongst the stars, Presley was special.

> The cult heroes were Brando's menacing biker hipster hero, Dean, the sensitive, mixed-up kid, but the prime masculinity model was Memphis's Elvis Presley. The working-class Southern boy from the wrong side of town with sexy, black movements and voice, spoke beyond the United States to working-class youth everywhere. The butch image of the ted set off his dandyism to protect his masculinity – elegance was no longer ladylike. (Brake, 1985, p. 73)

With his death, his status as a major entertainer began to be transformed so that Elvis came to symbolise something separate and 'holy'. When fans and journalists alike adopted such language and titles as 'The King', shape was given to these barely articulated feelings. They gave the impression that life without Elvis would be different, not just for his fans, but for all his contemporaries. An authority-figure was dead. This carried the implicit threat that a dominating role model who had enlivened and regulated the social behaviour of the young postwar generation had been removed from the scene.

Alongside the eulogies for the dead hero and the 'passing of an era', there simultaneously emerged an intense interest in the precise manner of his death and the details of his funeral and interment. This was at first largely an American phenomenon; it parallels the American fascination with the mystery surrounding the circumstances of the deaths of Monroe and of President Kennedy. The sudden death of a figure who symbolised so much of American popular culture needed explanation; the examination of the details would enable acceptance of the death and facilitate the mourning.

Beneath this apparent need ran the fear that looking at the details of the death might produce a different conclusion. If Elvis was dead, then his supporters had themselves to confront the fact of death and to accept the transitoriness of their youth and its hopes and dreams. The denial of the facts of his death might negate the threat of transitoriness, if there were sufficient clues to make plausible the survival of Elvis as a role model.

As this double fascination grew, anniversary tributes and commentaries came, for a time, to be dominated as much by obsession with the details of his last hours, as by his preceding life. His friends and former companions provided intimate details. Within days of his death, members of his former bodyguard claimed that he had died not from heart failure but from a cumulative overdose of the 'prescribed' drugs which he had been taking for some years. Presley had been publicly associated with President Richard Nixon's anti-drug campaign. The inconsistency thrown up by his bodyguards' 'testimony' offered rich materials for an industry of insider stories, yet provided few problems for those engaged in writing his memorials: they were concerned to emphasise the positive features of his life and death.

Presley's funeral received almost royal attentions. Flags flew at half-mast in the states of Tennessee and Mississippi. Memphis police estimated that 100 000 people gathered on the day of his burial, many of them in tears. The body was displayed in an open copper coffin at Graceland whilst fans, who had been queuing long hours, processed past. The body was driven, with an escort of white Cadillacs, Presley's favourite car and the proper American tribute, down the renamed Elvis Presley Boulevard (re-named for him during his lifetime) to Forest Hills cemetery, three miles away. Police, sheriff's deputies and National Guardsmen were deployed at the ceremony to control the crowds and to keep the ceremony private. Nevertheless, crowds gathered; wreaths were torn apart as flowers and written messages were collected as precious relics.

Within a few weeks, the number of fans visiting the graveside and searching for souvenirs and relics made it necessary to move the bodies of Presley and his mother back to the garden at Graceland where they rest today, alongside other close family members. Here, in a setting that leaves no doubt that the memorial is to someone of great importance, pilgrims offer prayers and gifts, and some seek, and believe that they find, miracles. The area where Presley is buried offers some of the characteristics popularly associated with the contemporary American way of death. The Presley family graves are close to a 'Meditation Garden'. A statue of Jesus with arms outstretched stands near playing fountains and coloured lights. The area is surrounded by elaborate wreaths with poignant and detailed messages from fans; there are poems and prayers to and for Elvis.

Attached to the wreaths and painted in flowers, images of Elvis depict him at various stages of his career: in army uniform, in Hawaiian costume from his film days, and in his famous white spangled suit from the Las Vegas seasons. Such images suggest it is impossible to separate the obsession with Elvis and his death from an understanding of the perceived successive meanings of his life as a cultural innovator. Elvis has a significance far beyond his music and films. His life story has elements of 'rags to riches'; what is fast becoming a hagiography draws a picture of, variously, the martyr and the poor boy who lived to become the fulfilment of the American dream.

Elvis Aaron Presley was born in Tupelo, Mississippi, in January 1935, the only surviving child of poor white sharecropper parents. His twin brother, Jesse Garon, was stillborn and buried in an unmarked grave in Priceville cemetery. He was never forgotten, either in the public legend that grew around Elvis, or in family memory. As a child, Elvis apparently visited the grave frequently; as an adult he repeatedly referred to him (Guralnick, 1994, p. 13). Brought up in the Bible Belt of the Deep South he attended the local Pentecostal church, the First Assembly of God, known as the 'holy rollers', and imbibed the music of country and western, gospel and blues; music from both the black and white vernacular traditions.

Although poorly educated, he was launched in his career in the mid 1950s, becoming known for his singing and his spectacular way of dressing. His music, appearance and way of moving his body while he sang, earned him the reputation of the 'white boy who sings like a black'. At a time of racial segregation and Ku Klux Klan activities, those promoting him were able to move popular black music into the white charts. Presley's stunning looks and his overt sexual gyrations made him the obvious candidate for the unofficial leadership of the new generation of teenagers. These had, for the first time and in large numbers, money to spend, and were seeking an identity that would separate them from their parents and from older singers like Perry Como or Bill Haley. Elvis was a hero and role model for young men and women alike, offering each a different way of relating to their own images of sexuality and rebellion. Elvis combined elements of the macho, overtly sexual style and the romantic, graceful lover. In the macho, young men could find a role model, and in the romantic, young women could dream of love both illicit and dangerous, but ultimately, as his songs and films showed, conventional in its outcome, that is, marriage.

He speedily became a spectacular public success. In his life he demonstrated what to some were apparent contradictions, but which were characteristics rooted in his upbringing and culture. Thus this sexually dangerous rebel was non-smoking, non-drinking, polite to his elders and, above all, devoted to his mother. When his military service papers arrived, Elvis responded willingly, although there was some media anticipation that he might resist. Fans wept as his celebrated hairstyle received the attention of army barbers.

After release from the army his career entered a new phase and he made a series of films generally considered to have done little justice to his talent. Nevertheless, he played in these films many classic roles from American history; he was, among others, a Cherokee Indian, a cowboy, a river-boat gambler, a racing driver, a circus performer. In each he finds a love, risks losing her, suffers at the hands of wicked and devious people, but finally triumphs through and wins his bride. The film parts were all 'goodies'; in each picture America's innocent son is revived to tell the same story. Elvis 'died' in his first film, 'Love Me Tender', and Colonel Tom Parker, concerned about the impact this might have on fans and the box office, apparently vetoed any further screen deaths. (At the time of Presley's demise, he was to ensure that death need make no difference to the star's career. Although he calculated correctly in financial terms, he lost his own connections with the Presley business after the family brought a successful lawsuit against him.)

Presley re-emerged as a stage performer with some of his old passion and launched himself into a career of concerts in the great entertainment centres of America. New rituals were constructed to stress the separate and special nature of this star. This was the time of the white spangled suits. The theme music from the film '2001: A Space Odyssey' heralded Presley's sudden and almost magical appearance on the stage. The custom arose that, after the performance was over, the public address system would announce that 'Elvis has left the building'. This stimulated a feeling as if a holy presence had been withdrawn, leaving the hall and the people within it empty of their idol.

Meanwhile, during this third stage of his career, his dependence on prescribed drugs increased, with consequent and considerable weight gain. When he died, aged 42, he was obese, and barely recognisable as the wild rebel of the 1950s. Nevertheless, at his death, his fans recalled and celebrated not only his youthful glory but the later years of apparent decline. Although his admirers might have been expected to select only his representative youthfulness, the stories of Presley as drug-ridden, incontinent and unbalanced, have not deterred them.

The focus concentrated both on his last hours and the funeral. As fans examined the death of their hero, they had to contemplate their own death. Reluctant to face their own mortality, they challenged the fact of their hero's death. Accustomed to his appearance and withdrawal during his life, they transposed his reappearances beyond his death. Was Elvis really dead? Shortly afterwards, the suggestion emerged that it had not been Elvis Presley displayed in the copper coffin and now buried at Graceland. If he was not dead, where was he? If alive, might he be encountered, as on the road to Emmaus or Damascus?

Queries were raised about the details of his funerals. Inconsistencies were discovered in the published accounts. Some fans regarded these as a therapeutic curiosity; others found it evidence of a resurrection. For those who perceived the anagram of Elvis/Lives, the very inconsistencies were interpreted as clues, provided by Elvis to his fans to reassure them of his survival. The marketing of T-shirts asserting 'Elvis is Alive' strengthened the plausibility structure for believing such accounts.

Thousands of fans viewed his body. For some of these, his facial features were not recognisable from those they knew so well from the films and photographs. The coffin itself is reported to have been exceptionally heavy, even for the overweight Presley. Significant questions were asked about the post-mortem and death certificate. These questions continue to be pursued by the press, some 61 years after his birth and 19 years after his death. These have been formally pursued by the authorities in Memphis, but without conclusive results.

On the Graceland tombstone, Aaron is misspelt. For those seeking clues, the misspelling of the middle name is read as a message that he is not really inside. Presley's own interest in religion and use of the mystical prompted others to believe that he had planned to fake his death and had chosen a date with special significance. Peter Eicher decoded 2001, the popular title of the music associated with Elvis' later performances, taken from Richard Strauss' 'Thus Spake Zarathustra'. Elvis' own interest in numerology would allow him to calculate that the numbers of his death date (written as 8.16.1977) total 2001 and signify to his fans that this was his chosen date to disappear (Eicher, 1993, pp. 9–10).

Some believe that Elvis, seeking to escape the pressures of his daily life and its isolation, planned his escape by faking his death. The 'body' in the coffin was perhaps a wax model which, with the necessary cooling unit, explained the excess weight. Alternative stories claim that an Elvis lookalike, already diagnosed as terminally ill, was brought to spend his last weeks at Graceland. It was his body that was displayed in the copper coffin. These stories had precedents in American pop culture. 'The likes of Glenn Miller, James Dean and Buddy Holly are also said to be lying comatose and horribly disfigured in remote sanatoriums [sic]' (Clayson, 1992, pp. 89–90).

The fascination with his death (or its elaborate hoax) began to take two distinct forms. There were, firstly, those who believed Elvis was alive. Secondly, others argued that he had died. This latter group sought explanations and looked for targets for blame. They told stories from his '100 last days'; and sought specific and physical details of his last days and moments, which included his reading of religious books. The targets included his family, the members of his bodyguard, and his personal physician, upon whom particular suspicion centred. Had they caused Elvis' death by their neglect? Or had they, perhaps, colluded in his 'escape'?

Once Elvis was argued to be alive, sightings were reported in many countries of the world. At first he was seen performing ordinary tasks, like shopping. Photographs were also published, purporting to show his face peeping out of a Graceland window, watching the pilgrims visit his tomb. Although it was some years before the reports began to be collected and widely published, they date from the time of his death. Kalamazoo (Michigan) where Presley had performed in 1973, emerged as the site of the earliest and most significant sightings. Accounts of brief sightings progressed to more complex encounters in which Elvis imparted advice, help or healing. He would appear as suddenly as he disappeared. TV and radio phone-ins all over America registered Elvis sightings (see, for example, Eicher, 1993).

Whatever the reality of the situation, the making of the myth progressed steadily. If Elvis could appear to be dead but remain alive, then anything was possible. Just as 'Bobby', a character in the popular TV soap 'Dallas', was brought back from the dead by the device that the scene of his death had merely been a dream that the viewers had, for several episodes, shared, so Elvis' death might have been a 'trick'. Given such media models, then the untimely death of the bearer of American youth and dreams might be an issue people could ignore. The happy ending might, after all, be achievable. In real life, as in fiction, death could not detain our hero. With one bound, he was free.

Elvis' death was a kind of liberation. Commemorative plates and mugs promised him 'Peace in the Valley' and 'A Closer Walk with God'. Not only could his famous youth be restored, but he could also be, in death, everywhere and with every fan. Elvis the man of contradictions quickly entered the realm of mythology where conflicting stories about his life and death could be constructed and maintained. Elvis' death made him accessible to fans in a way that had not been possible during his lifetime. Isolated in his lifetime by his manager and by the practicalities of being a star, he had been separate and untouchable. Fans could now visit his graveside, enter his home and view his possessions at close quarters. The purchase of souvenirs enabled them to own, relic-like, a small part of him. In the first 12 years since Graceland was opened to the public 12 million people visited Elvis' home. At Elvis' death, then, his star's transcendence was replaced by his divine immanence.

The creation of the star by his manager, Tom Parker, and his increasingly extreme isolation behind the gates of Graceland, had added to the mythology built around him. At his death that mythology was given full expression by Parker's marketing techniques. Commentary joined with tribute to identify Elvis as 'special' and 'different' and, implicitly, 'holy'. The hagiography was ready to be written, not by monks and scholars, but by journalists and fans. Elvis' death had ended his isolation. It allowed fans, critics and bystanders access to the 'real Elvis', who now belonged to anyone who wished to claim him. The additional chance that he might still be alive, even though fostered by the media and other commercial interests, made it possible for any fan to meet him, anywhere, anytime. Elvis, the inspiration who 'lifted the spirit' of those who listened to his music, and Elvis, who never died, together became someone larger than life.

One specific group which demonstrates a desire to affirm a continuing identity with Elvis is his impersonators. They are found in many countries, and are from different classes and ages, including the middle-aged and very young children. Some are professional entertainers, most are not; there is at least one famous American female Elvis. The majority live out their lives dressed and speaking like Elvis the performer. Their imitation excludes Presley's life as a recluse with a drug habit. They stress Elvis' 'good works' and love for his fans. Asked why they have adopted their role, one frequent rationale is that 'the spirit of Elvis was too big to be contained in one person'. They also, not uncommonly, claim that they are offering fans a service and are, in the process, 'getting closer to Elvis'.

One point of contact that brings fans 'closer to Elvis' is in Memphis where there is a 'Church of the Elvis Impersonators'. There weddings can be performed by look-alikes. Bridegrooms are often dressed as Elvis. The words of the liturgy bestow the blessing of Elvis and the promise that he will be with the couple in their married life.

One catalogue of professional entertainers lists 64 Elvis impersonators (Cahill, 1991). Their semi-sacred devotion, as well as their art, is apparent. 'In the beginning there was the word and the word was Elvis' (Clayton Benke-Smith, quoted in Cahill, *op.cit*, pp. 12–13); 'If he had lived, Elvis would have brought peace to the world' (Ken Welsh-Elvis Eagle, quoted in Cahill, *op.cit*, p. 118); 'And from that night on I knew the trail I must blaze would be the Elvis trail, however right or wrong that might be' (Janice K – the Lady Elvis, quoted in Cahill, *op.cit.*, p. 68). Whilst one of the entries is for 'Little Elvis', aged five, copies of the mystical Las Vegas model predominate over the rebel rocker. 'Little Elvis' dresses in Las Vegas style.

The majority of fans appears to believe that Elvis, in the words of 'Mouse', is 'dead bodily' but that he lives on in his music. The identification of his good qualities and, in particular, his generosity, leads fans all over the world to see him as a role model and, through fan clubs, to collect and work for charity. In conventions, in music and film festivals and in impersonations, they 'get close to Elvis'. Many report feeling his influence on their lives and testify to the peace and sense of closeness to him that these activities bring them.

The mixture of the belief that he is not dead and that he lives for his fans has taken Elvis Presley's name and image into a wide number of areas of popular mythology. Greil Marcus described 'the dead Elvis' as a 'cultural obsession' and gives evidence of Presley's ubiquitous presence in popular culture. For Marcus it is Presley's death which allows him to slip pervasively into popular imagery as 'when he died, many people found themselves caught up in the adventure of remaking his history, which is to say their own' (Marcus, 1991, preface).

The ultimate experience for most fans is a visit to Graceland; an opportunity to lay a flower on his grave, and to spend some quiet time in the Meditation Garden adjacent to the Presley family graves. This is a particularly special experience around the anniversary of his death, when thousands of fans from all over the world queue in a candlelight vigil, and when the grounds of Graceland are stacked high with wreaths and flowers.

For many, even for those born after 1977, the question of whether or not he is alive is irrelevant. Elvis has entered popular culture as a major icon and his image appears all over the world, on T-shirts, in shop windows and in stained glass. Rowland Scherman, among others, has recorded some of these images with the claim that 'Elvis is everywhere'. Scherman's photographs show Elvis in locations all over the United States, seeking to demonstrate that 'Elvis' presence is palpably among us' (in Pollard, 1991).

The Chicago settings include a McDonald's hamburger bar, where Elvis is the focus for the decor, and a bar displaying a newspaper cutting which declares that Elvis' statue has been found on Mars. Scherman shows car stickers inviting Elvis to 'phone home' and drivers to 'honk if you love Elvis'. A TV screen invites viewers to apply for the daily recipe, the 'Elvis Sandwich'. There are cafes, banks and hotels named after Elvis, and T-shirts proclaiming 'Elvis for President'.

Marcus has offered a more complex set of cultural images (Marcus, 1991). His collection provides references likening Elvis to Christ, to Hitler, and to both simultaneously. He records stories of 'Presley-burgers' made from his stolen body. The Elvis of Marcus' record is bizarre: he is powerful and omnipresent, but his supernatural persona is satanic rather than Godly.

Fans have their own preferred image of Elvis. For Elvis impersonators worldwide, the preferred image is the Las Vegas white spangled suit. The US Mail has chosen a stamp showing the young Elvis; the preference was made after a poll which gave the public the choice between images old and young. The necessity for the vote indicates the range of popular images. The images of the ultimate Elvis, in his decline and in his death, have both been ignored. Whilst the revelations about his decline and the circumstances of his death, purportedly on the toilet seat of his bathroom, have sold profitable books, they have left his crown untarnished. Elvis is a fallible saint, and his fans, perhaps discreetly aware of their own failings, suppress the fallibility of their icon. This may increase their relevance.

Sightings continue. A hospital patient reported that Elvis' visit to her bedside led her to recovery (*Cannock Mercury*, 24 November 1994). There have been further challenges to the coroner's report, with a group of prestigious Memphis citizens lobbying for the case to be returned; they claimed that 'the whitewash continues'. Elvis has been seen kneeling at the graveside of Jackie Kennedy, and in the New York Yankees' stadium, calling for the end of the baseball strike. Elvis is recently reported to have rung President Clinton, a known fan, on his private line, promising a comeback. Apparently, the FBI successfully identified Elvis' voice pattern. Elvis jokes and rumours were fuelled in 1995 by the media's promotion of his sixtieth birthday.

Whether or not the highly lucrative industry around his estate could survive his second coming is uncertain. In any case, it may even be irrelevant now. The obsession and the fascination with Elvis, both from fans and from the general public, continues to grow. Elvis embodies something of significance for fans and the power he gives them transcends his death, whether by his existence in hiding or from beyond the grave.

Elvis Presley's death and the responses to it offer an opportunity for further investigation. They offer insights into contemporary American attitudes to death. For, whilst it is clear that the Elvis cult is an international one, his religion has been founded in America and our 'cultural obsession' with Presley takes its imagery, its language and its meaning from America.

Elvis is important to America because he fulfilled an American dream. He was the poor boy born in a shack, who became, not President, but King. His sudden and premature death was a challenge as he embodied so many people's identity and aspirations. The mixture of mythologies articulating their attitudes to Elvis allowed them either to deny his death or to sanctify it. Thus, for many, Presley's death took on a spiritual meaning which the 'facts' of his last days are manipulated to reinforce. If Presley's life lent meaning to his fans, his death should receive an explanation too, otherwise meaning is evacuated. One such explanation is that he died a martyr's death:

he died either as a victim of his fans' need of him, or at the hands of an entourage who exploited him. Thus, whether the chosen image of Elvis is young and beautiful, or ageing and overweight, each can occupy a place in popular imagery and culture. Elvis the victim can represent both the shame and the hope of his fans.

The death of Elvis is an American drama, a soap opera with continuing episodes. The reluctance of his disciples to accept the reality of his death permits them to conceptualise him either wandering the States in disguise or reigning as a saint in the Christian heaven, or as a god in some other pre-, post- or non-Christian pantheon such as Marcus describes.

All the myths deny the reality of his death. Either Elvis has tricked death, or he is the martyr, to his manager, his wife or his fans and, having thus died for them, he lives on in their hearts and his music. Either way, the place of Elvis as a partner in a relationship has been strengthened. Dead or alive, they feel liberated by him. The singer Mojo Nixon wrote,

> I think people wanna [sic] believe Elvis is alive, because if Elvis, the American Messiah, the New World Royalty can die, *then so can they*. Our culture loves to pretend that death doesn't happen, and when the point man for post-war liberation goes down the tubes, the collective anguish and denial is amazing. (Quain, 1992, p. xiv)

The fascination with Elvis raises questions about the contemporary construction of the meaning of death in America. The postwar generation was socialised in conditions where death, in childhood and in the home, was unfamiliar. American citizens, unlike Europeans, had no experience of civilian bombing (see Wilkinson, chapter 10). In addition, the exposure of American children to regular death scenes on television trivialised death and made it unreal to the viewer, as part of the magic world of entertainment. It was reported from a meeting of the American Academy of Paediatrics in 1971 that

> by the time a child in the United States is fourteen years old, he can be expected to have seen, on average, 18000 people killed on television. (*The Times*, 19 October 1971)

Popular culture, promoted by the media and by entrepreneurial capitalism, depends upon entertainment stars who are simultaneously representative and separate. Elvis, of all stars, encapsulated this. This brief excursion into the impact of Elvis and his death makes no claims to be other than a speculation on some possible meanings. It can be asserted that, as an agent of cultural and social change, as the product of highly skilful commercial promotion, and as the 'right' person, emerging at the 'right' time, Elvis is part of the social history of the postwar generations. His career was marketed deliberately to promote him as a cultural icon, and particularly as one with overtones of the Jesus of Christian scripture. The motifs of common humanity and divine defeat of death seem to have been deliberately adopted in the selling of Elvis.

The myths that have grown up and been promoted since his death ensure that his past is continually represented. He has been used as a weapon in his fans' personal attempts to evade the fact of death. The stimulation of interest in resurrection appearances by Elvis has been a deliberate tool in his promoters' marketing strategy. Otherwise, whilst it is possible to identify why Elvis, and not another star entertainer, was so dominant, it is less easy to identify why his presence is so abiding. It would be interesting to speculate on whether the Elvis cult will last, and, if it does, what its future theology will indicate about his death and its meaning. The post-mortem life of Presley mirrors the post-mortem beliefs of post-Christian American youth. Elvis, the product of the Bible Belt, has been partially equipped with features from the Biblical narrative of Jesus. The next youth cult hero to die so famously may be immortalised and marketed on a different charismatic model.

REFERENCES

M. Brake, *Comparative Youth Culture: the sociology of youth culture and youth subculture in America, Britain and Canada*, (London: Routledge, 1985).

M. Cahill (ed.), *I am Elvis*, (New York: Pocket Books, 1991).

A. Clayson, *Death Discs: Ashes to smashes. An account of fatality in the popular song*, (London: Gollancz, 1992).

P. Eicher, *The Elvis Sightings*, (New York: Avon, 1993).

P. Guralnick, *Last Train to Memphis*, (London: Little, Brown and Company, 1994).

C. King, 'His Truth Goes Marching On', in Reader, I. and Walter, T. (eds), *Pilgrimage in Popular Culture*, (London: Macmillan, 1993).

G. Marcus, *Dead Elvis*, (London: Penguin Books, 1991).

M. Pollard (ed.), *Elvis is Everywhere: Photographs by Rowland Scherman*, (New York: Clarkson Potter, 1991).

K. Quain, *The Elvis Reader*, (New York: St Martin's Press, 1992).

12 Actuarial Visions of Death: Life, Death and Chance in the Modern World

Lindsay Prior

> Of death, and many are the ways that lead
> To his grim cave, all dismal ...
>
> Milton, Paradise Lost XI 468–9

SCIENTIFIC REPRESENTATIONS OF DEATH

It is, I think, above all through the work of Phillipe Ariès (1967, 1974, 1983, 1985) that we have come to recognise the historically variable forms which social representations of death might take. Ariès, of course, studied representations of death in such widely diverse fields as cemetery architecture, paintings, literary accounts, poems, funerary iconography and funerary ritual. For him, the changing forms of such phenomena revealed historically changing sensibilities toward death in the western world – from the tame and public death of the early Middle Ages to the invisible and forbidden death of the twentieth century. One class of social representation which Ariès did not study, however, was what might be called scientific representations of death, and it is this latter type of representation upon which I wish to concentrate here. Scientific representations emerged out of diverse nineteenth-century scientific sources and may be linked to such phenomena as the rise of anatomical pathology, the development of probability theory and the birth of modern epidemiology. In essence, they were representations of a calculable, and determinate death and to that extent they stand in stark contrast to the vision of random, feckless and capricious death which, according to Huizinga (1924), so haunted the inhabitants of pre-modern Europe.

I intend to examine scientific representations in terms of the context of modernity, and what is these days called postmodernity (Bauman, 1991). In fact, I hope to demonstrate that nineteenth- and twentieth-century images of death are very much tied up with the notions of a controllable and calculable universe – a universe which can be supposedly mastered through human praxis. To that end I shall first of all examine the ways in which nineteenth-century Europeans developed notions concerning the expectation of life, and then examine some of the ways in which twentieth-century Europeans have sought to deconstruct death.

MODERNITY AND THE EXPECTATION OF LIFE

In a moment I shall be looking at the interrelationships which exist between our concepts of chance and probability and our understanding of human mortality. The connection of death with luck and chance, however, is probably as old as the notion of chance itself. It was certainly a connection which Ariès recognised, and in his pictorial work (1985) he draws our attention to a number of sixteenth- and seventeenth-century paintings in which chance appears prominently on the canvas. Thus, dice in particular, together with other metaphors for death such as skeletal bodies and timepieces, were frequently used to symbolise human mortality (Ariès, 1985, plates 260, 281, 283). And this vision of death as chance was also mixed with a further image of death as inexorable fate. Thus in plate 285 of the Ariès work, we can witness the Burgmaier spouses staring mournfully at their own rotting skulls – duly reflected in a hand glass. In plate 257 on the other hand, it is an insect-headed death which leers at a young woman and her newborn child (from Hans Grien's sixteenth-century portrait), emphasising not merely the inevitability of death but also its ubiquity. Indeed, in the pre-industrial world it seems that death could strike arbitrarily at any age. Thus in Hans Holbein's woodcuts of the dance of death (1538) we see death snatch at one moment a healthy child from the hearth, and at another a robust woman from a nunnery. And these portraits of death's meandering served as a common point of departure for numerous European artists.

Taken together, then, the pre-modern portraits present a vision of a random, unpredictable and untamed death; of a death which can strike anyone, anywhere, at any time whatsoever and with equal possibility. What is more, the target of death is quite distinctly the isolated individual rather than any collective entity such as an age group or a community. It was, in other words, singular human beings who were selected for death – and it was consequently the isolated child, the personable young woman, the cripple, and the frail middle-aged spouse who appeared in the paintings and drawings to which I refer. Towards the end of the seventeenth century and specifically in the eighteenth and nineteenth centuries, however, we begin to stumble across a new image of death. It is an image formed in the mould of modernity; that is to say, an image which places calculation and predictability at the centre of the picture and which thereby elides the older concepts of randomness and uncertainty.

This switch of focus is rather neatly encompassed in a paper of Karl Pearson's published in 1897 in which he called upon the dance of death once more in an attempt to explain the vagaries of mortality (Pearson, 1897). Pearson represented death as a marksman firing at people crossing a bridge – but in his world it proved not only possible to calculate (with precision) the hit rate of the marksman, but to assess (with considerable accuracy) the marksman's margin of error. More importantly, perhaps, it was easy to see that it was the rate of mortality which interested Pearson – that is, a property of populations rather than individuals; and the fate of a collective entity rather than the fate of singular persons. Pearson's focus on the death rate was, of course, characteristic of nineteenth-century statistical practice, and in his discussions of the rate, Pearson also alluded to another feature of nineteenth-century mathematical thinking, namely the idea of probability.

During recent years, various historians of mathematics and statistics (such as Crombie, 1994; Daston, 1988; Hacking, 1990; and Hald, 1990) have argued about the existence of what they call the revolution in probability theory. The arguments relate to the appearance – from the 1660s onward – of a new concept of chance. In terms of the latter, chance was conceived as something calculable and determinate rather than as something shrouded in fate and mystery; consequently it was argued that chance belonged to the realm of things which could be examined and discussed in a scientific manner. This newly emergent science was developed by such mathematicians as Fermat (1601–1665), Pascal (1623–1662), Christian Huygens (1629–1695), James Bernoulli (1654–1705) and de Moivre (1667–1754) – though Leibniz and Euler in addition to numerous others also played a role in the crucial developments. In essence the new way of considering chance rested on the fact that it was possible to put precise values on what had previously been considered to be indeterminate outcomes. Thus the chances of getting two sixes with two throws of a six-sided dice were to be calculated as (1 in 36); the chances of four sixes with six throws as (1 in 125); and the chances of selecting, say, a card with a face value of less than five from a full pack of 52 as (4 in 13) and so on. This kind of precision even encouraged de Moivre to believe that he could rid the world of the superstition that there was any such thing as luck in human affairs (de Moivre, 1718).

The nuances of classical probability theory need not concern us here – they have, in any case, been dealt with more than adequately in the scholarly work of Daston (1988) and Hald (1990) in particular. Suffice it to say for now that classical probability theory tended to focus mostly on expectations of outcome and equiprobable *a priori* probabilities (that is, probabilities of the type associated with the throw of a dice, the toss of a coin or the drawing of a playing card). Interestingly this was so even when probability theory was applied to what we now call the expectation of life, so Huygens for example considered the life table in terms of a lottery composed of 100 tickets, whilst De Witt held to the assumption that the chances of dying in any six-month period were equiprobable.

This latter reference to life tables, of course, touches the hub of our own special interests – namely death. For it is quite clear that studies of mortality and studies of probability move hand-in-hand throughout the seventeenth, eighteenth and nineteenth centuries. So much so is this the case that Daston (1988, p. 126) has argued that, 'any account of the mathematical theory of risk in this period must begin with why, when, and how contemporaries kept track of death'. Indeed, the history of probability theory provides an interesting example of the ways in which what we now call social science has influenced and, to a certain extent, fashioned the content of the natural sciences. For it is quite clear that studies of human populations encouraged a revolution in mathematical thinking about chance events. This was so in the sense that the study of populations provided both data for the study of *a posteriori* probabilities, and then encouraged mathematicians to reformulate what it is we mean by the word 'probability'.

As I stated above, the first revolution in probability theory focused on equiprobable outcomes and (associated with this) subjective expectations. The elemental gambling problem, for example, resolved itself into the question as to what a person could reasonably expect from two, three or more throws of a dice (turns of a card, draws from a lottery (Huygens, 1692)); and it was presumably in this subjective sense of expectation that Ludwig Huygens spoke of the 'expectation of life' to his brother, Christian, in 1669. Even in terms of this early framework the appearance of death was of course cloaked in a modernist garb, but it was truly in the nineteenth century that the modern sense of expectation of life came into play – and with it, a newly developed and specifically nineteenth-century sense of chance.

The new concepts of chance, death and population are represented in a new object. That object is the life table. Both the history of this life table and its individual elements deserve our attention. Its history is to be partly located in the mathematics of the various individuals to whom I have already referred, and partly in the empirical concerns of demographers and epidemiologists including Halley (1656–1742), John Graunt (1620–1674) and William Farr (1807–1883). From our standpoint, what is most important is the recognition of the fact that it was bills of mortality which provided the raw materials for the analysis of a set of chance events which were clearly patterned and orderly. In fact the compilation of bills of mortality into tables by the likes of Petty (1623–1687), Graunt, Arbuthnot (1667–1735) and others at first served to underpin the vision of death as something calculable and regular. When the Huygens brothers transformed the data from mortality tables into smooth geometric curves, the vision of human mortality as an orderly, regular and predictable event was even further assured. And it seems safe to say that from that point onward, death was divested of its capricious nature. The irregular and random dance of death would be no more.

To understand how this new vision of death was constructed, we need to examine the concept of long-term relative frequency.

Consider the following series (A):

(A) 1   0   1   0   0   0   1   1   1   0   1   0

This pattern of ones and zeros may be seen as representing individual events – such as births among a group of women, or deaths among a population, or accidents among a group of children. In each case, an event either occurs or it fails to occur. And from (A) one can derive another series (A'). This second series is a record of the relative frequency of the events occurring in (A) thus:

(A) 1   0   1   0   0   0   1   1   1   0   1   0

(A') 1 (1/2) (2/3) (1/2) (2/5) (1/3) (3/7) (4/7) (5/7) (5/8) (2/3) (3/5)

We can see quite clearly that the fractions in the second series change quite wildly as the proportion of ones and zeros alter in the first series. In the long run, however, (A') is assumed to settle down – let us say to (3/5) or 0.6, and during the late nineteenth and early twentieth century that long-term relative frequency came to be interpreted as the probability of an event's occurrence. Similarly, it was the study of the total number of years lived divided by the *total number* of people, that came to be understood as the expectation of life. By contrast, for most of the eighteenth century and earlier, expectation of life had been interpreted in terms of one's personal expectation of years left to live.

The new interpretation was neither easily developed nor rapidly adopted and its ultimate acceptance (during the twentieth century) depended on the emergence of a whole series of specific steps. Among the latter one would have to include the acceptance of Poisson's (1781–1840) 'law of large numbers' which highlighted the appearance and mathematical significance of stable ratios in a series of events, and Fechner's (1801–1887) theory of indeterminism (see Heidelberger, 1987), which placed emphasis on the 'collective' as opposed to the individual, (that is to say, on series such as A' rather than A). Above all, one would have to refer to that paradigm shift in nineteenth-century western European thought which argued that individual events could only be comprehended in the framework of groups events (Kavanagh, 1993) and which denied any place to irregular and unpredictable occurrences.

This latter point is, perhaps, best illustrated with reference to the history of sociological thought. For there can be little doubt that between 1835, when Quetelet published his *Essai de physique sociale*, and 1898 when Durkheim published his *Le Suicide*, the primary focus of sociology was on the group properties in terms of which individuals and their behaviour could be understood. The details of this focus have been more than adequately summarised by Ian Hacking in his *Taming of Chance* (1990), and here I will simply quote Durkheim who argued very firmly that the regularity of statistical patterns 'implies the existence of collective tendencies exterior to the individual' (1952, p. 318). These collective tendencies were 'as real as cosmic forces' (1952, p. 309) and constituted the subject-matter of sociology. More importantly, it was clear to Durkheim, as to many others, that individual behaviour (here suicidal, there criminal or ritualistic) could only be properly comprehended in the context of such collective forces. That, of course, was a lesson which had been learnt from Adolf Quetelet (1796–1874) who had sought to develop various laws of human development based on the observation of statistical regularities and especially the distribution of empirical values (such as heights) around a mean – thus emphasising the significance of a population of values as against the particular and singular.

This focus on populations was quite naturally at its sharpest in the study of demographic patterns. I have already mentioned the change in our understanding of the expectation of life, from personal expectation of years left to live to the sum of the total number of years lived divided by the total number of people in a society and there were, in addition, numerous other changes in our assessment of life and death. Many of these surfaced in William Farr's English Life Table 'Number 1', (published in the Fifth Annual Report of the Registrar General in England, 1843).

English Life Table No. 1. was by no means the first life table, but it was the first to incorporate the concept of a death rate, and also the first to apply mathematical concepts of probability to patterns of death in an entire nation (as opposed to a town or city). Farr's primary genius, however, lay in his use of simple ratios – such as the number of deaths per 1000 living – and he devised ratios for births as well as for deaths and calculated age- and sex-specific ratios as well. (The most important age-specific ratio – the infant mortality rate – was not however calculated until 1877.) Farr considered the death rate as an accurate measuring instrument – rather like a thermometer – and referred to it as his 'Biometer' (see Eyler, 1979). But as well as simple ratios, Farr also drew upon the principles of calculus to compute the elements of the life table. Indeed we can see in Table 12.1, an excellent example of the way in which elements of probability theory surfaced, for the starting point of 100000 implies that we can compute the probabilities of living from one year to the next. What we have here then is what might be called an actuarial vision of human existence and a new statistical device for studying society. The chances of life and death have now become calculable, and a detailed matrix of existence has materialised such that we can compute the mathematical expectation of life. We can also conjecture that the life table is a device which assisted in underpinning a significant cultural shift in attitudes toward risk. For as Lorraine Daston (1987) has suggested, this mathematical vision of order and stability facilitated the middle-class adoption of systems of life assurance. The certainty of death was still guaranteed, of course, but one could now plan for the event in a rational and systematic manner. Life and death were no longer a gamble.

Naturally Farr was not the only moral scientist to apply mathematical devices to the study of human populations; and during the nineteenth century there were numerous attempts to discover the functions which describe the curve for the proportion of a birth cohort who survived to each age. De Moivre had, of course, opened the bidding as early as 1724 with the adoption of a simple linear function (arguing that population growth or decay could be modelled on a straight line). But by 1825 Gompertz (1779–1865) had recognised the usefulness of the exponential function for modelling populations, and by 1860 William Makeham (d. 1892) modified the Gompertz function with a general chance factor so as to devise a more complex mathematical equation. (For a discussion of these issues see Smith and Keyfitz, 1977.) In the twentieth century this search for a general function to describe population growth persisted – Lotka's renewal equation (Lotka, 1932) and the construction of the logistic equation stand as two examples – though none proved to be entirely satisfactory. In any event it is clear that during the nineteenth century the general uncertainty of death was removed and mortality took on a mathematical stability which was unrecognised in the pre-industrial world. Chance, of course, remained on stage but it now ruled over a new 'empire' (Gigerenzer et al., 1989).

The life table, then, is one of the most significant representations of life and death that our own culture has produced. It not only expresses a vision of life as a rationally calculable object, but also provides a set of background expectancies of normal, natural life spans. It forms an essential part of that mesh within which death is explained. Those who report on and who analyse death – especially in the medical community – are dependent on it for their everyday judgments of what is and what is not a normal, natural death.

THE DECONSTRUCTION OF DEATH

In 1839 the Registrar General for England and Wales published the First Annual Report. Among other things the report documented the causes of death which afflicted the entire nation, and in subsequent years similar reports were published for Scotland (1854) and Ireland (1869). These days of course, the publication of annual mortality reports extends around the entire globe – if only in the form of the World Health Organization's Annual summary.

The emergence of mortality reports in general depended on two things: first, a concern with what Foucault once alluded to as the bio-politics of populations (Foucault, 1978) – a subject upon which we have already touched; second, a concern to differentiate and classify diseases. The eighteenth-century nosologies of Sauvages and Cullen are essential precursors in this respect to the more familiar nosologies of Farr (Registrar General in England, 1839) and Bertillon (1893). But, as one might guess, since diseases can never be classified as 'natural kinds' (contrary to the claims of the realists), each nosology necessarily reflects the cultural context of the age in which it was written.

When William Farr introduced his nosology of diseases in the first Annual Report for England and Wales (1839), he explained that,

> The primary divisions of a Statistical Nosology should evidently be founded upon the mode in which diseases affect the population: whether they are generated and prevail only in particular localities (endemics), extend like cholera over nations (epidemics), or are propagated by contagion; whether they arise in an isolated manner (sporadically) from ordinary causes, and sources existing in the organisation itself; or whether they are caused by violent means. (Registrar General, 1839, 16:69)

If we dwell on this quotation for a moment we cannot fail to note how the concept of an anatomical seat of disease is almost entirely absent from the classificatory logic. Unusually, the guiding principle of taxonomy is something other than anatomical space (though the concept of seats of disease did figure in the second tier of this nosology, and became dominant in later revisions of the schema). The reason lies in the fact that the nosology is nestled in a historical cusp which marks off two radically different styles of medical thought.

Farr (as with his friend Florence Nightingale), adhered closely to a miasmic theory of disease. Among other things, this latter entailed the supposition that pathology originated in the odours which emanated from putrefying organic materials. Farr therefore tended to focus his attention on such factors as the role of geographical space, atmospheres, topographies and material circumstances in generating or impeding the flow of disease. For example, his category of 'zymotic' disease encompassed those types of disorders which we call infectious – but, in the very nature of the term zymotics, the presence of infection was linked to aspects of environmental conditions.

Zymotics as a nosological category held fast until 1901, though its inclusion had been under threat for many decades. The threat came from the increasingly popular germ theory of disease which hypothesised that the spread of disease was somehow linked to the spread of microbes rather than the spread of miasmas; and although it is not possible to date the appearance of the germ theory of disease precisely, it is possible to argue that it dominated the last quarter of the nineteenth century. Naturally, as theories of disease changed so did the names of diseases and thereby their place in the nosological mesh. Yet one set of considerations which did, to a certain extent, remain constant from the publication of Farr's 1843 nosology to that of the International Commission in 1901, concerned the role of human anatomy in classifying the causes of death; for both Farr and his heirs laid a significant emphasis on the human body as an Atlas of human disease, and in this respect even the 1839 nosology marks a significant break between the ideas contained in the eighteenth-century nosologies as compared to their nineteenth- and twentieth-century counterparts. Indeed, the principles which had been enunciated by Sauvages in his *Nosologia Methodica* (*c.* 1772), and by William Cullen in *Synopsis Nosologiae Methodicae* (1785) had both been drawn from a discourse of pathology which attempted to define disease in terms of its origins rather than its localisations (Foucault, 1973), and had thereby tended to associate and conflate conditions which Farr considered to be unrelated.

The emphasis on the localisation of pathological lesions was of course most fully developed in the medicine of the Paris Hospital during the early years of the nineteenth century (see Ackernecht, 1967), although these practices are of interest to us only in so far as they influenced the classification of disease according to anatomical site, and thereby promoted the human body as a frame in terms of which diseases could be differentiated. As I have already suggested, the emphasis on the localisation of pathology did not lead abruptly to the exclusion of such things as miasmas and zymots from the classification of diseases, but it is clear that as the nineteenth century progressed anatomy came to dominate taxonomy. The apogee of anatomical thinking was not, however, reached until the 1890s when Bertillon introduced his nosology (see, for example, Bertillon, 1903); and it was, more or less, Bertillon's system that was adopted for the International standards in 1901 (Commonwealth of Australia, 1907). Those standards were revised regularly and updated during the twentieth century to the point of the tenth revision (1993) which is currently in use.

These international nosologies and nomenclatures of disease are of interest primarily because they represent a cultural vision of human disorder. Within the broad framework, of course, individual diseases come and go, but the basic principles of analysis remain familiar, and with that in mind, I have somewhat arbitrarily selected (in Table 12.2) to outline the classificatory framework of the ninth revision (1977) as it was applied to mortality in Scotland during 1985. Whilst looking at the Table one may be usefully reminded of Foucault's claim that, if for us

> [T]he human body defines, by natural right, the space of origin and of distribution of disease. ... this order of the solid, visible body is only one way – in all likelihood neither the first, nor the most fundamental – in which one spatializes disease. There have been, and will be, other distributions of illness. (1973, p. 3)

Thus, we can see quite clearly that the nosology contained herein takes as its starting point the human frame and builds on it an anatomical geography of disease. Of the 17 great orders contained in the nosology, 10 are clearly related to anatomical seat. Diseases of the genitourinary system sit next to diseases of the digestive system; diseases of the circulatory system next to diseases of the nervous system. Furthermore, many of the sub-divisions in the nosology (such as those for neoplasia) depend on even finer anatomical distinctions – here the liver, there the brain, yet again the kidneys, lungs and pancreas. The causes of death therefore are not only discovered in human anatomy, but are further classified according to anatomical parts. The human body in this sense serves both as a site for discovery and as a frame for classification. It is in this frame that the language of causation is developed and elaborated; and in terms of Table 12.2, we can see that the majority of deaths in Scotland were attributed to such things as Diseases of the Circulatory System (mainly Ischaemic Heart Disease, and Acute Myocardial Infarction), Malignant Neoplasia, and Diseases of the Respiratory System.

I shall return shortly to consider the causes of death contained within Table 12.2. For now, however, I would like to draw attention to the fact that between 1839 and 1993 the basic (nosological) framework of mortality reports have usually been supplemented – to a greater or lesser degree – by a consideration of numerous 'collective' factors and their influence on mortality. For example, the influence of age on mortality was systematically examined in 1865, (in the 25th Annual Report of the Registrar General for England and Wales) though age-specific measures of mortality make a first appearance (in England and Wales) only in 1877. Social class analysis of mortality (restricted to infant mortality) appears in 1913 (Szreter,1984), though the Registrar General for Ireland had published social class data on the Dublin population as early as 1886 (Humphreys 1887). Occupational mortality makes an early appearance in 1851 (in the fourteenth Annual Report for England and Wales) though the analysis of death by occupation as distinct from industry only truly appears in the 1920s, side by side with the emergence of the concept of industrial disease (Registrar General, 1927).

These supra-individual concepts of class and occupational division (together with earlier ones such as 'healthy districts') were used not simply as supplementary descriptive aids to mortality reports, but also as building blocks for a distinct architecture of explanations. This latter produced explanations which sought the origins of death not merely in individual bodies, but in wider social and environmental effects – such as those which might flow from class, inequality, poverty and unemployment. The tables which cross-tabulate infant death rates by social class, for example, emerged out of such a discourse – that is to say, one which addressed itself to populations rather than persons. It was a discourse which in many ways ran counter to the personalised schemes of explanation which characterised anatomical pathology, and interestingly it would seem as if this extra-personal dimension to death is these days reinterpreted in line with a distinctly late twentieth-century vision of illness and mortality.

In any event, death in twentieth-century western society was (and is) to be initially explained and described in terms of disease processes which are firmly located in human anatomy and physiology, and the incidence of such processes has been gradually normalised and standardised through the use of statistical manipulations. The results of such standardisation are available in tables and reports of the kind to which I have referred. But what is really important to remember is that this form of reporting does not simply offer us a reflection of empirical processes occurring in actual populations, but serves to determine and fashion the facts it presumes to report upon. In short, the conceptual structure of the reporting sets the limits within which relevant causes of death can be discovered and selected and thereby the limits in terms of which we can come to comprehend death.

Data on populations are of course ultimately derived from data on persons. In that sense, the life table and the report on mortality depend on the occurrence of specific and singular events in the population – the deaths of individuals. At every such event a medical Cause of Death certificate is normally completed by a medical practitioner or medico-legal investigator. In fact the medical certificate of cause of death embodies a logic of causation which is well worth examination. This is because the certificate lays down both the structure of an explanation and also a set of rules about what is and what is not an acceptable cause. As in the case of the mortality report, the format of this certificate has also been designed in terms of international standards (WHO, 1968) – standards which themselves have undergone various transformations during the twentieth century. For example, in 1912 it was stated that heart disease must take precedence over diseases of the respiratory system as a cause of death (see HMSO, 1912), whilst in 1948 it was agreed the underlying cause of death should be selected as the cause of death (see WHO, 1949). But leaving those considerations aside let me summarise the explanatory rules which are implied by the format of the modern death certificate.

Rule 1. Death is a product of pathology.
That is to say, that cause of death will always be a disease process which is in some way evident in the deceased person's body. It might take the form of a diseased artery, a carcinoma, or a respiratory infection – but for every death there will be pathology.

Rule 2. Death is a physical event.
Consequently, a cause of death can always be located in some anatomical site or other.

Rule 3. A cause of death is a visible thing, susceptible (in theory at least) to detection by sense-data.
That is to say, that one ought to be able to see the diseased anatomy at post-mortem. (Though post-mortem dissection may not be considered appropriate in every case.)

Rule 4. A cause of death is always a singular event, (though it might exist as part of a sequence).
Causes of death are always singular and sequential through time. It is always possible to cite one disease process which either precedes or determines the sequence of other such processes.

Rule 5. A pertinent cause of death is usually one which is proximate to the event.
That is to say that primary causes of death are never distant, and are always present at the moment of death.

As I have outlined elsewhere (Prior, 1989), many of these principles and assumptions are unrealistic (in the sense that they fail to reflect the complications of individual deaths). Nevertheless, it is in this reduction of death to its pathological essentials that we locate what Bauman (1992) has referred to as the deconstruction of death.

By using such a phrase Bauman intends to draw our attention to the fact that in the modern world, the explanation of death (one of the great imponderables of life) in terms of a set of distinct and limited number of disease forms helps to generate the illusion that death can somehow be controlled. That is to say, since death is caused by disease and since, in theory, all diseases are conquerable through human praxis, then death itself is conquerable. For example, the WHO nosologies which we have previously considered list some 999.999 forms of disease, injury and causes of death – each one of which is in theory curable, or surmountable. (The reader may be delighted to hear that 'old age' is not included among the 999 causes – see WHO (1977)). It is then but a small step to conclude that 'in theory', death itself can be cured; that once we have fathomed out the causes of cancers and pneumonia and wasting diseases we will have overcome death itself.

Nowhere is this line of reasoning more forcefully expressed than in certain forms of late twentieth-century public health discourse. These are commonly characterised by two major themes: first, that ill health and its ultimate consequences (early death) are avoidable; second, that the key to good health lies within the grasp of the actions of individuals. So death and misfortune can be avoided if people behave properly – eat the right things, exercise properly, stop smoking, and so on. (This is undoubtedly the message contained in the British government's *Health of the Nation* (1992) document.) Death it seems stalks only those who are careless – this despite the fact that the mortality rates of those who are careless of their health and those who are fastidious remains stubbornly similar (viz. 100 per cent).

CONCLUSION

Near the turn of the present century Max Weber introduced to the world his notion of rationalisation (see Weber, 1930). And although this is neither the time nor the place in which to explore the nuances of that concept, it can be claimed that among the essential characteristics of the rationalisation process were listed the expulsion of notions of mystery and wonderment from the everyday world of human action, and the consistent attempt to reduce everyday events to their technically controllable and predictable forms. In examining scientific representations of life and death, I hope to have demonstrated that such a rationalisation process has clearly been at work in our own spheres of intellectual interest. For death has indeed become a predictable and in many respects a technically controlled event. (In that sense one might even see the rise of the hospice movement as an inevitable expression of the Weberian rationalisation process.) Indeed, it is only when the established expectations of life are defied – as with the deaths of children or deaths of young adults from disease forms such as AIDS – that those of us who live in the war-free zones of the world are in any way shocked at the capacity of death to strike in its hitherto random and senseless fashion. And it is, perhaps, only under such conditions that we can even begin to glimpse the image of death which once haunted the inhabitants of pre-capitalist Europe.

The Changing Face of Death

Table 12.1 Births, Deaths and Marriages
English Life Table – (No. 1.)

Age	Living	Males	Females	Dying in the next year	Males	Females
0	100000	51274	48726	14631	8170	6461
1	85369	43104	42265	5267	2716	2551
2	80102	40388	39714	2710	1370	1340
3	77392	39018	38374	1853	954	899
4	75539	38064	37475	1338	679	659
5	74201	37385	36816	1047	542	505
6	73154	36843	36311	834	432	402
7	72320	36411	35909	676	346	330
8	71644	36065	35579	563	278	285
9	71081	35787	35294	469	223	246
10	70612	35564	35048	392	179	213
11	70220	35385	34835	364	179	185
12	69856	35206	34650	351	178	173
13	69505	35028	34477	415	218	197
14	69090	34810	34280	463	237	226
15	68627	34573	34054	497	240	257
16	68130	34333	33797	507	246	261
17	67623	34087	33536	514	250	264
18	67109	33837	33272	521	254	267
19	66588	33583	33005	529	259	270
20	66059	33324	32735	537	264	273
21	65522	33060	32462	545	268	277
22	64977	32792	32185	552	273	279
23	64425	32519	31906	561	278	283
24	63864	32241	31623	569	283	286
25	63295	31958	31337	576	287	289
⋮						⋮
90	1140	481	659	311	135	176
91	829	346	483	242	104	138
92	587	242	345	182	77	105
93	405	165	240	135	56	79
94	270	109	161	96	40	56
95	174	69	105	64	25	39
96	110	44	66	42	16	26
97	68	28	40	26	10	16
98	42	18	24	17	7	10
99	25	11	14	9	4	5
100	16	7	9	6	2	4
101	10	5	5	4	2	2
102	6	3	3	2	1	1
103	4	2	2	2	1	1
104	2	1	1	1	1	1
105	1	–	–	1	–	–

Source: Registrar General in England. 'Fifth Annual Report', *PP*, 1843

Table 12.2 The Causes of Death by sex of deceased and
nosological category. Scotland. 1985.

	Nosological Category	Sex of Deceased Male	Female
	All Causes/All Ages	31147	32820
I	Infectious and Parasitic Diseases	140	138
II	Neoplasms	7496	7122
III	Endocrine, Nutritional and Metabolic Diseases and Immunity Disorders	316	407
IV	Diseases of the Blood and Blood Forming Organs	77	104
V	Mental Disorders	356	609
VI	Diseases of the Nervous System and Sense Organs	377	433
VII	Diseases of the Circulatory System	15423	16896
VIII	Diseases of the Respiratory System	3605	3551
IX	Diseases of the Digestive System	887	1151
X	Diseases of the Genitourinary System	355	542
XI	Complications of Pregnancy & Childbirth	–	9
XII	Diseases of the Skin and Subcutaneous Tissue	19	70
XIII	Diseases of the Musculoskeletal System and Connective Tissue	64	205
XIV	Congenital Anomalies	133	132
XV	Conditions Originating in the Perinatal Period	129	117
XVI	Symptoms Signs and Ill-defined Conditions	149	136
XVII	External Causes of Injury and Poisoning	1621	1198

Source: Derived from *Annual Report 1985*. Registrar General for Scotland.
Edinburgh. HMSO, 1986.

REFERENCES

E. H. Ackernecht, *Medicine at the Paris Hospital, 1794–1848*, (Baltimore: Johns Hopkins University Press, 1967).

P. Ariès, 'La mort inversée', *European Journal of Sociology*, (1967) 8:2:169–95.

P. Ariès, *Western attitudes toward death from the middle ages to the present*, (Baltimore: Johns Hopkins University Press, 1974).

P. Ariès, transl. H. Weaver, *The hour of our death*, (Harmondsworth: Penguin, 1983).

P. Ariès, transl. J. Lloyd, *Images of man and death*, (Cambridge, Mass.: Harvard University Press, 1985).

Z. Bauman, *Modernity and ambivalence*, (Cambridge: Polity Press, 1991).

Z. Bauman, *Mortality, immortality and other life strategies*, (Cambridge: Polity Press, 1992).

J. Bertillon, *Nomenclature des maladies*, (Paris: Montrevain, 1903).

Commonwealth of Australia Bureau of Census and Statistics, *The nomenclature of diseases and causes of death as revised and adopted in 1900 by the international commission*, (Melbourne, 1907).

A. C. Crombie, *Styles of scientific thinking in the European tradition*, vol. II (London: Duckworth, 1994).

W. Cullen, *Nosology: or a systematic arrangement of diseases by classes, orders, genera and species*, (English tr. Edinburgh, 1785).

L. J. Daston, 'The domestication of risk: Mathematical probability and insurance 1650–1830', in L. Krüger, L. J. Daston and M. Heidelberger (eds) *The probabilistic revolution. Vol. 1. Ideas in History*, (London: MIT Press, 1987) pp. 241–60.

L. J. Daston, *Classical probability in the enlightenment*, (Princeton, N.J.: Princeton University Press, 1988).

Department of Health, *The Health of the Nation. A Strategy for Health in England*, (London: HMSO, 1992).

E. Durkheim, *Suicide. A study in sociology*, trans. J. A. Spalding and G. Simpson, (London: Routledge and Kegan Paul, 1952).

J. M. Eyler, *Victorian social medicine. The ideas and methods of William Farr*, (Baltimore: Johns Hopkins University Press, 1979).

M. Foucault, transl. A. M. Sheridan, *The birth of the clinic*, (London: Tavistock, 1973).

M. Foucault, transl. R. Hurley, *The history of sexuality. An introduction*, (Harmondsworth: Penguin, 1978).

G. Gigerenzer, Z. Swijtink, T. Porter, L. Daston, J. Beatty, and L. Krüger, *The empire of chance. How probability changed science and everyday life*, (Cambridge: Cambridge University Press, 1989).

I. Hacking, *The taming of chance*, (Cambridge: Cambridge University Press, 1990).

A. Hald, *A history of probability and statistics and their applications before 1750*, (New York: John Wiley, 1990).

M. Heidelberger, 'Fechner's indeterminism', in L. Krüger, L. J. Daston, and M. Heidelberger (eds) *The probabilistic revolution. Vol. 1. Ideas in history*, (London: MIT Press, 1987) pp. 135–47.

HMSO *Manual of the international list of causes of death*, (London, 1912).

HMSO *Annual Report of the Registrar General for Scotland. 1985*, (Edinburgh: HMSO, 1986).

J. Huizinga, *The waning of the middle ages*, (London: Edward Arnold, 1924).

N. A. Humphreys, 'Class mortality statistics', *Journal of the Royal Statistical Society*, (1887) L:2:255–92.

C. Huygens, *Laws of Chance: or a method of calculation of the hazards game etc*, (London, 1692).

T. M. Kavanagh, *Enlightenment and the shadows of chance*, (Baltimore: Johns Hopkins University Press, 1993).

A. J. Lotka, 'The growth of mixed populations. Two species competing for a common food supply', *Journal of the Washington Academy of Sciences*, (1932) 21:461–9.

A. de Moivre, *The doctrine of chances: or, a method of calculating the probability of events in play*, (London, 1718).

K. Pearson, *The chances of death and other studies in evolution*, vol.1. (London: Edward Arnold, 1897).

L. Prior, *The social organization of death. Medical discourse and social practices in Belfast*, (Basingstoke: Macmillan, 1989).

A. Quetelet, *Sur l'homme et le développment de ses facultés, ou Essai de physique sociale*, vol. I (Paris, 1835).

Registrar General in England, *First Annual Report*, (London: Parliamentary Papers, 1839) vol. 16.

Registrar General in England, *Fifth Annual Report of the Registrar General*, (London: Parliamentary Papers, 1843).

Registrar General in England, *Supplement to the twenty fifth Annual Report of the Registrar General*, (London: Parliamentary Papers, 1865) vol. 18.

Registrar General for England and Wales, *Decennial Supplement. 1921 Part II. Occupational mortality, fertility and infant mortality*, (London: HMSO, 1927).

B. de Sauvages, *Nosologie methodique*, (French tr. Lyons, 1772).

D. P. Smith and N. Keyfitz (eds), *Mathematical demography: Selected papers*, (Berlin: Springer, 1977).

S. R. S. Szreter, 'The genesis of the Registrar General's social classification of occupations', *British Journal of Sociology*, (1984) 35:4:522–46.

M. Weber, 'Author's introduction', in M. Weber, transl. T. Parsons, *The protestant ethic and the spirit of capitalism*, (London: Unwin, 1930).

World Health Organization, *International statistical classification of diseases, injuries and causes of death*, 2 vols. sixth revision (Geneva: WHO, 1949).

World Health Organization, *Medical certification of cause of death. Instructions for physicians*, (Geneva: WHO, 1968).

World Health Organization, *Manual of the international statistical classification of diseases, injuries and causes of death*, 2 vols. ninth revision (Geneva: WHO, 1977).

Subject Index

Name Index